from
J. Scully

On Directing Shakespeare

ON DIRECTING SHAKESPEARE

Interviews with contemporary directors by Ralph Berry

HAMISH HAMILTON

HAMISH HAMILTON LTD

Published by the Penguin Group
27 Wrights Lane, London W8 5TZ, England
Viking Penguin Inc, 40 West 23rd Street, New York, New York 10010, U.S.A.
Penguin Books Australia Ltd, Ringwood, Victoria, Australia
Penguin Books Canada Ltd, 2801 John Street, Markham, Ontario, Canada L3R 1B4
Penguin Books (N.Z.) Ltd, 182–190 Wairau Road, Auckland 10, New Zealand

Penguin Books Ltd, Registered Offices: Harmondsworth, Middlesex, England

First published in Great Britain 1989 by
Hamish Hamilton Ltd

British Library Cataloguing in Publication Data:
CIP data for this book is available from the British Library

ISBN 0–241–12689–4

Printed in Great Britain by
Richard Clay Ltd, Bungay, Suffolk

Contents

List of Illustrations

A Midsummer Night's Dream, Peter Brook, Royal Shakespeare Theatre, 1970 (*Shakespeare Centre Library*)

Timon of Athens, Peter Brook, Bouffes du Nord (Paris), 1974 (*Béatrice Heyligers*)

Adrian Noble (*Clive N. Totman*)

As You Like It, Adrian Noble, Barbican Theatre, 1985 (*Stephen Macmillan*)

Macbeth, Adrian Noble, Barbican Theatre, 1987 (*Ivan Kyncl*)

The Plantagenets, Adrian Noble, 1988–9 (*Richard Mildenhall*)

Bill Alexander (*Aldwych Theatre*)

Richard III, Bill Alexander, Barbican Theatre, 1985 (*Reg Wilson*)

Model of set for Alexander's 1986 Stratford production of *A Midsummer Night's Dream*, (*William Dudley*)

A Midsummer Night's Dream Bill Alexander, Royal Shakespeare Theatre, 1986 (*Ivan Kyncl*)

The Merry Wives of Windsor, Bill Alexander, Barbican Theatre, 1986 (*Reg Wilson*)

The Merchant of Venice, Bill Alexander, Barbican Theatre, 1988 (*Ivan Kyncl*)

Declan Donnellan (*Robert Workman*)

The Tempest, Cheek by Jowl, 1988 (*Robert Workman*)

Twelfth Night, Cheek by Jowl, 1986 (*Robert Workman*)

Cymbeline, Peter Hall, National Theatre, 1988 (*John Haynes*)

Sir Peter Hall (*John Haynes*)

The Winter's Tale, Peter Hall, National Theatre, 1988 (*John Haynes*)

The Tempest, Peter Hall, National Theatre, 1988: Prospero, Ariel and Act IV, Scene One (*John Haynes*)

Michael Bogdanov (*Gino Empry*)

The Wars of the Roses, English Shakespeare Company, 1988: Falstaff and Doll Tearsheet, Richard III and Jack Cade's rebellion (*Laurence Burns*)

Preface

This book has its origins in a letter which appeared in *The Times* of London on 13 October 1971. In the controversy that followed Peter Brook's brilliant and astonishing *A Midsummer Night's Dream*, Jonathan Miller wrote:

> Mandarin bardolatry is on the move again, I see. Your correspondents who attack Peter Brook's *Dream* have systematically misconceived the task of the theatrical director and by implication, therefore, have failed to understand the relationship that exists between tradition and the individual talent. According to them the director should modestly efface his own personality and allow the text to speak for itself.
>
> One might sympathise with this dogma if the text in question contained, in addition to the speeches that comprise it, additional clues which specified the sort of diction that would count. Given the fact that Shakespeare left no collateral instructions it is hard to imagine how one would ever know that one was in the presence of a version wherein the text was speaking for itself. How would the characters speak in such a performance? What accents would they use and where would the proper emphases fall? How would the cast stand and what would they all be dressed in? What does a fairy look like and in what way does his utterances differ from those of ordinary mortals?
>
> Even if the author were alive to tell us it seems doubtful whether he would be able to give a satisfactory answer to all these questions. And even if he were able to stand up and object to certain interpretations of his own text it seems quite likely from what one knows of living authors that he might be

pleasantly surprised by other equally startling departures from the orthodox version.

The mystery of Shakespeare's genius lies in the fact that innumerable performances of his plays can be rendered, few of which are closely compatible with one another, most of which, however, are at least congruent with the speeches as written. Since we can never know which one of these corresponds with Shakespeare's original intention the director must satisfy himself with the task of trying to improvise a set of people who could all convincingly mean *something* by the speeches assigned to them. In order to do this he may put the play into a new period and even set it in an entirely novel circumstance.

The point is that the act of dramatic interpretation consists of a journey backwards through time in the effort to find some significant historical ground upon which to raise an eloquent representation of human conflict. Success is then rated, not by the degree to which the performance approximates to an entirely unknowable state of Shakespeare's mind, but by the extent to which the text now speaks with more or less coherent vitality. It may be that this elusive vitality is best arrived at by setting the plays in the author's own period or possibly in the period from which he took the original story.

However, if one is going to be consistent about this and not merely lapse into a mock Tudor antiquarianism, it will soon become apparent that elements will have been introduced which will almost certainly strike the modern audience as esoteric gimmicks. What was a fairy to the Elizabethan audience? Surely not the gauzy Pre-Raphaelite creature of yesteryear. Few of us believe in fairies now and yet there *is* something intriguing about the concept of a supernatural world that lies beyond the reach of common sense.

Brook, I think, found, to many people's satisfaction, an objective correlative of this notion which, while it may have violated Shakespeare's unstated thought upon the matter, fulfilled a version of what he did actually write down.

We accept without question the successive transformations

of scripture throughout the history of painting and see nothing odd, vain or arrogant in a painter who sets his Annunciation in a mediaeval Flemish town. Shakespeare himself wrought the same changes upon antiquity, not because he arrogantly supposed their stories to be smaller or thinner than his own imagination but because he realised that one of the tasks of art is to overthrow the tyranny of time and to recreate a universe within which the dead converse at ease with the living.

With the passage of time Shakespeare's plays have quite properly assumed the status of myths and it is the honourable fate of all great myths to suffer imaginative distortions at the hands of those to whom they continue to give consolation and nourishment. The story of Oedipus existed before Sophocles changed it again, and when Freud incorporated the tale into his theory of family conflict he was merely adding another substantial chapter to a tale whose telling can never be finished. So let it be with Shakespeare.

I found this an eloquent and striking statement of the licence a director demands for his art. In his insistence on the priority of the text, with all its vitality, over 'Shakespeare', Miller placed matters in a perspective fresh to me. It was at once clear that his letter demolished many spurious criticisms of modern directorial methods. But other, more reasoned, questions remained. I resolved to know more about these matters, which I had previously encountered largely as a member of the audience in Shakespearian productions. And so I conceived the idea of interviewing a small group of leading directors, in England, the Continent and America, with the aim of investigating their approach to Shakespeare and their salient methods in producing him. Together, these men would, I hoped, create a unique collective answer to the question, 'What *is* Shakespeare today?' This is the record of that investigation.

These interviews compose, in effect, an extended conversation about Shakespeare in the theatre today. There are recurring themes, but I did not seek to impose an oral questionnaire upon the pattern of encounter. The interests of each director guided the movement of conversation. Certain questions which I put to some would have been irrelevant to others, or at least implicitly answered elsewhere. And there are, naturally, a great many questions which I did not ask. A successful director is by definition an exceptionally active man and I did not seek to prolong discussion of any issue beyond a point which might strain the courtesy of my hosts. Moreover, I was not bent on a work of stage history: so I ruthlessly suppressed any inclination to ask questions on the marginalia of productions, on the lines of 'did you double the Ghost and First Grave-digger?' The allusions here to any given production are illustrative of a directorial approach to Shakespeare. They are not, in themselves, the subject of investigation. The prime aim is an increased understanding of the relations between Shakespeare, today's theatre and ourselves.

Introduction

The problems of discourse commonly arise from a word which is used in diverse senses. Such a word is 'Shakespeare'. Two main senses are discernible in discussion. They overlap, naturally, but I believe that most people give an underlying emphasis to their use of the term. 'Shakespeare' is in the first place a man, a classic author: one has an image of a face, a beard, an expression. In the second place, 'Shakespeare' is shorthand for the works of Shakespeare: one recognises a bound volume, play texts, the foundations of a production. Certain consequences flow immediately from one's election of the prior sense. If a man, Shakespeare has, it is felt, some rights over his plays and us. He is the greatest English writer and the greatest playwright of whom the world has record. We owe him our devotion, and in preserving and reperforming his plays we serve him. Such an attitude escapes into the realm of aesthetic theory, and insists that the intention of the author be of prime account in the interpretation and presentation of his works. But if Shakespeare is purely text, then different considerations apply. We do not serve a man, we excavate or exploit a quarry. The plays cease to be expressions of intention, or attempts at communication; rather, they become material. Whether or not we make open use of Cocteau's provocative '*textes-prétextes*', the term he applied to his Shakespearian productions, we accept that the umbilical cord linking the man and work is severed. I exaggerate these attitudes to make their import plain; most people do not approach the matter with this kind of logical finality and traces of the alternative attitude are doubtless present in even the extreme proponents of one or other. The most dedicated servitor of Shakespeare will readily concede that he built multiple meanings into his texts and the most ruthless practitioner of the quarry-text school may yet feel that he is accomplishing a higher intention, a willed meaning, of Shakespeare. Still, for practical purposes, the conflict is there. One can simply choose sides, if one wishes, and leave it there. But the conflict is so perennially fascinating, the issues so broad and subtle, that one should surely wish to investigate further. To choose sides too early is to evade the challenge.

Let us take the assertion (as it is often phrased) that directors should permit the text 'to speak for itself'. That is impossible. To begin with, the text itself is a massive variable. For half the plays of Shakespeare, our sole source is the Folio, published seven years after his death and seen through the press by his literary executors. The remaining plays exist additionally in single play text (Quarto) versions, a number of which are evidently corrupt and highly untrustworthy. Often the better Quartos are at variance with the Folio and we cannot be sure that the Folio represents Shakespeare's final thoughts. Standards of typesetting and proofreading bear little relation to those of the present day, and we have no original to check: saving a fragment of *Sir Thomas More*, no manuscript in Shakespeare's hand survives. It is agreed that there are numerous corrupt and dubious passages in even the best-preserved of the plays we have. Then, the texts are by modern standards starved of stage directions. These directions are usually limited to straightforward details of entrances and exits, and factual statements of non-verbal actions: *Throws him a purse*, and so on. There is nothing at all corresponding to the interpretative annotations with which a contemporary dramatist will interlard his dialogue. What we have are the words and the major actions: no more. And this is only the beginning, for the texts that we have cannot, in many instances, be presented in their complete versions. It is a question of length. There is no particular reason why *The Comedy of Errors* or *Twelfth Night* should not be played in their entirety. But *Hamlet*, in a conflation of the second Quarto and the Folio texts, would last over five hours. Much the same applies to *King Lear*, *Troilus and Cressida*, *Anthony and Cleopatra* and others. Whatever the playing time audiences were accustomed to, whatever the speed of performance, these texts have always been cut heavily and always will be. How, then, does one cut? The playing version that the director selects bears always the imprint of his own mind. There is no way of making a neutral cut. One can try to arrive at a 'skeletal' play, the residue corresponding, if one likes, to Shakespeare's extended stage instructions; but there is no certain means of identifying this playing version. Tradition is no sure guide. The Polonius-Reynaldo scene in *Hamlet* (II, i) is usually cut, but a director is perfectly at liberty to argue that it throws indispensable light on the play. No scene in *Antony and Cleopatra* is more easily spared than the Ventidius-Silius dialogue (III, i), yet its *Realpolitik* is a fundamental perspective on Antony. In sum, a Shakespeare production in its simplest formulation – the words and actions presented to the public – must be governed at many points by the decision of the director. There is no other authority to appeal to.

All this is obvious enough. The real problems now begin to emerge, for the words of the text as chosen have to be delivered by actors who have certain physical characteristics, who are apparelled in a certain way, who speak their lines with a certain emphasis. *Meaning*, broadly, is the product of what the audience perceives as emerging from these immensely complex events. And there is no escaping the responsibility for directing, i.e. determining these events. Jonathan Miller's question goes to the heart of the matter: 'What does a fairy look like?'

What, indeed? Most of us, I suppose, would, if appealed to, conjure up an image of the children's book illustrations on which we were brought up. It is unnecessary to argue in detail how potentially misleading this must be. In visualising a style of illustration, we assume a reality of connection. We see, perhaps, a visual contemporary of Shepard's *Wind in the Willows* or Beatrix Potter. These matters are rooted in the culture of every nation and must surely be well removed from the reality that 'fairy' connoted to the Elizabethans. There is no question of a 'correct' translation of 'fairy' for modern audiences: the imaginative leap has to be made by each director. Peter Hall, for instance, brought into being a group of earth-stained urchins.

But we cannot expect 'fairy' to accomplish the task of effortlessly defining itself for us.

Words, in fact, are the critical obstacles that the modern interpreter of Shakespeare has to overcome. The problem is paradoxically more exacting for the British and Americans than for any other nation. The reader who is formally engaged in translating Shakespeare into a foreign tongue gives each word a special consideration. The normal Anglo-American reader assumes that he is perfectly familiar with the mass of Shakespearian vocabulary. He therefore retains his energies for the difficult or obscure terms. He looks up 'provulgate' or 'hugger-mugger' and finds out what centuries of scholarly labour have made available. He does not look up 'court', or 'honour', or 'art' – indeed, there is nothing to look up. But these are precisely the trap words, the words that we retain with similar meanings but which rest on assumptions and attitudes that have long grown obsolete or changed radically.

'Court' will make the point as forcefully as any term. As Konrad Swinarski explains, his productions of *All's Well That Ends Well* and *A Midsummer Night's Dream* rest on a central conception of 'Court'. It is the grand image of Shakespeare, for him. Now, for the average Anglo-American of our day, 'Court' is purely a decorative appendage to the political and social life of the capital. Its doings are as chronicled in the Court Circular, and take up a little daily space in *The Times* and *Daily Telegraph*. The Elizabethan sense of 'Court' as the centre of power in the land is now scarcely accessible to us. With an exercise of the historical imagination, we can appreciate that the Court in *Hamlet* is a dangerous and politically charged milieu, with its quota of careerists, ministers and executive power. We will normally fail to realise that 'Court' in this sense has any relevance to the comedies. But the Elizabethan recognition of 'Court' as the Government, the one place where all the great careers were to be made, could scarcely have been neutralised simply because they were watching a Pleasant Comedy. The resonances are there in the text, waiting to be sounded. Swinarski's perception that 'Court' is 'Government' is a central reminder of the difficulty with words, that they imply questions and issues yet permit evasion. Words become a formula for divesting events of their meaning.

The director has to recreate meaning, to reactivate the decaying, amorphous words of the text. He is not an historical scholar (though he must be in touch with the discoveries of scholarship) and he is not a restorer. His task is to identify for his day the vital elements in a text and to communicate them. Every production of Shakespeare presupposes a national group which is the predominant audience. (Of course, a summer production in Stratford may play to a largely international audience, but my essential point remains.) The meanings latent in the text have to be actualised with that audience in mind. A Coriolanus founded on the overtones of an English public-school upbringing is a perfectly valid conception, for an English audience. To an audience unfamiliar with English ways these particular meanings would fail to resonate; but there are always alternatives. The militaristic side of Coriolanus' upbringing finds echoes in the social structure of many nations and tribes, but happens not to be a strong English tradition. Even so simple a term as 'soldier' needs a specific (and not a generalised) audience before it can be satisfactorily defined. (Consider what 'soldier' connotes to a Japanese, a Swede, a German, an American.) The point is that meanings are not lexical absolutes, to be animated by the players. Meanings are generated by community and history; the audience participates in and establishes them. The audience does not, as it were, blankly spectate at a set of visual and aural images. Thus the director has to enter into that audience's bloodstream, to be aware of the images that compose the present and the past of the community – its felt history, that is to say. But this leads us to the decisions that a director takes in presenting a play of Shakespeare.

The director makes three cardinal decisions in presenting a play of Shakespeare: he chooses the play; he determines the playing text; he creates the metaphoric vehicle for the production, the ambience generated by setting and costume. I came to believe in the course of this enquiry that the most important decision is the first. Its significance is normally obscured by the sheer mechanics of mounting a production. Much of the Shakespeare we see is put on in a festival or repertory theatre and the choice of play is circumscribed, often determined, by factors of cost, actor availability, the need to ensure heavy box-office activity and so on. In these circumstances the nominal canon of thirty-seven or thirty-eight plays can sometimes shrink to *Hamlet* and *Twelfth Night*. Michael Kahn, Trevor Nunn and Robin Phillips have much to say on these matters, which should be sympathetically received. But I point to the occasions where a leading director, of established reputation, has virtually a free hand to select his play. And now the choice becomes all-important, for he will not select a text until he senses its mysterious affinities with the movement of the times. While he has no doubt an active and personal engagement with a play, he has additionally the sense that certain chords in it can be made to vibrate with a peculiar intensity in the contemporary mind. To vary the figure, the director becomes the barometer of society.

Let us illustrate. The most dangerous, the most politically vibrant play in the canon was once *Richard II*. That is because it deals with a deposition. It is on record that a performance of *Richard II* was staged, at the instigation of Essex's followers, as a direct preliminary to an attempted *coup d'état*. 'I am Richard the Second, know ye not that?' said the old Queen to Lambarde. But today nobody regards the play as an anti-monarchic manifesto. It has become an existentialist analysis of a human being stripped of his exterior appurtenances, reduced to the ultimate problem of defining himself. The 'meaning' – the thrust of the play – has changed radically. Other plays come and go with the flux of politics: *Julius Caesar* and *Coriolanus* periodically supply analogues with dictatorship and class conflict. (A version of *Coriolanus*, Dennis's *The Invader of his Country*, once supplied a topical commentary on the Old Pretender.) Some plays have simply had to wait for their audiences. *Troilus and Cressida* (with *Measure for Measure*) is now one of *the* plays for our times – almost all the directors whom I conversed with expressed a special interest in it – yet until a generation ago it had virtually no stage history whatever. It is too early to say so with confidence, but perhaps *Timon of Athens* will come into this category; it is certainly possible that Peter Brook's production at the Bouffes du Nord (October 1974) heralds a wave of interest. The history of Shakespeare on the stage is full of instances where plays, neglected for years, have suddenly been re-established as centres of contemporary interest. But on the whole, the most fascinating exercise of the director's barometric function lies in his choice of a play that is already popular. He then displays a facet of the text that has not been properly understood and he demonstrates that *this* is the play for today.

Thus, the *Henry V* of a generation ago was a strongly nationalist statement, classically formulated in the Olivier film. This remained true for a number of years after the war. The Royal Shakespeare Company's production of the mid-Sixties demonstrated – what is indeed true – that the text contains a latent anti-war statement and this version was given full weight. It is now, as I guess, the orthodox view of the play. One need not labour the point that what was possible in 1964 was impossible in 1944: and vice versa. The text does not change, audiences do. Or again, the Peter Hall/David Warner *Hamlet* of the same period showed him as a student. This, oddly enough, is what the text actually declares Hamlet to be. But the image of Hamlet as an apathetic, alienated graduate student provoked considerable reaction from those accustomed to the Renaissance prince. The younger generation took very much to *their* Hamlet. Here a production crystallised a generational division, a further movement of the times. And finally, there is the rigorously postcolonial *Tempest* of Jonathan Miller in 1970. (He restaged the production on the same principle in 1988.) This view indisputably reflects a real concern of the text, yet until very recently nobody knew what decolonisation was like; it had never happened. The production, and its audience, had to wait for the events of the 1950s and 1960s. It is, then, a complete naïveté to speak of the 'meaning' of a Shakespeare play as an entity that can be defined, established and placed on record in perpetuity. The play is changed by the act of selection, which implies the social context of the new production. In selecting the play, the director undertakes to guide his audience to an area of contemporary consciousness and enlarge its understanding.

The choice of play should be recognised for the paramount act that it is. In every way, this act governs the next decision, the determination of the playing text. This is not, I think, a matter on which one can usefully generalise. The plays themselves are so diverse in nature, and we ought to accept Peter Brook's distinction between the plays which are very elaborately written and those which are very tightly organised. The Brook *Midsummer Night's Dream* was based on an uncut text; Trevor Nunn has never directed an uncut Shakespeare. Miller cuts freely, Swinarski most unwillingly. Kahn cuts less and less. Practice is extremely various. We should, however, identify the nature of cutting. Essentially it is an affair of cutting the crystal, of presenting an object so as to reflect light at the desired angles. If, for instance, Shylock's soliloquy of I, iii, 42–53 is cut ('How like a fawning publican he looks! I hate him for he is a Christian . . .'), together with Jessica's testimony that he had often sworn he would rather have Antonio's flesh than twenty times the money, the effect of this is to reduce sharply the element of predetermined hatred in Shylock's attitudes and throw the weight of his later conduct on to the disaster of his daughter's flight with a Christian. These cuts neither mutilate the text nor go against its grain, but they do prepare the way for a more sympathetic treatment of Shylock allied to an ironic and sceptical view of the Venetians. And this strategy, naturally, is related to the prior decision of play selection. Broadly, a contemporary audience is well able to see the scales adjusted more in favour of Shylock than past audiences; it is a central possibility in the text that Shakespeare's infallible tact has left open. Cutting, then, should emphasise a certain quality, a certain source of vitality, in the full original. This is not to deny that cutting can be brutal, capricious, insensitive. Its function is nonetheless to illuminate, and not lay waste, the original text.

It has to be added that cuts of a certain magnitude are necessarily a phase in adapting, even rewriting, the original text. One can scarcely hope to mount the three parts of *Henry VI* in their entirety, though Terry Hands did for the RSC in 1978. So one solution, as in John Barton's version for the RSC, is to reduce three plays to the length of two. The English Shakespeare Company adopted this solution for its *Wars of the Roses* (1986– 89). So did the RSC, in the version that Adrian Noble directed as *The Plantagenets* (1988–89). This requires some rewriting of transitional passages and expository material. A talent at least for pastiche is indispensable here. Beyond that lies the full-scale adaptation, as in Giorgio Strehler's massive *Das Spiel der Mächtigen* (*The Game of the Mighty*), which is formally announced as 'by Giorgio Strehler after Shakespeare's *Henry VI*'. Evidently such productions extend the history of Shakespearian adaptations, which is more enduring than is generally realised. (Shaw, for example, was brought up on Colley Cibber's version of *Richard III*.) I know of no general criteria for judging such adaptations: each one is a separate enterprise, and will be judged on the skill and tact with which the adapter interprets and reanimates the vital essences of the original text. The Barton *Wars of the Roses* was widely acclaimed, yet the same author's version of *King John* was as widely criticised. Strehler's *Das Spiel der Mächtigen* had a prolonged success. On a smaller scale, Trevor Nunn admits to enjoying writing a line or two himself (for good technical reasons) and is positive that no one ever notices. Practice, clearly, is extremely diverse and wide-ranging in its expedients. It seems best to regard cutting as one side of a coin, on the obverse side of which is rewriting and adapting.

The stage setting and costumes comprise the metaphoric vehicle, or ambience, of the production. In the mode of choice which the director makes here his entire philosophy of production will be revealed. On no issue did I encounter a greater diversity of opinion. While the categories are not watertight, the major possibilities open to the director are: Renaissance; modern; a historical setting that is neither Renaissance nor modern; and eclectic. Each has its rationale.

(i) Renaissance

The immediate possibility for most of Shakespeare's plays: to it can be added mediaeval for the histories and Roman for the Roman plays. The central idea is that the period of composition, or the period to which the author alludes, should be directly reflected in the costumes and settings. These in turn will reflect the language, the concerns and the assumptions of the text. This strategy has more resources than its apparently simple literalism would indicate. Negatively, it avoids virtually all problems of anachronism. (If a character refers to doublet and hose, that is what he is wearing. Malvolio's cross-gartering requires no translation.) It marries easily with a version of the Elizabethan stage, if that is the setting the director wishes. Unlike contemporary styles, it denies nothing in the text. It is powerfully retentive of meanings. Moreover, the policy need not be dogmatically historical-literal: it can tolerate *pourparlers* with eclecticism. The 1972 *Julius Caesar* at the Royal Shakespeare Company was staged in Roman costume, but in black leather (which is quite un-Roman) suggesting strongly the aura of Fascism. The Renaissance approach has distinguished advocates: Sir Peter Hall, for one, has always preferred it, and his baroque *Tempest* (1974) displayed facets of the text available only to a Renaissance production. In 1988, he chose a Caroline period setting for his revival of *The Tempest*. Swinarski found Polish Renaissance settings perfectly suitable for his productions. Kahn prefers to choose between Renaissance and modern. The simple, powerful strategy of the historical approach is never likely to be discredited.

(ii) Modern

The logic of Shakespeare flows easily into other channels and the contemporary setting is the most obvious of them. If Shakespeare is our contemporary, the argument runs, let him be presented in the costume of the present day. And indeed this brusque attack upon the relevance of a text is virtually guaranteed positive results. It immediately breaks through the mental barrier existing for many between (say) kings, queens and consuls and the present day, and appears to establish the authenticity of the production's credentials. Those knowing the text well, for whom the mental barrier is no problem, will nonetheless be engaged and gripped by each piece of modern translation that the director introduces. The approach undoubtedly communicates rapidly and directly to a large portion of the audience. Against this are some losses. A part of the original text will make no sense at all. References to swords, horses, clothes and so on must be cut, ignored, or left in as a distracting presence. Much has to be denied in the text to shape up the present-day analogies: and this denial may be altogether too sweeping. Shakespeare, in Patrick Cruttwell's phrase, is *not* our contemporary* and in seeking to establish the converse proposition one can damage irrevocably the fabric of the text, which is sustained by a web of assumptions and attitudes confined to Renaissance thinking. And this in spite of the genuinely illuminating analogues that a modern setting, always prolific of stage invention, can supply. I recall a *Love's Labour's Lost* which opened with a group of students dreamily passing a marijuana pipe around. This is not a bad analogue to the state of fantasy into which the Navarrese courtiers are sunk, a state destined to be challenged and refuted by the realities of the later stages. Still, this invention evidently fails to grip (say) the concept of 'fame', or for that matter the known unwillingness of students to banish women from their academies. The danger is always that an immediate point can be made vividly and tellingly, but that it relies on a set of assumptions about our own society that the remainder of the text cannot sustain. There is a direct and irreconcilable conflict between the text and an overt, physicalised translation into modernity. On the whole, the approach seems best adapted to the comedies, where the gains usually outweigh the losses. The mode is out of favour for staging the tragedies

*'Shakespeare is not our contemporary', *Yale Review*, (1969). Cruttwell was responding to Jan Kott's now classic book, *Shakespeare Our Contemporary*.

and indeed there is something curiously dated about the phrase
'modern-dress *Hamlet*'. But there is always the chance that current events will supply a set of analogues so compelling that the
director can accept the invitation to make open use of them.

(iii) Period Analogue

This is the rationale for the choice of an historical setting
other than the present, or Renaissance/mediaeval/Roman. Logically there is little real difference between (ii) and (iii). In practice,
this species of historical period-analogue has great resources,
simply because the field of choice is so enormous. We need,
however, to keep in mind the distinction that Michael Kahn
draws between '*décor*' and 'concept'. By '*décor*' he means a
period style that is chosen for its visual elegance and offers a
purely cosmetic way of dressing up the text. 'Concept' means
that in pointing to a particular set of national and historical
circumstances via the costumes, the director marks close and
striking affinities with the realities of the text. A production
based on period analogy must be judged on its orientation to
décor or concept; but these are not exclusive categories. They are
best thought of as composing a spectrum.

Beginning at the *décor* end of the spectrum, I instance a *Love's
Labour's Lost* patterned visually upon *Les Très Riches Heures du
Duc de Berry*. Elegant and appealing, the costumes contributed
primarily a mood, an aura. It is hard to detect more than the
broadest of analogies between the courts of Navarre and the Duc
de Berry. The production was in fact innocent of genuine reflection upon the text. That is not a criticism but a statement of
category: the production had modest aims and accomplished
them successfully. Or take Kahn's Risorgimento *Romeo and Juliet*
(Stratford, Connecticut, 1969), for which naturally he had an
entirely realistic appraisal: the Italian setting was congruent
with the feuds of the period and supplied many possibilities of
display and invention. That was sufficient and required no de-
fence. But the more ambitious enterprises seek always to turn
local visual opportunities to conceptual advantage. Not in-

frequently, a Shakespeare comedy is set in the early nineteenth century. Now the advantage of this is that the lovers can take on the mode of Romantic posturing. The strategy works well for *Twelfth Night* and *The Two Gentlemen of Verona*, where Orsino and Valentine can be got up to look like Byronic heroes. This broad allusion to the cult of Byron genuinely expresses a reality of the text – Orsino and Valentine are both *poseurs* – and the costumes help to explain the play, as well as dress it.

Peter Brook's historic Watteau *Love's Labour's Lost* (Stratford-upon-Avon, 1946) rested not on a few well-taken opportunities, but on a central conception: that the world of Watteau is the ideal visual analogue to the world of Navarre. The Watteau *fête champêtre* comprehends, if you like, anti-festive forces and these forces are symbolised in the alienated figure, who may be Watteau, present in the painting. This corresponds with Mercade and all he stands for. 'The words of Mercury are harsh after the songs of Apollo.' (Shakespeare surely means the collocation of Mercade-Mercury to reverberate.) Thus the production, though of course highly decorative, was not *décor*. It was an act of criticism of a very high order.

All period analogies, of the non-decorative order, are acts of criticism. When they succeed, they impose a permanent layer over the text in the minds of the audience. Tyrone Guthrie translated *Troilus and Cressida* into the Europe of the early twentieth century: the Trojans, English officers of the Household Cavalry; the Greeks, Kaiser Wilhelm's Germans. At one level, this concept covered a number of finely taken opportunities: Ulysses, Admiral Tirpitz; Helen, an Edwardian chorus girl married into the peerage, beautifully embodying the triviality that Shakespeare depicts in the nominal *casus belli*; Thersites, a war correspondent setting up his box camera and tripod. The voyeurism of Pandarus and homosexuality of Achilles translated easily into the idiom of the period. But more profoundly, Guthrie caught a sense of two societies in conflict, two nations locked in a war of values and attrition, and this in a period near enough to be poignant but not conveying the fatal dissonances of a contemporary war. Proximity can numb thought and stifle reactions. The Trojan War may be the poetic archetype of all wars, but in the minds of the audience all wars are not equal: 1914–18 is not the War of the Spanish Succession, nor is it Vietnam. Guthrie's immense theatrical flair propounded an insidiously suggestive vehicle for the thoughts and emotions of his audience.

Clearly, we are contemplating the fact that audiences have memories as well as sensory apparati. History happens and it changes people, partly because history is recorded and remembered. A Shakespeare production is totally within its rights in basing itself upon this central fact and appealing to an audience's knowledge of what has happened. Take Jonathan Miller's *Measure for Measure* (Greenwich Theatre, 1975). This exploits what is in effect a pun of history, that the city of Duke Vincentio is also the city of Freud. The pun would be meaningless, but for the play's unquestionable concern with sexual repression. Thus Miller, in setting his production in the Vienna of the 1930s, was able to throw a brilliant light upon a certain area of the text. And in this, he appealed to an ineluctable fact for today's audiences: we cannot un-know Freud. Robin Phillips' *Measure for Measure*, also of 1975, made the same point. Set in the Vienna of 1912, his production identified sexual repression as the core of the play. To this was added a distinctively 1975 awareness of corruption in high places and the feminist issue of Isabella's integrity (and not, as such, 'chastity'). The production was structured around the audience's sense of past and contemporary history.

A consequence of this approach is that strong light implies shadow, that certain aspects of the text can expect at best a neutral exposition. I do not think this a major drawback. The fact is that a Shakespeare text is so large and comprehends so many possibilities that a metaphor which illuminates a single major aspect within the two hours of playing time is fully self-justified. What is certainly desirable is that the director, in advancing his metaphor, should not make it so rigidly schematic as to exclude all unwanted meanings. The best directors will always play for additional meanings, for ambivalences and possiilities that go beyond the main outline of the structure. The suggestion can be stronger than the statement. Still, it is undeniable that separate metaphors can coexist peacefully within the same text. The Miller post-colonial *Tempest* and the Hall Renaissance *Tempest* are incompatible with each other, but perfectly congruent with the text: and that is all that matters.

The extreme of the *décor*-concept spectrum is, I suggest, occupied by history. Not a specific historical period, but history itself. This is territory claimed if not owned by the Marxists: the idea is that Shakespeare depicts a dialectic of historical forces that is unfolding to our present day. Really, this idea is a modern development of Samuel Johnson's view that characters in Shakespeare are not individuals, but species. Thus they are representative of social groups, or classes, in conflict. Naturally, this approach works best for *Coriolanus*, for Marxists the premier play in the canon. (Not, I think, since the 'Stavisky' *Coriolanus* in the Paris of 1933 has anyone presented *Coriolanus* as a *right*-wing play.) Other plays emerge well from the Marxist treatment though. If one views *The Merchant of Venice* as based on the critique of capitalism focused in the Antonio-Shylock debate of I, iii, then the whole drama can logically be developed as an ironic scrutiny of Venetian values. What, after all, is Antonio's position but the absurd claim that overseas investment is morally superior to taking straight interest on capital? (And this at a point in history when mediaeval denunciations of 'usury' were increasingly seen as irrelevant.) A Marxist *Merchant* is able to activate this contradiction, together with many low-toned ironies of the text, and play down the romantic, fairy-tale elements. Again, the early histories are fairly Brechtian. (And Brecht, be it added, was profoundly influenced by Shakespeare.) *King John* is a devastating analysis of kingship and the director is entitled to emphasise the alienation of the leading character in the Bastard's 'Mad world! mad kings! mad composition!' *Henry VI* is above all a disillusioned critique of the power process: and it contains, as Strehler points out, the only on-stage rebellion in the canon. What is always possible in the staging of these histories is that the audience should be made aware of the ongoing relevance of the action: and this, not through the crudities of contemporary costuming, but through subtler provocations. Giorgio Strehler seized on a passage of immense poignancy in *Henry VI, Part Three*: *Enter a* Son *that has killed his father, bringing in the dead body . . . Enter a* Father *that has killed his son, with the body in his arms.* This is emblematic drama, drama which reduces the conflicting forces to two compelling images. Strehler, in giving full emphasis to this moment, made his actor wear a beast's mask – which he tore off in discovering the body's identity, to reveal an anguished human face. The audience is confronted with the human reality of the Civil Wars. Among the other possibilities, an emphasis upon a 'chorus' figure, a flowing sequence of scenes in the epic continuum, a calculated 'demystification' of kingship, all these are ways of animating the fundamental Shakespearian detachment and irony. Every director must come to terms with his own conception of history.

(iv) Eclectic

And this may simply yield Peter Brook's position, which is that he is not interested in history. In that event, the main possibility seems the portmanteau category that I term 'eclectic'. The theory, as stated by Peter Brook, is that consistency of costuming is the enemy; it is a superimposed schema, both stifling and distracting. He wishes to create via his costumes 'provocations' that identify themselves with no one era or national situation. 'The necessity is that anything visual in a Shakespeare production should not confine the audience to a single attitude and a single interpretation.' This desire to keep the options open is characteristic of today.

Eclecticism may be wide-ranging, or fairly narrow-gauge. Michael Bogdanov's cycle of the history plays (1986–89) ranged from the Middle Ages to the twentieth century and I put to him the question:

Are you saying that you can have a kind of fluid eclecticism, in which one moves scene by scene from one period to another, or do you regard each actor as a one-off who inhabits his own individual world in his own individual costume?

The answer is yes, to both. You can have the eclecticism moving scene by scene, and you can have an individual moving through parallel to that, in one costume, through a whole series of different scenes with different costumes.

Bogdanov's *Richard III* was played in modern dress; the combat between Richard and Richmond was staged with swords and armour; at the close, the production reverted to contemporary, as Richmond made his TV address. Similarly, Ingmar Bergman's *Hamlet*, set in an indeterminate period, finished with Fortinbras taking over in a military coup. At the National Theatre, London (1987), this was an SAS raid. At the Brooklyn Academy of Music (1988), Bergman's Fortinbras became a Central American military leader in beret and jackboots. In each case the final speech became a photo-opportunity before Klieg lights, a microphone and a hand-held video camera. Thus the ranging of the production style led to a spectacular and specifically contemporary climax. To such directorial strategists as Bergman and Bogdanov, the combination of freedom and diversity of allusion is what makes the ultimate appeal.

Others are content to work within narrow-gauge eclecticism. Howard Davies' *Troilus and Cressida* (RSC, 1985) was set in the mid-nineteenth century, with specific references to the Crimean War. (Pandarus was discovered reading a Balkan newspaper.) But the soldiery wore American Civil War uniforms and the set suggested a crumbling mansion, the Tara of *Gone With The Wind*. The slaying of Hector recalled Manet's *The Firing Squad* (and thus, the execution of the Emperor Maximilian). So Davies' *Troilus and Cressida* conflated about a decade of history. The *All's Well That Ends Well* at Stratford, Ontario by David William (1988) made Helena a Charlotte Brontë governess of the 1840s or so, but set the Italian scenes in the American Civil War. Again, there was modest historical licence, but nothing to make the average theatregoer feel that any violation of decorum was taking place.

Eclecticism is not, however, a commanding doctrine. Sir Peter
Hall, for one, rejects it. He has always preferred to set his
productions in Renaissance (or mediaeval, or classical) costume.
Bill Alexander is happy to work with the period envelope, as in
his *Merry Wives of Windsor* (RSC, 1985) set in Macmillan's
England. Both Hall and Alexander feel, however, that a certain
adjustment of Renaissance styling is necessary. Hall makes the
point that the Elizabethan period is difficult for us: we have a
resistance to ruffs, farthingales, padded breeches and the like. He
finds that the Caroline era (1625 on) is much easier for the
contemporary sensibility. Alexander, too, wanted a Renaissance
Merchant of Venice but chose to set his production (RSC, 1987) in
the Jacobean era. (That is, some twenty to thirty years after the
play's date of composition.) Costume style reflects a wider perception, that the modern world begins to edge into view in the early
seventeenth century. Given the marginal licence that such adjust-
ments mean, these directors are prepared to work within the
tight limits of the period envelope.

Robin Phillips' position is of special interest. He has always
been happy with the period envelope, often setting his productions in the larger nineteenth century. It is for him a preferred
mode of discourse. He has recently said: 'I'm becoming eclectic.
I'm sure now that you can combine periods, that people can
accept it.' The key point is that audiences are changing and are,
I think, for a multiplicity of reasons prepared to accept eclecticism
as the central aesthetic of our times. If that is so, we can expect
to see more Shakespearian productions than ever coming to
terms with this truth.

In all this, the role of the designer has not been more than
glanced at here. It is obvious that productions at the major,
highly subsidised State theatres offer brilliant opportunities for
the designer. The need and the means for lavishness are both
present. The RSC made in 1981 the cardinal decision to encourage higher investment in production, i.e. to spend more
money on lavish production values. But it is easy to exaggerate
the importance of 'Designers' Theatre'. I think this for the simplest of reasons: directors appoint designers; designers do not

appoint directors. The role of the director as the central artistic entrepreneur is not to be displaced by the designer. Only the director can determine the 'super-objective' (in Simon Callow's term) of the production and, with Shakespeare, decide on its style as Renaissance, modern, period analogy, or eclectic.

These are the major strategies open to the director of today. In pursuing one, he further defines his interpretation of the current import of the text. It becomes the 'imaginative distortion', in Miller's phrase, of the original myth. The production itself cannot be judged on its supposed fidelity to the *Ur*-text of the myth, the words of the Folio. Rather, it must harness the myth's energies to a new pattern that holds meaning for us. I cannot discover a formula for judgment here. Certainly many productions are crude, eccentric, capricious, insensitive. The myth has been 'denatured'. But this is because most enterprises in most fields fail to reach high standards. It does not necessarily reflect a fundamental misconception of the challenge. Nor will the metamorphosis of the director into the chairman of the actors' board substantially modify the situation. And what, then, is the situation? One comes back, perhaps, to Peter Brook's saying that one needs a double attitude, of respect and disrespect – the dialectic is what it's all about. Trevor Nunn accepts 'loyalty' rather than 'fidelity' to the text as the best guide. Or perhaps one comes ultimately to the metaphors for Shakespeare that the directors choose. To Jonathan Miller, Shakespeare today is part of an expanding universe, dramatic matter continuously created out of fundamental substance created centuries ago. To Peter Brook, Shakespeare is energy. The role of Shakespeare is still to change the universal perception and in addressing themselves to his work the directors perceive it as life itself.

The Interviews

Jonathan Miller

Jonathan Miller has been directing Shakespeare since 1969, when he produced King Lear *at the Nottingham Playhouse and for the Old Vic. He has been an Associate Director at the National Theatre (1973–75) and was for two years in charge of the BBC-TV Shakespeare project. Since 1987 he has been Artistic Director at the Old Vic.*

Ralph Berry Is there, today, anything in your letter to *The Times* that you would like to single out or modify?

Jonathan Miller No, I think that in a way that is the best brief expression of the point of view that I hold today. I think that I could amplify and enrichen some of the points but that really is, in a way, my basic manifesto about Shakespearian production. Can I say in a sense that my basic idea springs from one notion which comes not from the theatre, but from linguistic philosophy? It comes from a rather striking phrase by the Oxford philosopher, Peter Strawson, who in an essay when he was commenting on Bertrand Russell's theory on descriptions tried to find a reason for the difficulties that Russell found himself in when trying to account for the meaning of certain sentences, which didn't refer to an actual historical personage but which nevertheless meant something and were not nonsense. And Strawson emphasises that the reason why Russell got into this difficulty was that he forgot something very important about propositions. He said that it is not propositions which mean something but the people who mean things by the propositions which they utter. And I think that in the theatre what one has is a series of texts very many of which are almost bereft of collateral instructions telling one what the characters are and what they mean by what they say. All that you have are the utterances themselves. What you therefore have to do is improvise, and discover and embody people or personalities who might convincingly and consistently have meant something by all the utterances which happen to be written down opposite their name in the texts which we have inherited from the past.

RB It is clear, then, that you do not think of the Shakespeare text as having single, absolute, final meaning at all. You think of a multiplicity of meanings which it is the business of the director to project, or rather that it is the business of the director to select one and project that. But presumably you would not issue a licence to anybody on this. You would believe certain meanings as projected by directors could be, how shall we say, wrong, misleading, inadequate, not fully, not reasonably in accordance with the original text that has come down to us?

JM Yes. I think that there are extremes when one knows that the text has been denatured beyond the point where anything satisfactory happens. It's not beyond the point of what the author intended – that, in a sense, is hardly what interests me. As I said in the letter, in a way the author's intentions are beyond guess. There is no way of finding out what he intended. Nevertheless there is a possibility of producing some sort of distortion or denaturing of the text. Now I can't produce any sort of recipe or a series of linguistic prescriptions in advance of any particular work which will allow one to say, 'This is what you mustn't do, ever!' Until an individual instance has been produced I wouldn't actually be able to say in advance how not to denature a text. I could say that certain given examples, once they had occurred, were instances of denatured text, but I couldn't tell in advance how not to do it.

RB Yes, I understand that. Could we move on to the question of how you personally go about the business of directing a Shakespeare play – what would you single out as the first step in the sequence?

JM Well, I think it varies from play to play. It varies from moment to moment in one's own career. I don't think there is, again, a set recipe or a series of ordered steps that one moves along in order to arrive at a full production. It happens in different ways, in different plays, as I say, according to one's mood. Sometimes one has a very large, generalised notion about the overall meaning of the play, that may be a moral meaning, in terms of the individual human motives of the play which one has discerned in the text, or it may be some rather emblematic theme which one has extracted from the play as a whole, or it may be something much less generalised. One may almost, in a sort of hallucinatory moment, have overheard in one's mind's ear two phrases out of the play spoken and inflected in a certain way which then act as a sort of nucleus, or a crystal, which then consolidate the rest of the text – that if a given line is being spoken in a certain way or a certain tone of voice, with a certain form or a certain inflection, then other inflections must follow from it in other parts of the text which one has not overheard in this way and, very often, a production will start from one hallucinatory inflection which one has overheard in one's mind's ear when thinking about it, or perhaps when not even thinking about it; it may just suddenly come out of the blue.

RB This inflection, then, is not something which in the first instance occurs in an actor; this is something that occurs to you personally, in your mind alone.

JM Often before I've ever met any actors and before I've actually seen a cast who might be used to inflect it in that way. It is like one of those spirit voices that suddenly speaks in the street and you hear it uttering a line in a certain way, and the way in which that line is uttered bends the rest of the play accordingly. I can give you an example. When I was going to do *The Merchant of Venice* – I was asked to do *The Merchant of Venice*, so that in a sense the initiative for doing the play in the first place was not mine, therefore I didn't approach the play with some generalised notion to begin with – but having been asked to do it the play entered my imagination at a subconscious level and without any prompting or intention or deliberation on my part. On one evening I wasn't doing anything in particular, but I overheard in my mind's ear Portia speaking the line 'the quality of mercy is not strained' and in place of the ringing feminine rhetoric of the familiar version, I heard and saw a brief flash in which I saw a rather boyish figure leaning forward over a table on one elbow saying those first lines in a rather irritable, explanatory tone of voice, as if trying to push something which someone rather stupidly misunderstood previously saying (well, I can't reproduce it accurately), 'the quality of mercy is not *strained*'; and in that tone, with the weight placed on 'strained' and the visual weight placed on 'elbow on a table', certain consequences arose. First of all, the visual image of the table meant that I could no longer place the scene in a courtroom. People do not sit and lean across tables in courtrooms, they can only sit and lean across tables in small chambers, like Justices' chambers, off the main courtroom. Once I had seen that, it meant that there were only certain settings which could accommodate the hallucination and this became a nineteenth-century setting in which someone could quite realistically plead a cause in a judge's room. Out of that suddenly the production began to take its form, from that tiny, unrepresentative nucleus.

RB So a production with you has a moment of conception and thereafter, the idea having formed, this idea is allowed to dominate the multitude of other considerations.

JM Yes.

RB Which you must then organise.

JM Yes, that's right and then, in a sense, the image of it is rather like a candelabrum, this central thing becomes the thing on which the whole thing is hung, and then there is a whole series of dependent ornaments which fall from that central conception. Although, in fact, as far as the play is concerned, it may not be a central conception, it's only central in that that was the one that initiated the first step. As the play then develops other interests may shift the emphasis, but the emphasis would not shift in the way that they had shifted had it not started in that particular hallucination.

RB What seems fascinating to me here is that your approach has, from the outset, destroyed the cliché. The cliché is that the speech is a setpiece, which has no context, it being the setpiece. You have, however, envisaged the speech within a context, and this at once overleaps the barriers between the original event and the production that had been formed over the centuries.

JM Well, in a sense I am lucky in that I am ignorant of the theatre. I have never been a theatre enthusiast; in the past I didn't go very much to the theatre and therefore I had no knowledge really of the standard ways of doing a play. Therefore, lines come to me and inflections, notions and ideas about the plays come to me without that decoration and corrosion of previous ideas. Now some people may look upon this as a drawback. They say, 'Oh well, you're actually an amateur in the theatre,' but I think, in fact, it is this amateur status which allows one to see the thing for the first time and in that way it is not so much fighting against a cliché, because I don't know the clichés very well. It is just simply that I haven't been exposed to them and therefore have not been seduced by them.

RB I see the great value of this. Could I ask you to elaborate one point that you made? You spoke of the table being a necessity of the production because of the original concept and that the concept became identified with the nineteenth century. Could you elaborate on the fitness of the nineteenth century for your production of *The Merchant of Venice?*

JM Well, of course, having committed myself to a nineteenth-century framework as a result of purely accidental exposure to an image, I then had to examine the congruence of that setting with the rest of the text and the more I examined it, the more it actually seemed more than congruent, but actually very illuminating. The nineteenth-century setting brought out and emphasised interesting features of the status of the intelligent woman, the woman stultified by the domination of men, the domination of fathers and suitors. A woman with enough intelligence to plead with great eloquence and success and wit and guile in a courtroom suddenly starts to vibrate with an interesting intensity in the nineteenth-century setting. Similarly the theme, albeit subdued and subtle, of the homosexual relationship between Bassanio and Antonio has a subtle and rich overtone without necessarily being explicit as in the relationship between Oscar Wilde and Lord Alfred Douglas. I didn't wish to see this as a *roman-à-clef*, and I didn't wish to illustrate the dilemma of Oscar Wilde and the homosexuality of Oscar Wilde, but very often in works of art they achieve their richness and their appeal because of the overtones which you strike when you use a certain image. Audiences who were, as it were, familiar with the tradition and the culture at large could scarcely avoid at least thinking, or bringing that colour of knowledge to the image that you supply, not because you wish to say specifically that this is Oscar Wilde and Lord Alfred Douglas, but that by being aware of the fact that it is similar to the situation of Wilde and Bosey the dilemma is somehow reinforced by being seen to be part of the general problem.

RB The historical context certainly makes a difference there. It's obviously true that, for instance, an eighteenth-century setting would achieve nothing for the particular points you had in mind.

JM No, I mean, I think that there are other slants, other ways of cutting the crystal which would bring out different sorts of appearance and illumination which the eighteenth century would do. I don't quite know what they are at the moment, but I can imagine something of interest in that setting. I can imagine something of interest in almost every setting that one chooses. I would say that one of the ways in which the greatness of Shakespeare shows itself is by the multiplicity of the settings in which he can be played off with profit and value.

RB One of the advantages of Shakespeare is that some three and a half centuries and a lot of history have elapsed since his death. The director, therefore, has an ever-widening pool of history to allude to.

JM Yes. You see, I think that one of the nice things about art is that history somehow presents itself to you as a simultaneous volume of events in which all events are happening at the same time, all equally accessible, all mutually referrable, and each individual item is enriched and complicated by the fact that it somehow implies every other event to which it is similar in that volume of history in which it takes place.

RB At the same time, however, history has to happen in order and some material must wait for its time. There seems to be an excellent example of this with your production of *The Tempest*. I take it that we have had to wait until the twentieth century to receive many of the possibilities in *The Tempest*.

JM Yes, I think that some of the notions of colonialism – and I am not thinking of the crude, radical view of the immorality of colonialism, but some of the ways in which we visualise the ironies of colonialism – have only become available to us since we have seen the break-up of the colonial system and of the colonial mind. This, in a sense, is a general point. It happens in disease; we can often only understand natural processes in dissolution, because in dissolution we begin to see the component parts and how they are related to one another. It's in disease that one understands health and I think that we can actually now by hindsight understand a great deal more of the relationship of white Europe to the black world. Knowing what we now know about the emergence of the black world and its revolt against white Europe, I just don't think that we would have had the conceptual apparatus, the cognitive skills, to visualise that until it began to break down. Now this is not because I wish to seize *The Tempest* or to hijack *The Tempest* and to fly it to a modern airport and make it do the work of anti-colonial radicalism; that would be, I think, a very crude and brutal thing to do. It is just that by bringing out that particular theme in *The Tempest* something rather rich happens which wouldn't occur if one simply played the romantic version of *The Tempest*, where both Caliban and Ariel are impalpable spirits or gross clods. I mean, I think that there is something very interesting also in seeing the trio of Prospero, Caliban and Ariel in the light of some metaphysical idea of the division of the human soul and the tripartite nature of the mind.

RB How did your approach to *The Tempest* come into being?

JM Well, it came into being in two ways. Very often I find that, although I spoke previously about not being exposed to theatrical clichés, I've been exposed to a certain number of them and certainly some of my moves in the theatre have been prompted by a revulsion against certain well-established clichés. Now the one which stuck in my gorge was the sequin-spangled, pointed-eared, flitting figure of Ariel on wires, his hands held stiffly behind him as he flew *à la* Peter Pan on and off the stage. This seemed to me to be sentimental and diminishing, and similarly the scaly, web-footed monster of Caliban just didn't tell me anything about anyone, it wasn't a monster which meant anything and it clotted my imagination and stopped it from thinking. But I had been reading some years before a book by an anthropologist called Mannoni, who had written on the revolt in Madagascar in 1947, and he had used as a metaphor, in order to explain the relationships of the very protagonists of the revolt, the image of *The Tempest*, and he saw Caliban and Ariel as different forms of black response to white paternalism. In Caliban he saw the demoralised, detribalised, dispossessed, shuffling field hand and in Ariel a rather deft, accomplished black who actually absorbs all the techniques and skills of the white master; the house servant, who is then in a position to assume political power when the white master goes back home. And of course we had this situation only a few years ago in Nigeria, with the skilled civil servant Ibos and the unskilled tribal Hausas. Now once again I wasn't using *The Tempest* as a political cartoon to illustrate the Nigerian dilemma, nor, as it were, to castigate modern colonialism or to expose the wickedness of Rhodesia, but to use the images of Rhodesia, Nigeria and indeed the whole colonial theme as knowledge which the audience brought to bear on Shakespeare's play. They could scarcely avoid thinking of that situation when the two characters were represented as blacks. Now by doing it in this way I hoped to bring them into a closer relationship with the whole notion of subordination and mastery which I think is one of the things which Shakespeare is talking about with great eloquence in that play. And I think he is also talking about, in a sense, infantilism and about the way in which maturity is only arrived at by surrendering one's claim to control the whole of nature. A child arrives at maturity by appreciating the reality principle and, after all, what is the reality principle? The reality principle is simply the understanding that there are certain things over which one has control and there are many things over which one has no control.

RB I think that the reality principle is certainly one of the immutable touchstones of Shakespeare's whole work.

JM I think that this in a sense comes out very clearly in this play, particularly if you slant it in this manner. After all, one of the most important aspects of the reality principle is that there is a limited control over other people's destinies, not just over the physical world, but over the moral world, and that certain infantile personalities flourish in the colonial situation because they meet people whose power to resist their will is diminished by their lack of skills. So you often get rather immature personalities flourishing in the colonial situation because it has in it people who cannot resist the superior technology of advanced society and Prospero achieves his maturity in surrendering his power over his slaves, in leaving the island and returning to the world in which he must actually face his peers and equals, in a society where everyone has access to the same skills.

RB And indeed he looks forward to surrendering his power to his children.

JM He surrenders three things: he surrenders the power over his own children, he surrenders the power over subordinates, or at least over helpless subordinates, and he surrenders this impractical desire for power over the forces of nature. By breaking his staff he is doing what the child really does after the age of five – he realises that his rage will not call down the tempest but only produce contempt.

RB You've spoken eloquently of your concept of *The Tempest* as of *The Merchant of Venice*. How do you now go about the business of translating your concept with all its ramifications into stage language that the audience will be able to pick up?

JM That's a very difficult question because again there is no prescription and no recipe, there is no advanced instruction that one can refer to. In the first place you simply elicit from the actors those inflections and tones which illustrate those moral ideas which interest you at the time. You do this simply by explaining to the actor what you feel the salient issues of the play are for you at that moment, making it quite clear to them that you do not regard this as the definitive, final interpretation.

This is simply a provisional hypothesis which, though eventually, necessarily superseded, must nevertheless convince them that for the moment it stands as a plausible one and they can illustrate it by standing in certain ways, bending their voices in certain ways and adopting ways of speech which they had not previously used. In addition to that you frame the production with all sorts of visual accessories which emphasise your point. Sometimes they may be elaborate emblems which you hope the audience will interpret correctly; even if they don't interpret in detail or explicitly you hope that they will create suggestive overtones in their imaginations which will assist their understanding in the direction which you feel is important. What I try to do is to create as much complexity and indeed, as it were, strategic ambiguity as I can in the production: ambiguity in William Empson's sense, that I choose a cluster of meanings which are centred around the salient issue, but which nevertheless are not just simply that issue alone. I think if you choose clear-cut, explicit lines, what you get is fairly boring, instructive theatre, whereas if you create clusters of meanings, so long as those clusters are centred around a salient point, then I think you get theatrical art, as indeed I think you get poetic art in this way; you create very carefully centred, rich clusters of related, ambiguous overtones.

RB Do the actors cause you significantly to modify your view of the play during rehearsal, or do they rather, as it were, add to your concept?

JM I think they almost always add to the concept. I can't think of any production in which I've departed from whatever it was that set me going on the play with enthusiasm in the first place. I don't regard the additions as accessory ornaments either; they are integral, in so far as if I accept them and incorporate them, then they are actually part of the bone and muscle of the production, and they are often bones and muscles which I have not conceived or anticipated before I've started; and the great mystery and excitement of rehearsing and directing a play is the discovery of themes and items and features which are congruent with one's first intention, consistent with it, but nevertheless not anticipated at the time when you actually had that intention. Now you may ask how that happens. I think that what happens is that the first step perhaps in successful directing or rehearsing is the telling of an eloquent story at the start of the rehearsal which creates a frame of mind, a tilt to the collective imagination of all those involved which makes it inevitable that whatever invention is thrown up within that group will be bound to enrich and enlarge the comparatively spare and simple idea that you had up till then.

RB This telling of an eloquent story: does this mean that you personally will address the company at length about the play and the meanings that you have perceived?

JM Yes. I mean, I will often start with a prepared speech, or relatively prepared, which I will then improvise as I go along on the first day. I tend to rehearse in a very haphazard and indolent way. I have never set programmes, I don't block very clearly as I go along. I think my rehearsals are marked more by talk and teabreaks than by what one would call hard, regimented work and the actual moments of rehearsal in a sense are glosses upon the conversations which are running throughout the period of rehearsal, rather than the other way around. They are not, as it were, breaks from the hard work; the hard work is a consequence of the conversations which we have had.

RB How, for instance, do you deal with a technical point on this level, when an actor asks you for guidance on some point such as: Claudius says, 'Have you heard the argument? Is there no offence in it?' To whom does Claudius speak this line and with what inflection?

JM Well, sometimes one has it very clearly before one starts, you know, because of the framework that you have established to begin with and that is pre-planned long before the actor comes to the text; that is not very often. In the case of *The Merchant of Venice*, it was as I described it, already set up before I began; it was the occasion for doing the whole production. But in very many cases we discover in the process of rehearsal to whom he must have said it because in a sense what we do jointly is to conjure up the person who meant something by that line and, once conjured up, he can only speak it in a certain way to a certain person. I often think of the process of rehearsal as being very similar to a spiritualist séance. The warmth and social incandescence created by certain kinds of rehearsal, by the conviviality which you establish as a director, favour the arrival of voices which will seem to have meant something by the lines which they then utter. I think of these characters in Shakespeare's plays, or indeed in anyone's plays, as absconded personalities who are not yet there, who have a script prepared in advance for them, of which we do not know the precise meaning until they are conjured out of the air and actually speak through the lines.

RB Are they absconded personalities in the sense that everybody is an absconded personality?

JM Not strictly. I mean that I think in a sense everyone is an absconded personality, that we do not know who any of us really are, but in this particular case we are deprived of even the slender possibility that we have in ordinary social life of getting to know them. We will never be, and no one ever has been, introduced to Hamlet. I think of Hamlet as a series of lines to which an infinite series of claimants arrives and competes for. I sometimes think of the Tichborne claimant. Hamlet is someone who might be someone, were there to be someone to claim him, and I think the job of rehearsal is to create a circumstance in which claimants will present themselves for examination.

RB Now we come to a slightly delicate area. To follow up your metaphor, it is quite clear that some claimants can establish an overwhelming case if they can arrange for certain parts of the evidence to be tactfully laid aside for the duration. I have known, for instance, Hamlets too delicate to enunciate the line, 'I'll lug the guts into the neighbour room.' What happens when you find certain portions of the text that are not as fully congruent as you would wish with the main lines of your interpretation?

JM I will sometimes cut them. I don't feel any guilt about this. The text is always there to be claimed by the next competitor who might be able to fit the role without such surgery, and I have cut things. I have often cut rather famous lines. On the whole I try to reinflect the lines in such a way that they can be retained and still be congruent with the features of the claimant that I am backing at that moment.

RB In a sense, of course, cutting is a direct and honest procedure. The alternative so often is to retain the line, but neutralise it or throw it away.

JM I think that actually there is no such thing as throwing away a line. I think that almost all lines that are supposedly thrown away are simply inflected in a way that they lose apparent importance or become unnoticeable. Nevertheless there is an active decision about how they are going to be inflected – so long as they are retained they are dealt with in one way or another. Often it becomes a very complicated problem this and you will often spend hours over one of these indigestible features of the text, which means fighting with the features of the claimant that you are backing.

RB In any event we know that surely Shakespeare's plays must have been cut consistently throughout the contemporary performances, as they are today.

JM I think that there are no rules or regulations about this at all. Each generation tends to regard certain lines as the crucial ones, but that is because that generation has decided to focus upon one particular plane of interest or meaning within the play and within that plane certain lines obviously assume a dazzling precedence. Another generation will focus on another plane within which a different set of lines will assume a precedence. Merely because certain lines have become very famous, so famous as to be almost part of the fundamental tool kit of little cartoonists, that doesn't mean that one is therefore obliged to choose the plane of meaning within which those lines have always had their precedence. I'm always moved by one particular story in connection with this. When the paintings of Vermeer were first forged by Van Meegeren in the late Thirties, early Forties, the artefacts that were produced were so convincing, so faithful, that they took in very large numbers of art experts. Thirty years later the same pictures were presented to art experts of some standing, admittedly in the knowledge that they were forgeries; and these art experts were puzzled as to how anyone was ever taken in by the forgery. Not only do they know that they're forgeries, but they cannot understand how anyone was ever deluded into thinking they were anything but forgeries. Now this is not simply because in the intervening thirty years connoisseurship has improved, certainly not by that amount, but as Gombrich points out, it is due to the fact that anyone wishing to forge Vermeer in 1940 has chosen to do so because he has seen in Vermeer values and interests upon which he will focus and which he will emphasise when producing his forgery. Someone looking at Vermeer in 1970 is forging a different object because he has decided upon certain values which for him are interesting, so that when even the purpose of the game is fidelity, fidelity indeed to the point of deception, departure from the original is unavoidable. And in exactly the same way, in producing a play, exactly the same thing operates. Each period focuses on a play and projects into it interests and preoccupations and prejudices of that time in such a way that even if it's trying to be faithful it will produce a different object to someone working thirty years later, with the same commitment to fidelity, but who is nevertheless forced away from the original version by his particular interests. Now if this can happen with a work of visual art, when after all you are going from one object of the visual order to another object of the visual order, think how much larger the opportunities for departure are when in a play you're going from an object of printed order to an object of the performed order.

RB Yes, indeed. What, then, do you understand, if anything is to be understood, by fidelity to Shakespeare's texts?

JM I really hardly think of the term at all. I think that fidelity is the job of forgers and of map-makers, and of engineers and draughtsmen. The job of the artist in the theatre is illumination and reconstruction, and the endless task of assimilating the objects of the past into the interests of the present, on the understanding that the physical artefact which is the occasion for such an enterprise will be retained in some place in its original form, so that it is available for anyone else who wishes to make a competitive reconstruction of his own. It's an expanding universe, there is no end to it, it is a continuous creation, rather as the cosmologists have shown us the universe is. I think that it may well be that in a thousand years' time we will scarcely recognise the reconstructions which have been wreaked upon Shakespeare and I don't think therefore that a thousand years later the vandalism will have grown larger; all that will have happened is that the universe will have expanded, and that literary and dramatic matter will be being continuously created out of fundamental substance created in the early history of the literary universe.

1973

Konrad Swinarski

Konrad Swinarski was the most eminent Polish director of his day. Artistic Director of the Teatr Stary, Krakow, he was famed for his productions of A Midsummer Night's Dream *and* All's Well That Ends Well. *He died in the Damascus aircrash of August 1975.*

Ralph Berry I'd like to ask you first, and very generally, why you choose to direct Shakespeare.

Konrad Swinarski I think it was a coincidence in the beginning. I was asked to do a Shakespeare play in West Germany and I did *Twelfth Night*, and then I got more and more interested in Shakespeare. The productions I've done here, in Poland, a *All's Well That Ends Well* and *A Midsummer Night's Dream*. I did them for many reasons. It was the third time I'd done *All's Well*. I'd done it once in West Germany and it was not really understood. I did it a second time in Scandinavia, in Finland, and I considered that it was still not understood. I went on working on it and did it for the third time in Poland; and then, suddenly, it was somehow understood. So my version of this play, or my vision of this play, belongs to this country and this people. I've discussed it with the actors here, and I could see the reactions of the audience. I've discovered that Shakespearian interpretation consists not only of reading Shakespeare, but means a kind of society that understands you and can accept this kind of interpretation, let's say a black interpretation of a Shakespeare comedy . . . Why did I choose this play? Because *All's Well* had its own tradition in our history of the theatre, and it was interpreted as a kind of fairy tale for years and has never been done since the war. It was my private interest to discover the play once more from the beginning, in all its depth and double meanings, and to produce it for an audience that could pick up all the double meanings of this kind of so-called black comedy.

RB If I understand you correctly, then, you are saying that it is not so much a matter of Shakespeare as a general playwright that interests you, it is rather the fact of certain plays by Shakespeare that seem to you at a given time strikingly relevant to the society that you have in mind.

KS No, that's not true, because what you do and how you do it depend on the immediate situation. Of course many other Shakespeare plays could be done here at the same time, but I just picked up *All's Well* and *A Midsummer Night's Dream* because I could cast the plays the way I wanted them. I just don't have the actors to do Shakespeare's tragedies here, otherwise I would have done them. I think that I could do other Shakespearian productions in Warsaw, where there are so many theatres, but you never find an entirely satisfactory cast in one theatre; you have the Hamlet in one theatre and then you have another twenty-two theatres to find the King.

RB Could you tell me more about *All's Well* and the reasons, apart naturally from the accidents of casting, that induced you to put it on?

KS Look, I think that life is not very funny, but I like to play with it, and I picked on this kind of comedy because I think it is a picture of a world that is very similar to the world I'm living in and collaborating with; and I'm trying to show its face.

RB How did you go about the business of preparing *All's Well* for the stage?

KS I think I read this play first in a very simple way, I mean comparing it with our conditions. Maybe it's not so simple, but it's a useful way of discovering all the human relationships in the play. Of course, for us a court is a court; in spite of being a socialistic country we have a feudal society, which means that the Court in our country is a kind of power which finally determines what is going on between people. And then I read in a Polish review from the early twentieth or late nineteenth century that it's a very dirty play that should never have been printed; the translator said that he respected Shakespeare so much that he has translated this kind of dirty play only because of his respect for Shakespeare, not for the moral sense of the play. I think it's an edition of 1897 (in Poland) and it fascinated me, what the translator called moral and what he called immoral in the play. And then I went on picking up all the 'immoral' things in that play. For that translator, no one was a positive person, there is no happy ending, and he discovered Shakespeare's plan with the title *All's Well That Ends Well*. *Nothing* ends well in this play, but he was not going to elaborate this idea, he simply gave his message to the audience, which one could read or not. The translator does it for Shakespeare, but he doesn't want to destroy people's vision of that wonderful poet. And that was somehow the next point I started with. Now, all the human relationships: the first thing I discovered is that the whole story between Bertram and Parolles is really a homosexual story, which is based on the intrigue of Lafeu to get Parolles for himself, to deliver Bertram from Parolles, and to be useful to the King in this way while suiting his own interests. And in this play, you have scenes where you discover all the relationships. In the first rehearsal, I suddenly discovered that the final scene works perfectly if you have a kind of tableau on stage, who is with whom, who is against whom, so that the only possible solution is for Parolles to be together with Lafeu for him to speak the last lines about the handkerchief, and 'Wait on me home, I'll make sport with thee.' Diana is together with her mother, Helena is with Bertram, and in between are the King and the Countess who are managing the whole business concerning the two young people, having their own interests to pursue. It was not easy to judge from the beginning if the whole set of relationships could be brought into a final scene on stage, but suddenly I realised that there must have been a rule governing the way people were placed on stage – where they were standing, what they were telling, in order to indicate that their relationship has been, let's say, arranged in the right way.

RB How, then, did you depict theatrically the final positions in the relationships – to take the main point first, how do you see the future as between Bertram and Helena?

KS I think it's obvious – she's pregnant by him, but she's not finding the happiness she was looking for. She has discovered that the desire to have him, to conquer him, is futile because in the end he will not be her husband really, merely a figure. Even though she's pregnant by him, she realises that he is not the main point and that what she has won is a part of a human career, but not a part of a human being.

RB And how did you project this on stage?

KS It is through the last entrance, when she enters the Court and she sees how Bertram is lying to the King in order to remain in good standing with him, which means that he cares much more for his future career than he cares for human feelings. At this moment she gives up, because she sees it has nothing to do with human feelings, it has all been a game in order to go on making a career in the Court before the King.

RB So the actress displays quite clearly her feelings that she has lost, essentially.

KS I tried to help her, because when she appears on stage being pregnant, let's say eight months gone, the Countess comes close to her and she immediately picks up her belly. It is a young human being discovering the world that older people prepare for something other than the fulfilment of young lives and young love. The older generation is fulfilling *its* life through renewing the family, via the son.

RB This is of course an exceptionally difficult play. From what you have said it seems that your Bertram is a rather unattractive young man and you do not try to conceal this.

KS No, he's not unattractive, but he is a young man who in the beginning is somehow faithful to his friend Parolles, but point by point he is broken by society, which means, in his case, by Lafeu, who wants to draw him away from his friend and make him want to be a good servant to the King. He wants to bring Bertram to a normal life – that is, to marry, have children and be a normal son of a feudal family.

RB This is a play, too, in which it is vital to assess the direction of the energies, if you like, which are generated by the peripheral figures. I am thinking particularly of the King, the

Countess, the Clown, Lafeu and Parolles. How do you see these figures?

KS So let's start with the King. I think he's somebody who's not very old, but he's old through his knowledge of the world. He knows that everything in this world can be managed in politics. He knows a great deal about war and knows immediately how to handle the war as such. He lets the young people go but he does not let the government participate in the war. He knows that the young people need the war as a kind of experience, but on the other hand he knows that the government doesn't have to participate officially. He knows all the feudal moves: when he writes a letter to the Duke of Florence and sends it through the French lords, it's a very diplomatic letter, saying I'm not going to oppose you or abandon you, but I'm supporting you only with young people, not with the state power. The young people are very willing to fight, because they are young enough not to know what they are doing; all they care about is the next year at Court and they can make their career only through fighting. It is their only opportunity. Or look at the brothers Dumain, who collaborate with the Court as in effect official spies – in the diplomatic service.

But back to the King: I think that he understands the world and that he doesn't want to direct the government, he wants much more to direct life. And then Helena comes, who belongs to a different kind of society and is a kind of bourgeois daughter. The physician, her father, the only one he believed in, is somebody he remembers with gratitude. And there are two reasons for him to help Helena. First of all, he does not believe in the distinctions between classes and the whole story about blood in the original sources is a story of human relationships out of class. And he respects new life as being something vital, as bringing society further on to a new stage. He treats Bertram as being the son of a friend. There is nothing told explicitly about the connection between Bertram's father and the King, but anyhow it must have been a very deep human connection, for he wants to make out of Bertram someone who could prolong the memory of his connection with his father, whatever it was.

He looks on Bertram as someone who needs to grow up but has sufficient life-force to prolong the family. I think he knows everything about the relationship between Parolles and Bertram: there are no straight lines about that, but when you make it clear on the stage it is apparent enough. The one who helps him is Lafeu. Lafeu is a kind of Minister of Interior Affairs and maybe more, because they have something in common. When Lafeu enters the scene (II, i) they talk about, let's say, mental and sexual relationships, and Lafeu tries to introduce Helena to the King. When he mentions the story of Pandarus ('I am Cressid's uncle/That dare leave two together'), I think that they understand one another very well. Now the King gives Helena her chance and he wants to find out what is going to happen. Of course it has to be arranged on the stage in a particular way and I have edited the scene showing how Helena cures the King; she does a kind of massage.

RB Did you depict the massage as having specifically sexual overtones?

KS No, like every massage it was half sexual! It was only half, but anyhow the King suddenly discovers that he can move and Helena brings him to the point when he gets up – she helps him to stand up. It continues like this: she starts to walk with him, then all of a sudden she starts dancing with him, counting the steps, one, two, three, four, one, two, three, four, then it turns into a kind of court dance with the whole cast. Naturally, I supported it with music, the musicians who belong to the Court suddenly arrive on stage and are terribly surprised when the King gets up, and they start to play. It's a big surprise for the rest of the Court too (as well as for Lafeu and Bertram); they immediately appear and see the King moving. But that is not the end of the King's story. In the fifth act, when he sees what he has accomplished as the new director of life, trying to find happiness for Bertram and for Helena, he discovers that his direction is completely false, that Bertram cares only for his career, while Helena discovers that she is only a point in a game which does not bring young people together in love. She has been used. And the King goes on playing in this comedy, but he knows that he has not created happiness, he has created merely a new mis-understanding in human relationships. In his Epilogue, he asks for applause, and is deeply in doubt about whether a human being can rule the country and can rule life. He asks the audience through their applause to help the life that is directed by a human being. And at the end it must be played in such a way that he visibly doubts this possibility of a human being creating and ruling his own life.

RB It seems to me that the King must have been the central figure in your production and that the King expresses the final position that you wish the entire production to take.

KS Not exactly, I wouldn't say that: the King is very import-ant, but I think the truth lies between the characters, because Lafeu looking at the King could still express his opinion and the Countess could express her opinion of the King's wishes in the same way. The King has the Epilogue and must therefore be the last person to speak. But we went on with a whole final scene where we played the King's desire to bring the people together, and he's giving up the hope of Diana and her mother to make a career in the Court, the bitter situation of Parolles coming together with Lafeu and Lafeu, shall we say, being the winner of the story. And the bitter situation of Helena and Bertram – they know everything about themselves and about each other, but they go on playing the game in order to serve the King. It was done in a kind of pantomime, they were all dancing together so it could be shown; and in the end the fool Lavache is left smiling over the whole situation, which through his experience he has known in advance and almost from the beginning of the play.

RB Lavache, then, is above all the man who knows.

KS Yes: he's very old, but he still doesn't know everything. I wouldn't say he knows from the beginning of the play what's going to happen. He knows every human relationship, between the younger people as well as the older ones. And of course he's danced with the Countess and he plays a game with her. She goes on playing a game with Lavache to satisfy herself – she is of an age where to be desired is much more than to be bedded.

Lavache has a real human feeling for the Countess and would like to have a relationship with her, but he plays the game that he is allowed to play. He cannot come too close, because in the feudal sense he is not a friend of hers, he serves her.

RB He's a surrogate courtier.

KS Yes, but in the feudal situation he cannot come too close. And of course you can play this game out (possible at that time), so that he even puts his hand under her skirt, whereupon she tells the offender he is going too far, because she would have to give up her position as Countess compared to a man from the lowest social stratum. But he knows the world and is experienced enough to go on playing that game. He knows that human life is based mostly on sexual relations, something which he expresses through many things in the play, and he is telling it to the Countess; she knows it but cannot accept it. He knows about the relationship between Bertram and Helena, and about the relation- ship between Bertram and Parolles, and exactly what Lafeu wants; and he knows about the letters the Countess writes, but his basic sentence is about the unfulfilled sexual relations be- tween human beings. That's why he is wise; that's what he cracks jokes about and everybody understands it has a double meaning. He really understands most of the human relations in the play.

RB So, in a play that seems to be concerned primarily with social values, the Clown is the most explicit representative of the idea that what matters most in human affairs is sex.

KS Yes: he knows it, and he knows also what can cover sex and cause people to fight with each other, fight with themselves, to try to maintain their social position, or ladder, or career. He knows that sex can be the motor, the first movement, but he knows also the relativity of straight sex in life. He knows all the circumstances, he knows what real love is and what corrupted love is.

RB What, overall, is your view of *All's Well?*

KS Look, I think when I compare this play with life here in my country, it's a kind of story, it might even sound a fantastic story which has a lot of black . . .

RB Humour?

KS Not only black humour, it has a lot of humour but it has finally undefined black definition. Its statement is that human nature cannot be ruled by human nature, that happiness in life cannot be solved by a good King, that war is a kind of human experience which can be very cruel; but finally all the people agree to go on lying about the world that they live in, making a compromise, making a horrible compromise, in order for life to go on in spite of being dirty, in spite of being undefined, and that is something that compared to the conditions I have lived in is a kind of realistic theatre.

RB And indeed, in the conditions that we have all lived in, I think, realistic theatre. You've concentrated upon certain very dynamic areas in the text, especially the areas of social hierarchy and government power, of sex and of the necessary compromises that society must make in order to function at all. And this approach to *All's Well* highlights the quality of the play that we rather crudely draw attention to, normally, by calling it a 'problem play' – in company, invariably, with *Troilus and Cressida*, *Measure for Measure* and sometimes with other plays of this period of Shakespeare's work. Can I ask you now to tell me something of your *Midsummer Night's Dream*, which I think you take as touching the areas of concern associated with the problem plays, but rather earlier (1595 or so) than we normally think of as the beginning of the problem plays?

KS Maybe for one reason, that I did *All's Well* first and *A Midsummer Night's Dream* later, I took a lot of the first experience into the second play. It was funny but bitter as well. Now what does the play mean to us today? First of all I've told you already that in spite of being a socialist country we are still a kind of feudal society, because there is still a ladder with somebody who is down and somebody who is up. And of course a court in Poland is immediately identified with some kind of governmental business and I did follow that line in a way because I turned the costumes into court from the Polish Baroque period. So they were Polish nobles dealing with Polish problems, because the problems of Egeus and Hermia and Helena and the young men are for us a conflict between the young and the old generations and the Court (of Theseus, in this case) has to solve the problem and has to decide whom it is for. For a long time he tries to get out of this difficulty and nature finally decides for Theseus what he has to be for. The young people in the end find themselves the way they would wish. But behind this is the story of Titania and Oberon, which has to be interpreted in my country in a certain way. Of course they are gods. What do gods mean to us? They are free. They live more than one human life and they have much more experience than one single life here can. All the mythological background is used to depict a couple staying together but having different interests in the world. Titania is now taking over the power in this, let's say fantastic government, having the fairies; Oberon has his fairies too, but they have already divided their kingdom into two parts, so that Oberon has the final decision in what he wants to do, but he cares much more for sensual life and the Queen, Titania, cares much more for harmony in the kingdom.

RB 'Harmony' you take to include the commitment to past relationships, which is the reason Titania gives for not handing over the changeling that Oberon desires?

KS Yes, I'd say Titania wants more and more control in ruling the country, and she cuts down every human sensual relationship – that's the reason why Oberon tries to punish her with Bottom. Now having these two lovers here is not a fantastic story, it is a sexual story and a political story in one. But I think the most important thing is of a kind that there hasn't even been in this country – there are still courts that are above us which have a different kind of independence, a different order of human behaviour: they are not bound to any other court any more. But in *A Midsummer Night's Dream* you have many levels, you have Titania and Oberon, you have the Court which is already bound to a situation and you have a third level, the craftsmen and working classes. To me, the main point became this: I could not understand why in *A Midsummer Night's Dream* the fifth act is just an epilogue. Everything is finished, they are in full harmony, having found each other, and the Duke's very happy because everything has gone the way he wanted it. And then you have the third group, the workers, who provide an Epilogue by putting on a show, but I still believe that Shakespeare intended to hold a mirror to the Court through the workers. Of course it is easy to identify symbols here, and we tried to show the Moon as a kind of allegory of human desires and human dreams, to show the Lion as a kind of governmental power and the Wall as being the older generation separating the young lovers. The moment you establish all the symbols like that, you can go on to state who does understand the real story, because on the one side Theseus understands everything, he understands the correspondence and who else could there be? I think Hippolyta understands them (but she doesn't respect them) and the man who wrote the play, Quince.

There was an actors' group with the man who wrote the play, consisting of Bottom, the man who plays Thisbe, and two or three more. They're not professional actors, they're amateurs, and they are delegated from the unions, which is natural enough here but which is also in Shakespeare's lines. They meet for the first time, and he looks at them and invents his play, scene by scene, for the first version of the play is different from the last one which he puts on in front of the Court. He uses one for the powerful Lion and one for the Moon – there must be something in their expression to cast them like that – and uses one for the Wall. They are not professionals, but they know that something can be accomplished in front of the Court, but they are frightened of going too far in case they are punished for it. The old man who writes the play, Quince, is completely aware of everything, and he is not frightened to put his vision of the world to the test in front of the Court. It might sound very complicated, but I think it *is* very complicated and very true to life. Now the man who plays the Lion, Snug, and the one who plays the Moon and the third one who is the Wall, they don't know what they are playing. Quince uses them and is glad they don't understand the meaning. He produces a play that is deeply linked with the story of the Court during the recent period, and you have the line and acting when Theseus comes and says, 'You are very well', because the line was punishing someone and they are brought by the Moon because human fantasy is not very useful in the Court. The young people follow Theseus' lead and are already completely corrupted by the Court. They only try to support Theseus in what they think is his opinion. But Theseus is wiser than the young people and he permits the play to be produced, even though it speaks the truth about the life of the Court. And he allows it to go on to the end, but when it comes to the Epilogue, he says, 'No epilogue, I pray you . . . But come, your Bergomask,' which to us is a kind of folk dance. Of course we dance folk dances everywhere when we don't speak the truth about the government. So it has a double meaning in my country: the folk dance is a substitute for the truth being told. The truth would be the Epilogue he never speaks. And I think it is the story of the man who wrote the play, who wanted to bring the truth to the Court as seen by the working classes, who fails in his bid to be a poet for the Court and to speak the truth. Because Bottom takes over the action and he gives Theseus the opportunity, 'Will it please you to see the epilogue, or to hear a Bergomask dance between two of our company?' and of course Theseus chooses the dance, and the idiotic dance is the end. Quince disappears and he has to go away because he has failed to tell the truth about the life of the Court, about life generally.

RB But what was the truth of the message that Quince wished to deliver to the Court?

KS I think it's a secret, but not such a secret! But the secret would be that he would say that every human feeling can be corrupted by state power. He never comes to this point in the play: they all disappear and the actors are very happy, because they were applauded by the Court. The only man whose tragedy it is is the one who wrote the play that could never come to the Epilogue. He showed a fragment of action, a kind of analogue, a story of what happened in the Court in the four preceding acts, but he could never speak the final position, which is what he thinks about this kind of world.

RB Can you elaborate the importance of this message that

Quince is trying to get over and particularly why it bears upon the whole theme of state power?

KS Look, Quince is to my mind very well informed as to what is going on in the Court. He knows about the two couples and he constructs a play from real facts which are happening in the Court – people must have known them, so he knew. He constructs a play, from known facts, which would have something to do with reality. The reality of the Court concerns couples and he has turned two couples into one couple. When he mentions Helen and Limander instead of Hero and Lysander, the association immediately comes out and he is clearly talking about the Court story which appeared two nights previously. Now, all these young people are present and are watching this play, and Theseus understands immediately that he is talking about what has happened in the Court. And he respects it, until the point when he has to compare it with the opinion of the young people about themselves, because they are already corrupted, having arrived at this point in their career at Court. They believe they are happy, they are brought by nature together and we know that it is not quite like that. And there is Hippolyta. She is not full of understanding, she wishes to punish the people for going too far, but Theseus allows them to go on telling the truth in the Epilogue and Bottom, being, let's say, a rather corrupted actor who cares much more for his career than for the message he has to deliver, gives Theseus his chance to choose the Bergomask instead of the Epilogue. It is a tragic exit for Quince. He did not come to the last words he wished to speak, because the action had taken over and the actors had taken over the message he wanted to deliver, the truth that he believed in and had wanted to say in his old age (thus I cast him); and he was allowed only to dance an idiotic dance in the end. And the Court applauds, because a dance is a solution for every situation – much more than an Epilogue is.

RB The play scene in A Midsummer Night's Dream is an anticipation of the play-within-a-play scene, the Mousetrap scene, in Hamlet, in that both scenes are really designed to elicit a certain response from the head of the government.

KS I think that it is a great invention of Shakespeare's, his creation of theatre scenes like that, bound to the basic design of the play, and I think that there is no real difference here between *Hamlet* and *A Midsummer Night's Dream*. His great invention is to compare life with the stage. He touches on so many levels simultaneously, by which you can discover that theatre-in-theatre, life-within-life, cannot come to the ultimate point.

RB One further point arising from your *Midsummer Night's Dream*. It is a classic instance of the difficulties confronting the director in a Shakespeare text: what does a fairy look like? What did your fairies look like and what did they represent?

KS In the beginning I tried to find a kind of Polish fairy, which does exist, but is very Romantic, mostly from the early nineteenth century. But then I looked for another solution. There is a dress of Queen Elizabeth which shows her like a snake, wise enough, like a human eye, hearing everything, having ears, and being able to say everything, having a mouth. So finally we decided to make fairies like a kind of, let's say, supporting part, like a police of the biological kingdom, where there is an eye, where there is an ear and there is somebody who is smiling, manufacturing a good atmosphere for the Queen. And we just used the biological parts of the human being in order to support the Queen. I did the same to Oberon with the difference that he has got his eye, he has got his smiling boy and everything like a part of the biological human being working for this kind of court. Now there is a big difference between Puck and the fairies from Titania's train, because the other fairies believe that serving their lady, Titania, is an act of homage and self-fulfilment, while Puck believes that by participating in everything he is much better than Titania's train. And – it's my invention, but there's no other good way of showing it – this Court of Titania and Oberon is surrounded by pieces of human sensuality, listening, looking, serving and doing whatever servants do in different courts.

RB So you see the Court of Titania as being the mirror image of the Court of Theseus? And generally, in fact, the Court would appear to be the grand image of Shakespeare's work that excites your imagination.

KS For several years, because this Court was much closer to Bosch than it has ever been to any other Romantic, nineteenth-century version. It had nothing to do with Goethe's imagination about the Romantic work. It became very biological and it was done by people who were perfect in body movement, because there is a special school we have here for physical training. They are all going to be sports teachers, but they have exercises in pantomime and in classical dance. So they are able to do everything, they somehow lose their bodily weight and become extraordinarily light and graceful in their actions, moving and behaving unlike normal human beings. They are very good sportsmen, very good dancers, very expert in pantomime.

Now, what about the fairies? I think the fairies, like the Christian angels, are sexless. they are completely fulfilled in serving somebody, they are much better at that than in living their own lives. The one servant, Puck, who is not completely sexless, is a personality who understands human relationships. Somehow he is sexless, because he cannot have the relationship between a woman and a man – he can participate, like a voyeur, but his greatest opportunity is to have the power of mixing up human relationships and he enjoys it, because this brings him closer to human nature, it gives him the satisfaction of feeling that he's not completely out of this world. It takes every kind of mixture in human nature to satisfy him, because he's a mixture of an unfulfilled human being and a kind of human fantasy. His satisfaction is that everything that goes wrong in human affairs, against human nature, brings his existence closer to the existence of human beings. We have a kind of parallel story. The Polish devils are like that – maybe there's no general definition of a devil, but still it's a feature of the Devil that he mixes up every extreme human situation in order to be supported, for his existence to be respected in this world.

RB How did you stage the final scene of *A Midsummer Night's Dream?*

The Tempest, Jonathan Miller, Old Vic, 1988; Max von Sydow as Prospero, Cyril Nri as Ariel.

Jonathan Miller

The Taming of the Shrew, Jonathan Miller, Barbican Theatre, 1988; Brian Cox as Petruchio, Fiona Shaw as Katharina.

Konrad Swinarski

All's Well That Ends Well, Konrad Swinarski, Teatr Stary (Cracow)

A Midsummer Night's Dream, Konrad Swinarski, Teatr Stary (Cracow)

Trevor Nunn

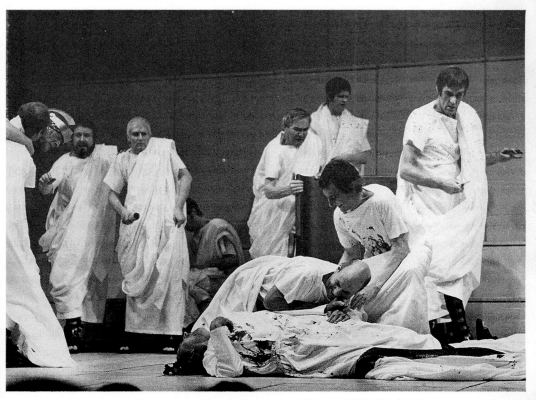

Julius Caesar, Trevor Nunn, Royal Shakespeare Theatre, 1972; Patrick Stewart as Cassius, John Wood as Brutus, Mark Dignam as Caesar.

'Indeed, you come near me now Hal,
for we that take purses go by the
moon and the seven stars . . .'
(*Henry IV Part One*, I.ii.13–14)

'I know thee not, old man. Fall to
thy prayers.' (*Henry IV Part Two*,
V.v.48)

Henry IV Parts One and *Two*, Trevor Nunn, Barbican Theatre, 1982; Gerard Murphy as
Hal, Joss Ackland as Falstaff.

Michael Kahn

Romeo and Juliet, Michael Kahn, Shakespeare Theater (Stratford, Connecticut), 1969; Donald Warfield as Paris, Roberta Maxwell as Juliet, Kate Reid as the Nurse.

Robin Phillips

As You Like It, Robin Phillips, Stratford Festival Theatre (Stratford, Ontario), 1987; Albert Schultz as Touchstone, Melanie Miller as Celia, Nancy Palk as Rosalind.

KS As a kind of promise. Because 'Give me your hands' does not mean only 'Please applaud', or 'We will be in harmony with you.' It can also be a promise for the future: when you applaud, we will tell you in future the whole truth of what we believe about the world. For many years, 'Give me your hands' has been staged in my country like 'Be with us' or something, or the actors will even give the audience their hands; but I think what he promises to say is a part of his truth, meaning that if you applaud us now, on the next occasion we will tell you much more of the truth. I think it is a kind of false understanding, or playing a game with the audience; when you applaud today's truth, tomorrow will be worse and better. And I think that's a double meaning of it.

RB And how did you project this concept in your staging?

KS A court is not only the prince and the princess, but consists of courtiers and people who manage affairs there. Now, I did *All's Well* before the *Dream*, which had these two brothers Dumain, so I invented, in the *Dream*, two people whose function is to take care of the Court, so that whenever the Court appeared they had to check if everything was OK. They were two actors who went through the whole play without a single line. Well, they were checking that nobody was around who could disturb the audition of the Court and finally when Puck was having his last monologue they felt something, they sensed that somebody was present about the Court, invisible to them, but still behaving on stage. They tried to catch this spirit, because they understood his lines but couldn't see him. At the last moment, when Puck speaks his monologue, they were trying to catch him, but as he was invisible they just caught each other's own hands. Puck disappeared without being seen – he just made himself small and disappeared between their legs. So they caught each other and they had looked at each other – what is the meaning of the words? – and they were looking around for him, and of course the audience was applauding after he'd asked them for applause. They were left without any solution, looking at each other – who is guilty? and why do the people applaud? – as the curtain was falling.

RB So the air is filled with disturbing questions at your conclusion. Perhaps we can consider now the general questions of fidelity to Shakespeare's text and the considerations that as a director you have in mind when you approach a Shakespeare text. Perhaps the first consideration for you, naturally, is the particular translation that you use?

KS We have quite a long tradition of Shakespeare in Poland, and the best translations – they're not adaptations – are from the late nineteenth and early twentieth centuries. These people were at least faithful to Shakespeare's text; even when they hated the plays I've been telling you about, they were faithful to the greatness of the playwright. Then we have many translations from the 1920s and 1930s, and the post-war period. They mostly try to adapt Shakespeare for a modern audience, without understanding the real meaning of the lines. It is a very vulgar business, because in the end they are taking the money and I have the feeling – when Dürrenmatt is adapting *King John*, for instance – that they make it simple for the vulgar bourgeois audience of today, in order to be understood. I think a part of the truth of Shakespeare is in between the lines, it's not in the words. And it is very vulgar to turn it into lines and to take money for that. I even hate – you might not agree with this – Bond's adaptations because I think it is something horrible, idiots writing for idiots. When you discover what is *under* the lines of Shakespeare, and when you go deeper and try to complete your world with the world of Shakespeare, you don't need new lines.

RB Do you cut the text much?

KS No, never, I've cut maybe ten to twelve lines of *All's Well*; and in *A Midsummer Night's Dream* I cut, in rehearsal, I think four jokes in the fifth act which don't work any more. But there were only a few lines I've cut.

RB That would be considered extraordinary fidelity to the text in England and America. What other Shakespeare plays would you especially like to direct in the future?

KS It always depends on the availability of the right cast. But the next play I would like to do is *Troilus and Cressida*, because I once started it, in Germany, and I gave up because I didn't have the cast for it. Then I would very much like to do *The Tempest*, but I still don't have the cast in my theatre in Krakow. Maybe in the future I can assemble the cast in another theatre, or invite actors to this theatre to do it. I would like to repeat *Hamlet*, which I did ten years ago in Israel, to make it under Polish conditions. I like many other plays as well! But I am bound to people I am working with, so I can only choose the plays I can really cast, and that's very difficult. I wouldn't do, say, *The Merchant of Venice* without the cast, and I don't have the cast here. But there are many other plays, many tragedies, that I would like to do.

RB It seems to me entirely logical that after your special concern with the problem plays, or the plays that relate to the problem plays, you should wish to direct *Troilus and Cressida*, *Hamlet* and *The Tempest*, which are profoundly sense representative of the problems in Shakespeare.

1974

Trevor Nunn

Trevor Nunn has been associated for most of his career with the Royal Shakespeare Company and has directed many of Shakespeare's plays. He was Artistic Director of the RSC from 1968–78 and is now Associate Director. Since this interview was first given, he has gone on to direct Shakespeare and other theatre in new and challenging ways.

Ralph Berry Can I ask you first about the general considerations that relate to the production of Shakespeare by the Royal Shakespeare Company?

Trevor Nunn The Royal Shakespeare Company works under a charter which demands that we should present the works of William Shakespeare at Stratford-upon-Avon. It doesn't actually state that we should present exclusively the works of William Shakespeare, but clearly the endowments that have contributed to the theatre's past and the subsidy that now contributes to the theatre's present welfare are really based on that one single directive. We are dedicated to the works of Shakespeare. To put it in a slightly livelier way, Shakespeare is our house dramatist. It's obvious that while such an instruction provides a great focus in our lives as artists, it also presents great limitations. Shakespeare wrote thirty-seven plays, perhaps had a hand in a few more. A theatre company operating in a market town requires to do five or six plays a year in order to keep a high level of box office turnover, which argues that we need to be going through the canon once every five or six years. But of course there are certain plays that are immensely difficult to redo that regularly; it's also true to say that there are certain plays in the canon that aren't worth doing that regularly.

Now when Peter Hall changed the Stratford Memorial Theatre Company into the Royal Shakespeare Company in 1960, the commitment in Stratford was largely a 'Festival Theatre' commitment. It was acknowledged that each year there should be some celebration of the bard and audiences arrived in Stratford very much as if they were on a pilgrimage. Peter's intention was to make Shakespeare live again and therefore it was vital that the word 'Memorial' was removed from the title. The sense of that theatre being a temple, hallowed, sacrosanct, demanding awed and religious response on the part of all who entered it, was anathema to Peter. And therefore he insisted upon one simple rule: that whenever the Company did a play by Shakespeare, they should do it because the play was relevant, because the play made some demand upon our current attention. Obviously there's a great danger that the demand for a play to be 'relevant' very quickly becomes a demand that the play should be topical. Nevertheless he urged us all to consider each of the plays in the canon as if that morning it had dropped through the letterbox on to the front doormat: and therefore, what had the play got to say, that very day. This was an approach which I personally found immensely refreshing and important. In fact, I first heard Peter talking about presenting the plays of Shakespeare when he came to Cambridge to do an annual lecture in the Senate House. I just happened to be passing the place – I dropped into the back row – and heard his theories of how he intended to run the theatre in Stratford, and how he would like another auditorium in London, and it all made a tremendous amount of sense to me. You see, the London auditorium is a further expression of that basic artistic stance, that is, for a company of actors to present Shakespeare's plays relevantly and vigorously, they need not only to be immensely skilled, but they need to be influenced by the writers of their own age, they must experience the influences of both ends of the writing spectrum. That is a cardinal belief the Company still holds. We still present new works and other classic plays in London, which are performed by the same actors who in alternate years go to Stratford and perform the Shakespeare plays. But here is the rub. To present the plays of Shakespeare relevantly, but also to present them (roughly) once every five or six years, is contradictory. It really is that central contradiction, that pressure, which I find most difficult and I think my colleagues find most difficult.

RB I wonder if you could elaborate that point. What is the particular difficulty about the five-year period – why is this an internal contradiction for you?

TN Well, let me give a few examples. When we did the production of *Henry V*, which came at the end of *The Wars of the Roses* sequence, recent productions of the play were still expressing a jingoistic patriotism which had been relevant to the immediate post-war situation. In fact my first contact with the play led me to believe that it was the National Anthem in five acts. The production that we did in 1964 in the midst of the 'make love not war' movements and the horror of the Vietnamese situation growing in intensity was a production which saw a play-within-a-play, a hidden play which amounted to a passionate cry by the dramatist against war. The scenes with the Archbishop of Canterbury at the beginning were presented as scenes of political cynicism.

RB Which they are, of course.

TN But which they had not previously been, or not in productions which I had seen. I think our production pointed to a disparity between the role of the Chorus and the events actually contained within the play itself. It showed us the Chorus as an Elizabethan/High Renaissance figure speaking eloquently, confirming exciting myths and fictions for an audience: the events which were then revealed in the play were very different, more real, harder, cooler, more ambiguous. Now, we haven't done a production of *Henry V* since 1964. We've revived that production, once in London, once in Stratford, but its life was finished by 1966. The difficulty that I now find is: how do we present the next *Henry V*? I still feel very much the same things about it. However, when a play is to be presented afresh, a designer to be approached, a director and designer to work together on a concept, the play to be cast – there of course needs to be some special excitement about the project. If I were to set up or direct a production of *Henry V* at the moment, I would only wish to repeat what happened previously. Now I know that that would be no good for my colleagues and it would probably be no good for the actors involved, and it would certainly be no good for the critics coming to see us after a number of years had elapsed. The difficulty is to avoid novelty but remain fresh. It's easy to respond to the necessity of putting a play on once every five years by saying, 'It's got to be different, we must find a new gloss on this play, there must be a different conception from last time.' But in that way the play is done superficially, is not really considered. There are many other ways in which it's difficult to meet that five- or six-year rhythm. For instance, Peter Brook's production of *A Midsummer Night's Dream* was so successful that I wouldn't now be able to get anybody else to do a production of that play in the near future, even if I forced them into the theatre at gun-point.

RB The play has been knocked out of the canon, effectively.

TN Yes. This was the case with *The Comedy of Errors*. In a season that I was setting up at Stratford it seemed to me that we could find another way into *The Comedy of Errors* if in presenting Shakespeare's four Roman plays we also (somewhat archly) put in *The Comedy of Errors* as Shakespeare's fifth Roman play.

RB Plautus cannot be too light.

TN In the event no one actually wished to do it, because Clifford Williams' previous version had been pretty near definitive. And consequently, after a long time, asking many directors what they might do with *The Comedy of Errors*, I arrived at the conclusion that we should do another revival, after a ten-year span, of Clifford's earlier production. Which was immensely successful. Perhaps that's an object lesson. We could revive much more of our work than we do. We tend to think of our work in the theatre in very much the way that journalists think of their work; I mean, it's something to be completed, shown to the public, screwed up and thrown away. We don't think of a production continuing to be meaningful for ten years. One part of the artistic conscience says that times have changed, society has changed, expression has changed: therefore the play must have changed. And another part says: but actually I don't think **differently about it.**

RB It might be useful to think of the analogy of the old movies here. Sometimes we can watch an old movie on TV – it's thirty years old and it's finished, it has no lasting vitality. Other thirty-year-old movies come out fresh as paint, they're good now because they were good then. They don't need redoing. We can adapt ourselves to the conventions of thirty years ago quite easily.

TN Yes, but of course manners and mores and morals do change radically and the pendulum swings, and with the thirty-year-old movie it can so frequently happen that one is watching a time very similar to our own, or which seems to have a very great bearing upon our own lives. Then there are certain old movies which just show us that the artists of the time were somehow bent upon escaping and not dealing with issues. They can't interest us. The total fictions of thirty years ago are really no more interesting than the total fictions of 300 years ago, or this year.

RB To take up the point you were making earlier though, you instanced several plays of which it seems that definitive versions have been done, for several years. But one can think of other plays in the canon that seem to have a special quality of elasticity; they are tolerant of new productions at very short intervals indeed, *Twelfth Night* for instance.

TN Yes, obviously the most important example of such a play is *Hamlet*. It seems to me that one probably could do a production of *Hamlet* every year, a totally different production of *Hamlet* – the play is that tolerant. But there's something very special about *Hamlet*. The major character's isolation and relation to another generation is a social situation, and a political situation that everybody recognises, and yet it's a situation that changes from era to era. I mean, the generation gap that exists now is quite different from the generation gap that existed three years ago. There are quite different misunderstandings between parents and their children – misunderstandings, fears, aggressions have always been there, but the nature of them and how they are expressed has changed. Therefore we are bound to find different things in that play every time we go back to it. Also it can be a different play for every actor who plays that leading role, because that role has got so much direct influence on the meaning of the play. *Twelfth Night* is capable of many different productions, in the sense that it is indestructible. It works even when people do appalling things to it, like saying, 'Wouldn't it be a good idea to make it about a country house society in the 1920s?' or when Jonathan Miller writes a long programme note about the neo-Platonism of the play and does a production to prove it. Actually, when all that's said and done, and we've got over the fact that his Gemini, as he called them, are wandering around with large red model dodecahedrons round their necks (having previously assimilated that they are wearing the loose white pantaloons of the Commedia clowns) the play survives – the human Viola and the human Sebastian refuse to be cabined and confined by an approach or a theory. I saw Peter Hall's production of *Twelfth Night*, and its autumnal setting and its melancholia seemed definitively right. He had touched a Chekhov-like centre in the play; it was unarguable. And when I saw John Barton's version of the play, it seemed to me that he had carried Peter Hall's perception further and in a less nineteenth-century or operatic manner – John Barton's production was much more stark, more of the Elizabethan playhouse – and yet, in showing us that Belch, Aguecheek, Malvolio, Feste, Orsino *and* Maria were all of an age who would bitterly understand 'Youth's stuff will not endure', he'd unlocked fully the dark and melancholic half of the play, in contrast to which, while 'golden time convents', Viola and Olivia and Sebastian play their games of disguise and romance. Recently it was suggested to me that we were quite wrong to think of *Twelfth Night* as an autumnal play: surely *Twelfth Night* is a winter play. Its relevance to the Twelfth Night festivities was not just that it was celebratory and joyous, but that Shakespeare clearly envisaged a bleak deep mid-winter situation, both climatically and emotionally – a much less funny play than tradition has made it. Immediately all kinds of images start to emerge from the text and yet, previously, every line of it seemed to be saying it's autumn and the leaves aren't quite dropping off the trees, and it's watery dawns and glorious sunsets.

RB I think those possibilities are certainly there. Another way of looking at it would be simply to focus on the title and point out that *Twelfth Night* is really two things; it is a feast and it is also the end to a feast. Consequently we can take the play as being either about revelry, or an awareness that the period of revelry is now over. And this of course can be projected dramatically in various ways.

TN When the celebration is over Orsino has failed to learn anything by his experience. It seems to me that while Belch and Aguecheek, Maria and Malvolio are all pushed out into reality, Antonio is not part of all that final celebration; he is excluded from the linking up which dissolves the lovers into the dream world. Feste then sings that final song, which is so urgently telling us that there may be twelve days of celebration, but we all must arrive at the end of *Twelfth Night*, and then what?

RB It's raining.

TN As my father always used to say when we had a few days' holiday, 'It's back to earth tomorrow,' and he used to say it four or five times during the final day when we were all desperately trying to enjoy ourselves. It's a strong, Puritan streak that exists in all East Anglians. It's very important not to enjoy ourselves too much, because of tomorrow!

RB But it was the play's statement too, I think. Malvolio would represent that principle.

Perhaps I could ask you to focus more closely on the particular issue that you've been talking about. We could put the question thus: why, in the end, do you choose a particular Shakespeare play for production in a given season? Setting aside, obviously, certain administrative pressures, the need to find parts for actors, the cost of relative productions, and so forth, that we well understand.

TN Can one really set those things aside? Because they are very real pressures and they do very largely control the choices in any given season. One thing that influences me very greatly in setting up a season is if a director has a particularly strong feeling for a play and (regardless of the last time it was done) if somebody is battering on my door with furious determination to do a play, I'm very well disposed towards it. I may say that happens relatively rarely. Directors are on the whole uncertain creatures, who require persuasion. Woo me. Woo me. Then one has to consider who is currently in the company, whom one would like to develop. And one has to consider whether, for a particular play, there are any of the great actors available. You can't embark on a *King Lear* without the certain knowledge that one of the great actors is going to do it for you, or somebody you suspect has greatness in him. It's a waste of everybody's time otherwise. Then of course one has either to achieve a balance and variety in a season of plays, or a coherence, some kind of intellectual coherence. The main examples of this would be the *Wars of the Roses* season, the long history season of '64, the late plays season that we did in '69 and the examination of the Roman plays. It's an approach that we would like to use all the time, but of course as anyone can work out, the number of related seasons that are possible in a collection of thirty-seven plays is strictly limited. There are many jokes that pass around the company, that we're going to do Shakespeare's Verona plays, or that we're going to do Shakespeare's Early British plays . . .

RB The Roman plays are a particularly fascinating project. Why did you want to put them on – in a group, which has never been done before?

TN I was interested to begin with that Shakespeare should have returned, on four separate occasions, to the same background, the same society and many of the same concerns for his plays. Many people have said that *Titus Andronicus* could as well be set in Renaissance Italy or Greece or mediaeval Britain. Its Romanness they say is not important to it. Reading it, I found myself disagreeing. I found that Shakespeare had made a very real attempt to surround the events of the play with a larger social and political situation: an empire in decline, its borders threatened by unknown and unknowable forces, Gothic hordes. It struck me that the figure of Titus is presented as emblematic and representative of the old Roman virtues under attack. And it struck me that actually no other society, in historical terms, has been able to make the point of waning military power, moral collapse, mockery of traditional principles and nightmarish violence unleashed. At the beginning of the play Titus talks about his twenty-five sons – 'half the number that King Priam had'. Now, how are we to take such a line? First of all, it designates Titus as the emblematic Roman military figure, the representative of a great tradition, part myth, part real, hence of course twenty-five sons, his own private army, all of them warriors, all of them dedicated to the service of empire and emperor. Secondly, one can read the line in a very naturalistic way as an indication of character. The man maybe has had many wives, women are totally unimportant to him and to that society, but the propagation of the family tradition is vital to him.

Of course, I began to ask myself the question: how accurate was this early picture of Rome? What did the collapse of the Roman Empire mean to the Elizabethans? To what extent was the play post-bear-baiting box office and to what extent a morality play, invoking the whole society and using Titus' story as a kind of image or parallel? I began to see two distinct movements in the play. Shakespeare shows us a society at breaking point, heading if not hurtling towards the cliff, as rigidity and discipline of a great past is thrown aside, reviled and mocked. But secondly he shows us just how damaging are those rigid disciplinarian principles when (to be upheld) they override a man's human, instinctive responses. Blinkered Titus kills his own son for a principle, refuses to bury him for a principle, gives away his daughter for a principle and accepts the execution of two other sons on principle. His awakening from a disciplinarian past is painful and moving, and, as in *Lear* later on, the old man cannot cope and loses his treasured reason. It was when reading that play that I was struck by the entrance of Aemilius, who says to the gibbering Saturninus that Lucius is heading towards Rome with an army of Goths, who threatens to do more for his revenge than Coriolanus ever did. And I suddenly thought, how current was the Coriolanus myth? Who was interested in that story when Shakespeare was writing *Titus Andronicus*? Who in his audience would have understood it? Where did Shakespeare get it from? If he was picturing the collapse of Rome, into a wilderness of tigers, into a brutal vengeful collection of animals, and here referring to a little known incident about the very beginnings of Rome, what was forming in his mind and what did he make of it? And really, from that beginning, I started to reexamine the three plays, *Julius Caesar*, *Antony and Cleopatra* and *Coriolanus*, acknowledging of course that there is a superficial relationship between *Julius Caesar* and *Antony and Cleopatra* because they share some of the same characters, but they're written in very different styles. It occurred to me more and more that Shakespeare seemed to be finding, by using the Roman background, Roman imagery, the opportunity to make free comment about political issues he just wasn't able to when writing the English history plays. There was always the overriding factor of having to support the Tudor dynasty, though of course the kind of true king/false king arguments that run through these plays is fascinating. Nevertheless, there clearly is no *freedom* for the dramatist to express himself and in the Roman plays he does go much further. Now Shakespeare, like all great dramatists, finds it impossible to write about a character other than from the point of view of that character and consequently he's no propagandist. And I certainly didn't do these plays to try to prove that Shakespeare was in any sense presenting finished and coherent political conclusions.

RB I think there are really two theses here, which I personally find very convincing. One is that Shakespeare's plays are among other things dramatic notebooks, in which he alludes in code form, if you like, to unwritten plays he's going to get around to later. Your Coriolanus reference in *Titus Andronicus* seems to me a persuasive example of this. And the other thesis is that Shakespeare has a certain idea of Rome that remains, very broadly, a constant in his life and Rome is, among other things, a way of writing about political problems in such a way that they are virtually free from censorship, they are not taken (perhaps) to allude to contemporary England.

TN Having started on this line of enquiry, I wanted to present just the three plays, *Julius Caesar*, *Antony and Cleopatra* and *Coriolanus*, insisting of course that there was no special chronological significance about them; there was nothing of the history cycle in them. But it seemed to me that it was a great shame not to examine *Titus Andronicus* again too, so I decided to do all four, really in a manner of open enquiry. I was not expecting to find clear relationships between them, but I wanted myself and the actors to *find out*. It seemed to me that it would be a pretty dry and academic exercise to take the plays in the order in which they were written. That couldn't have had a great deal of interest for the actors – they had to believe in the real situations in which they were involved, not the literary relationships, and consequently for them to feel that there was some kind of historical connection between the plays was, I think, a good and productive thing for them. They did a great deal of background work which I think helped the plays in performance. Of course it's inevitable that, having presented the plays in one season, there should be comparison with the *Wars of the Roses* sequence, although no comparison is possible.

RB Essentially, the *Wars of the Roses* formed a narrative, and the Roman plays, whatever else they are, are not a narrative. They are ways of opening out, spatially, areas of political action and conduct.

TN Yes. Of course, they all introduce the theme of the disparity and friction between private and public. I mean, private morality and public necessity. I think the biggest contribution that we made in doing the plays was to reveal more of the character of Brutus and the position of *Julius Caesar* in Shakespeare's development. I began to understand that it was much more closely related to *Hamlet* than I had previously reckoned – to realise that Brutus was faced with the problem of assassinating his best friend and therefore has to make a moral/political choice.

RB I found your *Julius Caesar* startlingly original in at least two major ways, in terms of character presentation. Your Caesar was the first I've ever seen who's really struck me as being dangerous, an enemy to the state. Every other Caesar has appeared to me as a sort of company chairman, who's a little bit over the top, and the Board are getting rather restive about him. He doesn't really seem that much of a problem. He does in your production. And the other is Brutus. Every other production I've seen takes at face value the adjective that is applied to him constantly throughout the play, 'the noble Brutus'. Your production questions this. And taken together, this sheds a flood of light on the play for me.

TN Yes. Brutus himself questions his nobility. He questions himself and his own actions constantly. When at the height of the tent scene Brutus turns on Cassius and says, 'I shall be glad to learn of *noble* men,' it's a vicious taunt at Cassius, but I also think it's an indication of the self-revulsion that is in him. We were able to find a complete continuity for the character by questioning that endlessly repeated adjective. Viewed through Cassius' (myopic) eyes, Caesar is fundamentally *ignoble* in wishing to retain and consolidate power. The aristocratic tradition is otherwise, a commitment to preserve the idea of equality and freedom – as John Wood (who played Brutus) once pointed out, freedom for Cassius to dislike Caesar publicly without fear of arrest. Both Brutus and Cassius die amidst uncertainty, but they know that a whole era has come to an end. 'It is *impossible* that Rome shall ever breed thy fellow' – because Rome has changed. 'Our day is gone,' says Titinius. The opportunists and empire builders have taken over. So far as Caesar is concerned – I was reading recently a review by Bernard Crick who, writing about the plays, lamented that we had chosen a simple and naïve Mussolini-like solution for the character, and pointed out that the problem Shakespeare is dealing with is less obvious than that. It seems to me he has put his finger on the difficulty with the play in performance. If one doesn't suggest that Caesar is fast becoming a military dictator – I mean, that after the civil war he has total control of the army and therefore cannot be removed; he can't be voted out and he's not going to move over to let somebody else enjoy that power he has fought for – if one doesn't suggest that military power supports him and if he doesn't in some way embody the military power, then obviously we get to the moment of his assassination and we just think that it's dreadfully unfair and dreadfully unnecessary that so many people should set upon a harmless, defenceless senator.

There's a great deal of evidence in the play that Caesar has reached a point of dangerous insanity, not only from the number of times that he refers to himself in the third person and as an institution, not only in the terrifying 'Northern Star' speech just before the assassination, but in little references like the one from Casca, 'There was more foolery yet . . .' What happens to the two tribunes? This is something that I haven't picked up in any previous production – maybe that's because I wasn't concentrating – but Casca says that Marullus and Flavius, the tribunes of the people, 'for pulling scarfs off Caesar's images, are put to silence'. Surely he means they've been executed. It's been very sudden. Two men in high office have been executed and all they did was to pull down a decoration off an image which until last year no one was allowed to put up in the first place. Now that's deeply sinister and deeply disturbing: the cult of the individual leader has arrived, fascist control has happened. It can be argued that it's a tiny reference to it, but I believe that what Shakespeare is trying to do at the moment is to suggest that these things cannot be openly discussed; and why Brutus has to pluck Casca by the sleeve is because it is no longer possible to go up to Casca and say, 'Hey, what just happened?' It has to be secret, cloak and dagger. A police state is either in existence or is imminent, everybody is going to report everybody else. Can Cassius trust Brutus, who, after all, when the play begins, is a chief adviser to the supremo? Can Casca be trusted? Where does Artemidorus get his information from? So I think one has to be that graphic in a stage production. On the other hand we did try very hard to show Caesar's humanity – wherever it exists in the text. Again, it seems to me it's not Shakespeare's primary concern – at the beginning of the play we tried to present a relationship with Antony from the little suggestions of 'you and I like plays and Cassius doesn't' or 'you and I laugh a lot and Cassius doesn't', but actually there are no opportunities in the play for Caesar to laugh a lot. He's constantly disturbed by soothsayers, by prophecies and by premonitions of one sort or another; he is decidedly unrelaxed, fainting, angry, disputatious.

RB You worked in too that nice line that Jonson reports, 'Caesar did never wrong, but with just cause.'

TN I'm sure that's the original. If one does take that to be the line, it's the ultimate statement of the power-obsessed dictator. Papal infallibility, etc.

RB I'm glad you replaced that line. It was too good to be taken out just because Jonson laughed at it.

TN I get the feeling that something like that must have happened.

RB And *Coriolanus?*

TN *Coriolanus* really is my favourite play, and I am annoyed that I can't get it as clear and as good in performance as I want it. Here is the example of the mature Shakespeare adopting every possible point of view through his characters, approving of nobody, but rejecting nobody – and so allowing a complex debate to occur.

RB How did your actors experience the problems of the Roman plays? How did they react to the text and its difficulties? What did you find to be the major difficulties at the rehearsal stage?

TN We began in ideal circumstances. We had a four-week period in London with a totally available company, which is rare, a large bare rehearsal room and no restrictions on the scheduling of rehearsals or undue pressures of time. So we talked and we improvised a great deal. We improvised every single situation in *Coriolanus*, we improvised a lot of *Julius Caesar*, nothing more memorably than the assassination. I only wish I could have recaptured what happened in the rehearsal room when some of the actors were using texts and some of the actors, overwhelmed, were using the only words that occurred to them at the moment.

RB If I can speak as a member of the audience here, something special unquestionably did come through. What was particularly powerful about the assassination as you staged it was that the emotional effect came after the killing, rather than the event itself. The reactions of the assassins to the deed that they had done was the most powerful stroke of theatre.

TN That's exactly what happened at the improvisation. The incident was quick, many people had no time to move and some people genuinely thought that some joke was being played. We discovered why it could be possible for the Senate area to be surrounded by guards, yet for none of them to prevent the killing. The four guards were positioned quite close to Caesar. They had been told that their job on which their lives depended was to prevent any harm happening to Caesar at any time, but they still didn't move. We conducted a series of interviews after the event to try to find out from people, as it would be TV reporters trying to find out; what did they feel? What happened? Give us your version. And the guards were agreed that it wasn't their place to go into the middle of the Senate floor. That's where the politicians went, that's where the great speeches were given. Whatever happened there, it was not for them to interfere. But then we also discovered that once the assassination had happened, there was a long, stunned time, when nobody said or felt anything. Then there was pandemonium, which of course is exactly noted in the text. Shakespeare's naturalistic writing amazes me. He is so accurate. In improvisation John Wood desperately required to be able to say to everybody, 'Stand still,' he needed to impose some order or pattern. And then contradictorily, he had the feeling that everybody else must go away, for the double reason that the responsible people must now deal with the immediate aftermath, and if people were going to get hurt it should be himself and his colleagues and not innocent people. In the improvisation it became absolutely clear how different the assassins' attitudes were. Cassius just couldn't stop stabbing at Caesar. That's a much more emotive part of the improvisational process, but since there is more of a personal vendetta between Cassius and Caesar – this was the moment when it really got expressed. Cassius was crazed, frenzied and Brutus stopped him. In the tent scene Cassius threatens Brutus with 'I may do that I shall be sorry for' and Brutus replies, 'You have done that you should be sorry for.' That always seemed to us to be a paralysing moment. Brutus is talking about the assassination and what Cassius has revealed of his motives. I am not saying that is unarguably the meaning of the line, but in performance it could only mean that one thing to the actors.

RB These improvisations that you practise are obviously superbly effective at bringing out the inner truth of the lines, the energies of the drama, if you like. How did you deal with the more obviously technical problems of the text – I think of matters like verse/prose distinctions and the like?

TN In the Royal Shakespeare Company, we're very fortunate in having John Barton, who is a Shakespeare scholar, and who is specially talented in teaching actors and helping actors with difficult texts. Consequently, at the beginning of rehearsals for the Roman plays, we had verse classes and a great deal of Barton-led text work. Our attitude to the text has to vary from play to play, as Shakespeare's language varies from play to play – sometimes our attitude has to vary from scene to scene, because Shakespeare's language varies from scene to scene. We mustn't *generalise*. The modern actor confronted with a complex Shakespearian text generalises. He tries to suck out its emotional meaning; he re-presents the text with a generalised colouring of the words which he believes will somehow communicate that emotional meaning. And he won't be specific, he won't coin language at the very moment when it is emotionally necessary. I have done some work with a remarkable voice teacher called Kristen Linklater. Her most eloquent instruction is 'Don't colour the words; let the words colour you.' But 'letting' or 'allowing' is the most difficult process for an actor. It takes such a long time and such a lot of trust. The only satisfactory approach that I have ever found with a difficult text is to start with the totally naturalistic situation. To work at communicating that situation until language of greater complexity becomes necessary. Until the full text that Shakespeare has provided becomes necessary. Now words must be superfluous. Or decorative. What we do invariably with our actors these days is to work with Shakespeare sonnets. That highly organised, compressed speech presents every possible language problem, breathing problem and technical problem to an actor. But equally, none of the sonnets will work unless it communicates a human situation, particular, felt and experienced. Therefore each sonnet must be personalised and we challenge the actors to find the situation which would provide this expression, this language. We ask, who is it about, who are you talking to, in your own words what happened? We find in matters of phrasing, in matters of timing, in matters of feeling, the sonnet insists that the speaker doesn't generalise, so many different changes of tone and meaning occur within its short length. We discover that an actor very quickly gets a sense of how to use a rhyme, like a concluding couplet, because the rhyme is necessary to support some sense of finality, or uplift, or plangent melancholy; but because the rhyme is necessary, it must be acknowledged, it must be used. Now, though I say our text work varies from play to play, we do intensive work on sonnets at the beginning of each season and we also have poetry classes organised by our voice teacher, Cis Berry.

With *Coriolanus*, I found myself encouraging the actors to forget about the formal demands of the text altogether, to treat the *Coriolanus* text only as naturalistic speech; Shakespeare anyway comes closer in this play to naturalistic speech than in any other; first of all because of the amount of prose that exists in the play (the citizen text, the officers, Adrian and Nicenor, and so on) but also because of the particular quality of the verse. It is deliberately irregular, lame or long. It reads like well-organised, though tightly compressed, prose. It would be disastrous for the actors to try to regularise it, by marking each line ending, or pausing to preserve a pentameter beat, because actually what Shakespeare is doing is to work against the pentameter, to provide (especially for his trained audience, attuned to the pentameter) the effect of natural rhythms.

RB It's curious, isn't it, that here is a play commonly regarded as an extreme instance, in drama, of the class conflict, and yet you are saying that the prose/verse distinctions (with all that they imply) are perhaps less emphatic here.

TN I'm saying in *Coriolanus* the verse looks after itself. If it's not heavily marked – and you can't take an end-of-line pause in most of that verse, you just can't do it – you've got to follow its punctuation, its sense. It's surprisingly spare, it's the language of political debate and argument. Of course we are aware that the patricians are speaking a heightened speech, an organised speech, a highly selected speech, and that the plebeians are not. We are also aware that the tribunes are speaking aristocratic speech, which is beautifully judged by Shakespeare. But in that play I encouraged people not to get hung up on the text. I asked them to learn it with total accuracy – it's not a text that's going to look after itself if it's at all sloppily rendered. Whereas in *Caesar* I demanded that the speaking of the text was very disciplined, very strongly marked, and that time and again the end of the line was important to the meaning of the line, important to the next phrase. Oh, yes, *Caesar* is very different from *Coriolanus*. Just look at it on the page. For *Antony and Cleopatra* which is so rich, so blown, we did a great deal of work with Kristen Linklater, the voice teacher. We did some peculiar improvisations, like trying to express colours with sounds and then colours with words – very tactile use of sounds. I really wanted the actors to relish everything of the *Antony* text, to relish it like they were eating it. It's something quite sumptuous and succulent. I wanted the actors to be reluctant to let each phrase go. We didn't achieve all we set out to but we were on the right track. I really do think that the demands of the plays vary: work that one would do on *Love's Labour's Lost* would be totally different from anything one would say to a group of actors doing, say, *Henry IV, Part Two*.

RB This is a matter of the most piercing judgment and sensibility, this central decision as to what is the quality of the language of a given play that one ought to reach towards and then embodying it, so far as one can judge, in one's production.

TN It was terribly clear to me, in *The Revenger's Tragedy*, that the language is brittle and flinty and sharp and jagged and consonantal; all the work that we did was towards that. Voice classes used to go on where literally all speech was consonants and everybody's jaws were made to work overtime. Sometimes I got people to render certain sections in French, because in

French you have to use consonants more, you have to be more precise. I was also trying to reveal things of the tone of the play, people being vicious towards each other, cynical, mocking, hurtful to each other. I think a good deal of that communicated.

The text that I didn't trust, and should have trusted, was *Much Ado About Nothing*. I tried to overorganise the actors in those great flowing prose sections of the play, I tried to show them that there were all kinds of rhythmic things that were happening within their speeches and I think that I made something too artificial of the play. Instead of trusting its rhythms, I emphasised and demonstrated them.

RB I think that perhaps the difficulty with *Much Ado* is that there are not only several plots in that play, but that the plots come from different plays. And the characters speak a language which is on a different level. I am thinking especially of Claudio and Hero, who are really inhabiting a quite different world from Benedick and Beatrice. It's not one of the plays in which the language appears totally to envelop, uniformly, everybody in the play, as in *Romeo and Juliet* or the Roman plays.

TN The language of Claudio and Hero and (on certain occasions) of Don Pedro expresses a naïveté, a blinkered, romantic self-indulgence and that didn't sufficiently emerge in the version of the play that I did (on either occasion) because I tried to overorganise the prose. Actually the language of the play gets more difficult as its progresses, as the comedy becomes blacker – I have yet to see the play done with sufficient seriousness. 'Kill Claudio' is for real. Claudio's penance at the tomb mustn't be undervalued.

RB Could we think about textual matters generally and your approach to cutting? What are your general thoughts about a Shakespeare text, as it comes to you?

TN 'The two hours' traffic of our stage . . .' Cutting is always a dreadful thing to have to do, but I haven't done a *complete* Shakespeare play yet. The first production I ever did was *Hamlet* when I was eighteen and I only cut about fifty lines. But then it ran for five hours. Peter Brook only cut about ten lines of *A*

Midsummer Night's Dream, I think I only cut about twenty lines of *Julius Caesar*. When you approach the text of *Hamlet*, the cutting virtually is the production. What you decide to leave in is your version of the play.

RB So the question is not, do you cut, but: which play are you going to present?

TN Oh yes, in *Hamlet* that's certainly so. And to an extent in *Lear*. There's so much that has to be left out. I did a production of *Lear* that lasted for four hours and ten minutes, and I still regretfully had to take masses of the play out. Which leads me to suppose that the versions of the play that we now have don't necessarily represent playing versions. I don't think that everything was played in the Elizabethan theatre. We have discovered when we do a certain kind of rehearsal, running a scene very fast in order to get the actor's minds really tuned and their responses more flexible, that it's possible to play a Shakespeare text much faster than we usually do in performance. One is bombarded with words, one ends up by understanding what is going on. One feels replete, but one just hasn't concentrated on any of the details. Like speed reading, I suppose. So I sometimes wonder whether what's changed most of all in 400 years is the speed of the playing. I really do think that if we went back in the proverbial time-machine and saw Burbadge and Co, we wouldn't understand a word of what they were talking about.

RB Because they would be talking so rapidly?

TN And in a dialect that would distort the language to a degree much more than, for instance, a Geordie does in present-day English. I'm sure that when Burbadge talked about 'the dogs of *waahr*' and 'put up your bright *sworrds*, for the dew will rust them,' it would have been physically and musically thrilling – much more onomatopoeic, much more expressive than our present speech. We were talking about cutting, though. Not only do I think cutting necessary, but (unfortunately) it can become extremely enjoyable: the study exercise of making a slightly different scene from the one that exists on the page by linking certain speeches together or leaving a section out is most seductive. Occasionally what is required is a line here or two lines there, in order to make sense of a passage. So one has to write the line or two. That too is a wickedly enjoyable exercise. And nobody ever, ever notices.

RB Cutting, I suppose, highlights the central problem of fidelity to Shakespeare's text. What do you think of as fidelity to Shakespeare's text – if indeed this can be usefully defined, or described at all?

TN There is an approach to directing Shakespeare which is exemplified in the phrase, 'Wouldn't it be a good idea if . . .' and that approach upsets me. Any production of a Shakespeare play that I do, or my colleagues do, must start with the text. I must start with combing the text for its imagery, for its central ideas, for its visual ideas, and therefore I disdain the quick reading of the play which produces the superficial thought, 'This would work excellently as a Regency melodrama,' or 'This would be extremely pointed if we did it as a Chicago gangster show.' In that sense my loyalty to the text is total, because it is my starting point and my finishing point. But I am not a fundamentalist about the text, because my prime concern *must* be to make the plays work in a theatre to an audience living now. Therefore if I have to make cuts, if I have to make elisions, if I have to telescope, even – dare I say it – in certain limited circumstances, expand, I will do so. The *Wars of the Roses* is an excellent case in point, because it seems to me that *Henry VI Parts One, Two* and *Three*, and *Richard III* on four consecutive evenings would be a very gruelling experience. John Barton transposed, brought in sections of other plays, and in making the cuts and transpositions wrote certain sections himself. He has been totally honest about it and has published the result, and it's a fascinating document; it shows what happens to plays once they get into the playhouse, and are amended and reshaped – and reading it one gets a very clear picture of how the three or four different hands may have worked on the original. That's an extreme example of what we in the RSC are prepared to do with a text. Terry Hands did a version of *The Merry Wives of Windsor*; he put together all the Quartos of the play and I think he came up with something very remarkable. He actually sorted out the two sub-plots with a clarity that hadn't happened previously. I did a certain amount of such work with *Titus Andronicus* – we did more than a certain amount in *The Revenger's Tragedy*. But in *Titus Andronicus* I included two speeches in the version by using a mixture of other Elizabethan dramatists and myself; I think they work tremendously well, because they expanded and focused certain things that are intended in the original text but are presented obliquely.

RB So your watchword, then, would be loyalty to the text, rather than a kind of, shall I say, meticulous adherence to the letter of it?

TN Yes. I mean, I do get disturbed when people turn up at Stratford-upon-Avon and sit in the third row of the stalls, and as the play begins they open their text and follow partly the play and partly the text. That does seem to me to be a very sad thing for anybody to do at a live performance. The play is to be experienced, not to be checked.

1973

Michael Kahn

*Michael Kahn was Artistic Director of the American Shakespeare
Theater, Stratford, Connecticut, from 1969–74. In 1974, he
became Artistic Director of the McCarter Theater, Princeton, and
in 1986 was appointed Artistic Director of the Shakespeare Theater
at the Folger, Washington DC.*

Ralph Berry I'd like first to ask you about your work as Director
of the Shakespeare Festival at Stratford.

Michael Kahn Yes, we call it the Shakespeare Theater now,
not Festival, but that's not important.

RB Well, perhaps it may be important. You'll remember that
the Royal Shakespeare did change their name (from Shakespeare
Memorial Theatre Company) a decade ago and they felt it was a
good deal more than a facelift.

MK I think that we felt that dropping 'Festival' was also more
than just cutting out a word in our name, in that 'Festival',
although it has connotations of joy, of coming together in celebration of something, which I still believe the American Shakespeare
Theater should do, also has some connotations of being simply a
sort of less serious, mostly summer operation. And our goal
together for the AST is to move into a really year-round operation, and to mix productions of Shakespeare with modern productions and to create a company that works together for more
than four or five months. And to create an audience awareness
for more than four or five months. So we dropped the word
'Festival' for that reason, although I think the celebratory aspects
of the Festival we still like. We kept the name 'Shakespeare'.

RB There would obviously be very general advantages in a
more mixed, or balanced, programme: but specifically for Shakespeare, would you see a system producing more contemporary
plays as providing an advantage, in the Shakespearian context?

MK Yes, it has been in several ways. One is I think that one's muscles, both physical and intellectual, really are different – what one uses when one approaches a Shakespeare and a modern play – and I think that the refreshing of each of those at a given time only helps the other. And I think that the form you find in Shakespeare you can bring to a modern play and a certain freedom you get from a modern play you can bring to Shakespeare. I think any company that only does classical plays has a tendency to atrophy in a way; because there's so much work on technique, on even the most simple things like vocal production and physical stamina, that you can sometimes forget other basic things that working on a modern piece makes you do. Or even ways of thinking: if you do a very abstract or avant-garde piece, it makes you realise perhaps that certain logical ways of thinking are not necessarily true or helpful, and so you might notice that again in Shakespeare which you might not if you're not encountering other materials and other minds, other ways of writing and other ways of seeing things. I find it very healthy. With me, if I only did Shakespeare, if I wasn't able to go off some place else at the moment and do Harold Pinter or Sam Shepard or the kind of plays I do in the off-season, I would feel constricted in some way. I would like the experience that I'm having personally to be the experience of the company, together, because I would like to bring that sort of investigation to Shakespeare and vice versa. I know that I bring to Sam Shepard a kind of appreciation of the language, a kind of scope, that perhaps another director who doesn't do Shakespeare doesn't. And I would like to bring to Shakespeare, and with those actors together, some of those freedoms that I know are in Shakespeare but that one is forced to use when one is with Sam Shepard.

RB Do you find that directing Pinter has a bearing on Shakespeare?

MK Of course, when you're doing Shakespeare, you're terribly aware of language all the time. I find that there are all those things behind the words and around the words; what one does physically is important – and of course a good deal of what you communicate in Pinter is communicated in silence, either by doing something or by not doing something. And I think that in the productions of Shakespeare that's probably true.

RB When you come to frame up a season's programme theatrically there are certain administrative aspects that you have to bear in mind – you have to make fairly sure of audience appeal, you have to work within a budget and find work for certain actors, and so forth . . .

MK Yes, those things are already very difficult.

RB . . . Those are large factors, obviously. But beyond those factors, what makes you select a given Shakespeare play?

MK I've always tried never to do a play that doesn't engage me at that particular time. And I think that some plays of Shakespeare engage one at different times. I am more interested in some plays now than I was five years ago and less interested now in some plays than five years ago. And I think that it has to do with one's relationship to the world at that given moment, as to what concerns one the most. I think it's very personal and one can sense that there are times when certain plays are really *done*. I noticed that when, for instance, I did *Julius Caesar* and *Antony and Cleopatra* it was at the time when the Royal Shakespeare Company were doing *Julius Caesar* and *Antony and Cleopatra* in the same season. I think that's partly because both of us were interested in politics on the grand scale and it was a very political year; actually it turned out to be an election year in the United States, and one was concerned about leadership and public images. And so, *Julius Caesar*: which is not a play that I've particularly admired before, probably because it's that play that we're all taught in America in the ninth grade and it almost finishes us for good with Shakespeare. It's a play that I've seen many times and have never had any particular desire to do it. But then I reread it at a time when we were in the middle of an election and a complicated election in this country, because at the time I could find no candidate to vote for. Although my sympathies were for George McGovern I thought he would make a terrible President and my sympathies were not for Richard Nixon but I thought he would probably make a better President than George McGovern, although he was a despicable human being. I found politics to be an almost insoluble problem to deal with and I found that to be true in *Julius Caesar*. It interested me that in *Julius Caesar* everybody was right and everybody was wrong, and I thought that was really true and became fascinated by it. And then I followed that through to *Antony and Cleopatra*, although at a certain time *Antony and Cleopatra* stops being a political play and becomes another kind of play. There are times when everybody does *The Tempest* and I think this is because of its mystical appeal. For me, ritual areas of *The Tempest* are most interesting. And I honestly feel that right now everyone is going to be involved in *Lear*, that sort of cataclysmic universe, and I think that that's the play for now.

But I find that I respond very personally to plays and that sometimes (it's a little presumptuous to say this of Shakespeare) it's because a play helps say something a little more at a given moment, or, much more true of Shakespeare, a play helps you investigate something that you know is concerning you. You encounter, or have the chance to encounter in the play, a problem. I didn't think when I was doing *Julius Caesar* I was saying something about politics, but I felt in the working on it, the thinking about it, that I was beginning to deal through Shakespeare with responses to politics that at the moment were concerning me. And sometimes those other plays don't mean much any more. When I did *Love's Labour's Lost* in 1968 I was concerned with manners – we seemed to be in a time of superstars of one form or another whose fame was really based upon personality and modes of behaviour. That's not true right now and *Love's Labour's Lost* does not interest me now. I think it's a beautiful play, but I would not be drawn to *Love's Labour's Lost* now, whereas in 1968 we were involved in the Beatles and the Onassis and Kennedy ladies and Lee Radziwill and Mia Farrow and Truman Capote, and we had a series of popstars and jetsetters; a similar involvement in fashionability was really the germ for Shakespeare's writing it too. It fascinated me, but it wouldn't now, because I think the era of media pop stars is over.

RB So not only is there a very personal feeling of commitment that you have towards a particular play at a given moment, but also it's broadly social, you feel it (in part) because it's in the air. One director I know uses the image of the barometer – he says the director is the barometer of society.

MK Well, I used to say that I was worried if I didn't have my finger on the pulse of the nation. But I don't think that's necessarily what I mean. I think yes, that's true very often. (We don't really have to define 'society'.) It is interesting that many different plays are chosen by many different companies at the same time; it never ceases to fascinate me. Then you have the many plays to pick from. And aside from commercial considerations, that is having to do the one crowd seller, the audiences still come to twelve plays more than they come to others.

RB I think there's undoubtedly a 'viable' play at any one time. For instance, everyone I've talked to would like to do a *Troilus and Cressida* (again, even).

MK Yes. I would have preferred to do *Troilus and Cressida* two years ago. I said the other day jokingly that really we oughtn't to do *Troilus and Cressida* until there's another war. And therefore I hoped that *Troilus and Cressida* was no longer a play for our time. But I would have liked the opportunity to do *Troilus and Cressida* during the Vietnam War, rather than at the period of uncertain peace we're in now – as a warning, perhaps, yes, but I think it would have been even more immediate two years ago.

RB Perhaps we could think about the phase of implementing your concept of a text. You are talking, for instance, about *Julius Caesar* as a political play, which it surely is, much more than *Antony and Cleopatra*. How did you go about implementing what you understand to be the political aspects of *Julius Caesar*?

MK Well, I must preface this by saying that there are many things that I don't do any more when I'm working on Shakespeare, that I used to do. I no longer think that *Julius Caesar* has a particular point of view or that I would bring a point of view to *Julius Caesar*. What I found interesting about *Julius Caesar* was the fact that it was an investigation into, rather than a definition of, a situation. And so perhaps six or seven years ago I would have concerned myself with a decision: is Julius Caesar a fascist, or totalitarian – what *is* he? And maybe I'd have something to say there. Partly this was to do more with what I'm beginning to understand about Shakespeare, that what I really tried to do in *Julius Caesar* was to present a whole series of paradoxes. I thought that's what politics was, simply a series of paradoxes, and that *Julius Caesar* was both dangerous and at the same time necessary. And I kept coming to terms with that in my own life; a strong leader is often better than a weak leader, but a strong leader is also dangerous. And then in *Julius Caesar* you have a dangerous man who's a strong leader, but when he's destroyed so is the Republic. And that is absolutely extraordinary, that's an act of courage on the part of the writer to say that, to say that's the truth and that Brutus, who seems to be right, is also wrong. His intentions are right, his intellect is right, but at the same time he fails through a series of very foolish mistakes. Of course, at the time I could not help but think that George McGovern and Brutus were rather similar, but I didn't any longer say that I must make the audience know that Brutus *was* George McGovern. As a matter of fact I was very uninterested, and thought that if they went around thinking that Brutus was George McGovern and Caesar was Richard Nixon I would have done Shakespeare a disservice, because it would have made it another play. And so what I tried to do was to be true to the differences between each of those people, to try to make perfectly clear, so that they could exist side by side, what was valuable about Caesar and what was dangerous; that was the problem and there was no answer. It may be because I'm confused and it may be that I have fewer answers, but I tried to do a production which said: this is the problem of government and politics, that, side by side, exist the weak and the strong, and the good and the bad, and the possible and the impossible, and that so far we've not found an answer to that. And of course I haven't found the answer to that in life and I don't think the play does either. But I sympathised in that sense with every single character and I thought they were all also wrong.

  RB This is a fascinating illumination into the director's problem. But with that text, as with others, a point of decision has to be faced. Essentially, I suppose, the decision is on this question:

how do you project the part of Julius Caesar? How dangerous is
the man? Because if he is seen to be dangerous you have
resolved, or defined the problem in a certain way. If on the other
hand you present him as a rather harmless old gentleman, way
over the top in his career, then you have resolved the problem in
another way.

MK Well, I try to do both. I must say it was rather difficult. I
also thought, Antony really loves Caesar. One can say he's a
playboy of the time. But he's not a fool and he genuinely loves
Caesar. So to say that Caesar is simply dangerous is to deny the
fact that one of the most significant characters in the play – and
when we are doing *Antony and Cleopatra* with it, therefore the
most significant character because of the continuation of the
two plays for that season – has his strongest affections and
loyalties with Julius Caesar. So taking that as a guide, I felt, yes,
he's dangerous, he's a tyrant, he's vain, he's egotistical, but at
the same time he commands a genuine affection from someone
whom one is expected (by Shakespeare, in a sense) to respect.
And I had to come to terms with that and I did not want to say
that Antony therefore was a sort of H. R. Haldeman just being
loyal to his master. I thought, no, he's a bright man and certainly
bright enough, or emotional enough, to deliver the oration, and
keep right on going through *Antony and Cleopatra*. Caesar is
dangerous and yet at the same time he has kept Rome together,
and when they kill him, Rome falls apart. And Octavius is *not* a
better choice. Among other factors, the irony I suppose of doing
these two plays together is that you finish up at the end of
Antony and Cleopatra with another Julius Caesar, perhaps even
more dangerous, because he's young and has marched like a
machine right through *Antony and Cleopatra* from the sort of
green kid in *Julius Caesar* to somebody who destroys Antony and
Cleopatra, and who seems to have no human feelings whatsoever. So that I think the paradox of the plays is that you spend
all that time worrying, is Julius Caesar any good? And you kill
Julius Caesar and what comes about is actually a worse political
animal, which is Octavius; because I think that Octavius is
finally much worse than Caesar. I mean, he has no humanity –

it's shown in the galley scene, he has none at all. At least Julius Caesar was full of weakness and foible. No one likes Octavius in the plays and I suspect neither does Shakespeare. But that doesn't answer your question.

RB Actually it does, because I think you're saying that part of the meaning of a Shakespeare play lies in other Shakespeare plays, which I think is profoundly true, and that the problems of *Julius Caesar* are only partially resolved by the end of that play. They are further illuminated by the *fact* of *Antony and Cleopatra* and I think that most people, if they had to choose between Octavius and Caesar, would choose Caesar – I know I would – on the grounds that he is at least a human being, if a badly flawed one in human relationships. Whereas Octavius has no real human relationships (if we except his nominal counterpart, Octavia); he's simply a machine.

MK And I must also say that I was very involved in the idea of assassination. This is the country of assassins and so assassination as a political act was very important for me to investigate in that play. You see, where it leaves you is, do you go out and bomb Hitler? do you kill Richard Nixon? It seems perfectly sensible to say yes, you do go out and kill Adolf Hitler, but you don't kill Richard Nixon; and yet again, is Richard Nixon responsible for the killing of I don't know how many people in the Vietnam War? So violence as a political act concerned me and I continually faced my ambivalences about it. And I thought, so did Shakespeare. I don't think I was just presenting my own confusion as Shakespeare's; I thought, it's there. It seems perfectly clear that Caesar needs to be eliminated from the state and yet it also seems to be clear – I think that's why people don't like the second half of *Julius Caesar* – that it does present a sort of dissolution after the assassination. I think there is an implied criticism, or certainly a real investigation of what does an act of violence do to society? Does it save it? And the answer is clearly no. It may be necessary, but it doesn't save it. It changes it, but it doesn't solve the problem. And so it seemed to me to be false to create a Caesar who was just clearly Adolf Hitler. I mean, there have been productions where Caesar was clearly Hitler or

Mussolini. And I felt that that was simplifying the problem. Because we all know, yes, let's get rid of Adolf Hitler and seven million people might have been alive today. But to see Caesar as Hitler and Brutus as a liberal is simplifying that play, and making the audience much more satisfied because they know exactly whose side to be on, who to be sympathetic with and therefore to feel sorry for Brutus at the end. Brutus does behave quite badly much of the time.

RB It is, of course, possible for a production to detach itself equally from a protofascist Caesar and a liberal Brutus.

MK To detach itself: what do you mean by that?

RB To invite no sympathy.

MK Yes, of course – I suppose you feel the same about liberals and protofascists that I do! Yes, I guess what I'm really saying is that I'm struggling at the moment, really struggling with the fact that I am no longer sure that the director's job in Shakespeare is to interpret it. I'm terribly aware that all my productions interpret Shakespeare in some way, but I don't think that finally it's what I wish to explore, because I think that an interpretation given to Shakespeare reduces Shakespeare; and what is extraordinary about Shakespeare is that he is in a sense irreducible, that he is bigger and beyond. As you said last night, his is the greatest intelligence that one comes across. And to interpret that is to make it smaller somehow, to make it less rich, less resonant. I am struggling now with a way of organising a production, because obviously you have to go into a rehearsal and you do a production, and you do work with actors and you do open it. And it is finally a piece. But the problem is still not to deny, not to give up that extraordinary richness that you get in no other playwright in the world. It really is the problem that concerns me the most and I have absolutely no answer to it except at the moment to give up things that I used to do, to give up saying 'This is an anti-war play,' or 'This is a play about such and such a thing.' I feel that of course interpretation always comes in, because these are areas of any given play of Shakespeare's, as we said to start with, that relate to the reasons for choosing that play for production. And if you choose a play of Shakespeare's you are immediately making an interpretation. And then my struggle is to fight against making it just about that. Of course, I didn't like Julius Caesar as a character, when I read *Julius Caesar*, and of course I was somewhat more sympathetic to Brutus. And then I had to fight against swinging the play in that direction, because I don't think that Shakespeare has. I think that Shakespeare is infinitely more interesting than I am! As a person I see two sides of every issue, which sometimes leads to inaction, though I don't think I am Hamlet, but it does lead to a pause in my thinking or action. And I think that is true of Shakespeare, but he sees three or four sometimes. And I would like that to be true in the audience. I did a production of *Henry V* and I said to myself, what it was not was a pro-nationalist production. I thought it was trying to investigate what nationalism was, that it had its strengths and weaknesses, and that it did this, but it also did that; and people then went away saying this was an anti-war production. I don't think I specifically sat down to think of giving this impression. I might have. But now I would hope that if somebody went to see a production of mine and said this is an anti-war production – I would hope that that was what they got out of it, not what I necessarily was saying.

RB Yes, I sympathise very much with this account of the director's problem. Obviously, the director can never leave the duty of interpretation. Everything he does in his relations with the actors, say, is a series of decisions and the decisions must presumably be related, if only tangentially, to a central judgment. On the other hand, I can see that an overly thematic production, a production which too rigidly insists on negating certain possibilities in the text, is a way of approach that you feel has nothing for you now.

MK Yes, very little for me now. I think that at the moment I am really endeavouring to make the opposites in Shakespeare exist equally, or simultaneously, and it's very difficult to bring an audience along with you that way, because audiences so much want to be told what to think. One of the reasons, I'm afraid, that people have been going to Shakespeare for a long time is because in a sense they thought he would tell them what to think. And then they feel so insecure when they are not. When I went to school we were told that that was indeed what Shakespeare did. I mean, I think I was taught that Shakespeare was a moralist (something I absolutely don't believe in at all any more), that he had a firm sense of moral order and that one could go to Shakespeare to celebrate order. Well, there may be harmony or resolution in Shakespeare, but I'm not sure that it's order in the sense that I was originally brought up to believe. And I think audiences still go to Shakespeare because they know who's good and who's bad, and who to be sympathetic with; and I think that's not Shakespearian. And so I'm endeavouring to change them round! With the material by a writer who has become in the cultural pantheon a representative, in an odd way, of the *status quo*. And yet of course he is really revolutionary at the same time. That sets up a wonderful tension and it's all those tensions that interest me. To get the audience to come along with you, to feel that they're on an uncharted voyage, is what I would really like followers of Shakespeare to be, and I would like the audience to come in without their passports and without their maps; and think perhaps that if they crossed the sea they might fall off in the end, or they might possibly get to India. You know, I would like that sense of daring and very often one goes to terrible excesses in order to do that, which I've certainly been guilty of, but that is the method.

RB But the audience needs some bearings, doesn't it?

MK I'd like to give them *two*. I'd like to give them in one scene, one, and then I'd like to change it in the other, which is what I think is in the play and I'd like them to resolve that. Perhaps when they go home. I'd like it not to be so linear.

RB Perhaps we could think of this in terms of presentation of character, of the problems of psychology, which one has to arrive at with any character. Shylock, for instance, is clearly different in several major scenes.

MK A score of characters are like that. Shylock is, certainly, and Portia is too – the two major characters are.

RB So how do you approach this problem, that people appear to *be* somewhat different identities in different scenes?

MK This is a central question at the moment, because both actors and audiences have been trained to believe in a unified conception of characters, to look for that and when they don't see it to think something's wrong. Audiences think something's wrong – either the actor is not acting well or the play is not well written if they cannot pinpoint the essence of a character through unified behaviour. That is also true of our actors – especially in America – who are brought up to understand characterisation as behaviour in a certain way. Modern psychology allows us to realise that the self is really a series of identities. When I left my analysis – I must tell you this, that I left my analysis after four or five years, when I realised that the questions that were being asked of me by my analyst were, are you a Jew, are you a Christian, are you this, are you that? And I said those were not questions that concerned me and I realised that in Freudian analysis those were important questions, and I was unintegrated if I could not make those categorisations. I left my analyst. I felt that we were now getting into areas that I disagreed with and I was not going to pursue that. And I understand much better from people like Norman Brown, Herbert Marcuse and R. D. Laing that that is an irrelevant question. I think that's true of characterisation in Shakespeare.

And so, to get back to your question about Shylock; I no longer try to figure out why Shylock is behaving *against* his characterisation, when he behaves differently in one scene from another. I begin to go from the other way and say, all of those are Shylock. You see, I used to say, Shylock is such-and-such and when he behaves nicely or when he behaves meanly, it is uncharacteristic of him and therefore the other actor must *be* something to make him behave uncharacteristically, or, he must have a hidden motive, or he must – as we say in acting jargon – 'take a character adjustment' at that moment. Because his 'real' character exists in, let's say, the scene with Jessica. This is hypothetical, I do not believe this, but I've worked with a Shylock who did. He felt that the 'real' Shylock comes out in the scene with Jessica, when he's a good father, who really wants to protect his daughter and who is basically a generous man who is forced by circumstances to become a usurer, etc, etc. And so, when he is met on the Rialto and makes the suggestion about the pound of flesh – I've worked with a prominent and extremely able actor, who found a way that the pound of flesh was actually, at that time, a joke! And I think that's poppycock. I think that you don't say now, this is the scene where the real Shylock emerges and the other scenes are Shylock reacting to outer circumstances. I now prefer to say, no: these are contradictions in the character and the contradictions make up the character. That is, oddly enough, the hardest thing to get across to anyone. It is almost impossible to get that across to actors, because they feel adrift, for they too have been conditioned to say, 'I must find the line, the through-line, for the character.' It is almost impossible to get it across to audiences, because audiences don't like to feel that. They like to be able to say, 'So-and-so is such-and-such.' And I know it doesn't seem like a difficult process, but I promise you, it's the hardest.

RB This may well be one of the ways of defining Shakespearian drama. What I think you get in almost all other drama is this: either there is a clear-cut through-line for the actors to grasp, or there are certain disparities and contradictions in the behaviour of the characters which we suspect we can relate to the exigencies of playwriting, and perhaps, in a more-or-less disguised way, to the incompetence of the playwright. Whereas we still feel that the contradictions and paradoxes of behaviour in Shakespearian drama can nonetheless be related to a central self.

MK I think you must make a decision. Either you think that Shakespeare had a wonderful mind but was a dreadful playwright, or you decide that he had a wonderful mind and was a great playwright! If you think he was a great playwright, which I do, then you do not say to yourself, because this does not seem to make logical sense it's bad playwriting. I think you say no, then why is that then? That he is aware of what we are aware of now: that I talk to you now, and that I go and talk to my students, and then I go and talk to my teacher, and then I go and talk to someone that I'm in love with, and that you all meet together in a room and talk without mentioning my name, and you can come up with four different people. They are all me. And that is true about Shakespearian characters. When you asked me what one brings to another kind of play from Shakespeare – well, what I bring to Ibsen now is that I search for and relish contradictions in characters in well-made plays. And try to emphasise them, because I find that to be much truer than to say this is the given for that character. You see, it's very easy for me to interpret a play; it's the simplest thing for me to do, to say that this play is about this. I have been brought up that way. I went to school that way and wrote book reports about the author's point of view. I was taught to find out the spine of a play and the theme of a play, and interpretation is something that comes reasonably simply to me. And I have just come to the conclusion – I don't want to quote Susan Sontag but I am becoming *against* interpretation and I am continually fighting my desire to tie things up, and to categorise and to interpret. And I must also say that of course as a director, the minute you interpret a play everybody talks about your direction. They like it or they don't like it, but they sure as hell talk about you as a director. It's 'Michael Kahn's production of . . .', because all you have to do is to have a sort of concept they talk about. Part of the fun of it for me was doing that and I'm in the process of trying to free myself from that. Let's say that's where I'm about at the moment.

RB Let's consider one or two of the technical implications of this. How about period analogies?

MK Well, I'll tell you: I don't really believe in period analogies. I would prefer to do everything in the period it was written, I would prefer to do everything in Elizabethan or Renaissance and avoid making another reference, or inference through metaphors. I have done almost all my productions in Elizabethan dress or in modern dress and I have always been able to justify in my mind modern dress, because I keep saying to myself, well, doublets and hose were all modern dress anyway, when they put on a funny little thing over doublet and hose in *Julius Caesar* that really was modern dress. So it's all right to do things in modern dress, because somehow that kind of tension probably existed during Shakespeare's time. I don't really approve of taking another historical period. However, I'm about to do that with a play for the very first time in my life, with *Romeo and Juliet*. And this is only because I have an enormous feeling that the film has really investigated the visual aspects of the Renaissance so completely that there's no way for us to do it; so I just said I must think of it differently, I'm going to set it in another period. It's an English play, but Italy is always Italy. I looked for a period in which there would be a reason for a vendetta and I looked for a period in which there would be a genuine generation gap. I found this just after the Risorgimento, when families just didn't speak to each other. There was a *nouveau-riche* aristocracy that was on the side of the House of Savoy, and the Papal aristocracy was conservative and out of fashion, and so it seemed to fit in some kind of way. At least it frees me from feeling that I'm continually stuck, with everything reminding me of the Zeffirelli production and feeling the need to be different. You see, I've seen the Zeffirelli production twice and I saw the movie, and one of the dangers I'm now beginning to avoid is trying to see wonderful productions of Shakespeare. Nothing in the world could get me to do *A Midsummer Night's Dream* now. After I saw Peter Hall's production of *Twelfth Night* ten years ago, nothing could have gotten me to do *Twelfth Night*. When one sees a production that one feels at that moment is definitive – it doesn't change year by year, you know, so it takes a long while for something not to be definitive any longer. Zeffirelli's is the definitive Renaissance version of a play I find less interesting than many others, anyway. I don't think I'll ever see a definitive *King Lear*, thank God, nor will I do one, so therefore one can continually go to see *Lears*. But *Romeo and Juliet*, which I think is not nearly so rich as many of the other plays, is more obvious in many ways, much more simple; Zeffirelli really did, for me. Maybe ten years from now I'll think differently, but I've found I have to do *Romeo and Juliet* this year for those administrative reasons we mentioned earlier, so I've just had to get myself together and I've decided to set it in the nineteenth century, and so it will at least give me a back-door way of coming to the play. Also it will not make me feel that I have to be different or clever. If I did a Renaissance version I would be feeling, how can I do that differently? I hate it when directors feel they have to be clever. I would probably find myself always saying, 'Now how can I do that in another way?' and I don't want to deal with that, because I don't think that's very artistic. So I've put it in the nineteenth century, and I know therefore that people can read newspapers and smoke cigars and have sewing-machines; and I know the Nurse can now be at the sewing-machine during the speech when she says 'she stinted and said "aye"' instead of fanning herself as she does in every other production, and so that at least is a way of getting to it. Of course people will think it's a concept and really it isn't, it's just *décor*, but there you are!

RB Of course, it's not pejorative to call a concept 'decorative', it's simply a way of categorising it.

MK Many people do take a look at *décor* and think that's a concept; that's one of the reasons for getting rid of *décor*. I think those theatres such as Stratford, Ontario, that in a sense have no *décor*, are perhaps more able to get to the heart of a play than those theatres that, for each play, must come up with, 'What will this look like?' And you know, very often that time in rehearsal, when we're just in the rehearsal room with jeans or whatever it is we have on, is truer than when all of a sudden the fanciness comes in later on. And I think Peter Brook must have found that out, because while everyone talked on and on about the *décor* of the *Dream* – I've not asked Peter Brook about this – but it looked to me like a rehearsal room that I rehearse in, it looked like a white studio. It didn't look like an idea for *A Midsummer Night's Dream*, it looked like a place in which you would rehearse a production of *A Midsummer Night's Dream*. And all those wonderful props very much looked like rehearsal props. We cannot use the real props because of union regulations – it looked like they went out and bought those things in day-glo colours, and I suspect that that wonderful Sally Jacobs set is based on a room they rehearsed in, not an idea for the *Dream*. I have had that experience when a play has been truer to me in rehearsal when we have not had *décor* and have seen something else happen that has been not as good when the *décor* is on.

RB But do you think there's a serious case to be made when a production points to a real period, or a real historical analogy, and wishes the play to be interpreted through that analogy?

MK Well, I don't think you're going to learn more about *Coriolanus* by setting it in Napoleonic France. And to be honest, I don't think we're going to learn more about *Romeo and Juliet* by setting it in the Risorgimento, even though anyone who does know the Risorgimento might perhaps understand the feud. But I have seen a Napoleonic *Coriolanus* and to think of Coriolanus as Napoleon makes the play less interesting. I don't see what you get from it. It is easier for some people in the audience to assimilate, because they know more about Napoleon than Coriolanus. But it doesn't tell you a thing. It may tell you more about Napoleon, but it doesn't tell you any more about Coriolanus – it actually tells you less about Coriolanus. If you want to do a play about Napoleon, then maybe it's a good idea to do *Coriolanus*! But if you want to do *Coriolanus* then it's not a production to make at all.

RB I confess I rather agree with this, certainly with your instance, but for the purposes of argument let me push it a little further. Suppose we say that Shakespeare – what we call 'Shakespeare' – is ultimately intelligence and 'Shakespeare' for us is cognition, we know more all the time because history is evolving and we with it: why may we not allude to the more that we know?

MK I think any artist who's working does that. I don't think there's any way of not doing that. I think when you simply pick up the text and start to work on it, then your work is the sum of your experience. I don't know how you deny that. What you're asking me is how does one *physicalise* that? Now I think that that is unnecessary. It doesn't offend me when I see it, but I think that it has a tendency to change the issue. I don't see how any artist working does not bring to bear every-thing that he knows or perceives. The wonderful thing about Shakespeare is that he adds to your perception, in the same way that history does. I keep suspecting that although one says that the reason that audiences go to Shakespeare is because they love the poetry, or they love the pageantry, they really go because it actually does change perception. And if art has any function (and 'function' is a word I recoil from) it is to change or increase perception. I think that's what Shakespeare does and I don't think it's necessary, say, to set it in 2001 or an historical period to do that. One's sensitivity to situation, to character, to rela-tionships, to all of that, comes out of one's awareness and does not need to be concretised by information about the French Revolution, or about the Industrial Revolution, or about the 1930s. The *Julius Caesar* of Orson Welles is a famous production, but *Julius Caesar* is not about Mussolini. And that's all you see, a play about Mussolini. And actually the issue about Mussolini is probably easier to do than the issue about Julius Caesar.

RB You've been arguing all the time against a reductionist Shakespeare, against a reduced Shakespeare. How do you relate this strategy to the frontal difficulty of the text and cut-ting the text especially?

MK I'm cutting less and less and less. I'm terribly aware that when you cut Shakespeare, you immediately edit out the things you don't think fit and so you're immediately doing exactly what I disagree with. As a matter of fact, I'm going into rehearsals without edited script and the editing now – I hope my actors will forgive me – is very often to do with our inadequacies rather than Shakespeare's. I don't edit very much any more. I edited those musicians out of *Romeo and Juliet* partly for economic reasons. I'm perverse enough to think, wouldn't it be fun to do it, but it is also an Elizabethan joke and I must confess I find Elizabethan jokes less amusing. And so when they are really Elizabethan puns, I cannot really feel that anyone will care when I let them go. It's a great deal of money less on salaries, three fewer costumes, and also four minutes that the audience isn't going to understand anyway because they don't have any clues about Simon Catling and 'heart's ease' and all that. But I am editing less and that's because I am merely enjoying more things that don't fit in. And so we're getting longer and longer productions in Connecticut! But then you know I would no more dream of cutting out something from *Tristan and Isolde*. If you are bored with Shakespeare, you can overcome it; once you have, you reach some kind of ecstatic region; it's wonderful. It's like Buddhism, you arive at a changing of your time, the organisation of your rhythm – Shakespeare demands that of you. You come in with the rhythm that you had all day long, busying yourself in your office, a twentieth-century rhythm, and he asks you to change that rhythm. And that's very hard, you know; audiences want a play to match their particular kind of hurry and quickness and I think you can fight that. And if you change your rhythm, you change your sense of time and you come out with something else. That's why I begin to like all those impossible, in modern terms, orderings of Shakespeare's plays where you see one set of characters in the first scene and another set of characters in the second scene, then a third set of characters in the third scene; and the plot, *per se*, doesn't really get started till about the fifth scene. And of course you could cut, bang-bang-snap, into the situation, but those sorts of scenes have, I find, that ability to make the audience say OK, I don't expect this to go like a television show, I don't expect this to go the way my day at the office has been, I must succumb to this in some way. And I think that when you do you find the richness is there and you notice things you wouldn't notice otherwise.

RB In the necessary compromises that one makes between the plays and the audience, then, you are drawing I think the line more and more towards the play.

MK Yes, I think I always did, but I think that I brought something else – my 'ideas' about the play!

RB How do you approach the problems, for instance, of verse speaking? How do you mediate between the text and your audience in that way?

MK Well, as Americans, we have less of a tradition of a certain kind of verse speaking. We have not really heard very much verse speaking in that particular kind of way that wasn't poor and artificial. So at the moment part of my concern as a director is actually to get my actors to enjoy verse and to see it as the vehicle and the tool with which to deal. I'm still trying to get there with my actors and myself. Most American actors believe in a kind of emotional truth to plays and very often in some cases it is at the expense of the verse, or the verse is at the expense of the emotional truth. And right now, at this point in my life and in the company's life, I'm trying to find how to put these two together. But that is really my concern with words now, it doesn't really have very much to do with the audience, it has to do with our handling of it. Because we still sometimes are a little funny about that, we sometimes feel that when we speak verse we must do it as a purely technical thing; if we are also going to feel, we drop the verse. And I believe that both must happen. That is what I think eventually American Shakespeare will be. That is what I'm trying to find and so that is my concern – how to get us, that is the company and myself, really to enjoy, savour, use the verse and not feel it apart from the situation, in the life of the character. And that is a serious consideration now. And I think if I can find the answer, then I can truly call us the American Shakespeare Theater. Of course, people ask us all the time, what does American Shakespeare mean? It must mean something other than doing Shakespeare in America. I teach at Juilliard and I think my involvement there is how to mix technical facility with that specifically American desire to arrive at emotional truth. And I think that one can say that there's a difference between American acting and, let's say, British or Canadian acting. Great actors are great actors; they can somehow manage to do both. But there's a suspicion of words in America and there's an over-reliance on words in much of British acting, and I would like to bring the two together in the American Shakespeare Theater.

RB So what, ultimately, is Shakespeare for you?

MK It's the best play, the best playwright that one can ever deal with and for me it is the best way to investigate everything that one knows, and find out more.

1974

Robin Phillips (I)

*Robin Phillips was Artistic Director of the Festival Theatre at
Stratford, Ontario, from 1974–80, when he directed many
Shakespeare productions, and has retained his association with the
Festival.*

Ralph Berry You are the Artistic Director of the Stratford Shakespearian Festival Foundation of Canada. How much does this
word 'Shakespearian' commit you to Shakespeare, in any
season?

Robin Phillips We are, unquestionably, predominantly a
Shakespeare festival. We have a charter for our Foundation that
stresses that we shall promote the knowledge of, the awareness
of, Shakespeare; and the cultural and theatrical growth in
Canada through Shakespearian and other works, but predominantly through Shakespeare. I'm not sure that I agree with
'Shakespeare Festivals', or indeed with festivals related to any
specific author. But nevertheless that's what we are. Why don't
I agree with it? The problem of having to come up with a season
of Shakespeare plays is remarkably difficult. If you're not careful
you're left with a merry-go-round choice and the plays just
happen to come round again because it's now six years since
they were last done. And that's no reason for redoing it. It's
possible that when a play comes round again it's the right time,
but the biggest problem I have is choosing plays that seem to be
right for the time.

There are many factors that make a play right for its time, not
just to do with Shakespeare, but with what theatre is there for.
You have first to know why you're in the theatre, what theatre
is supposed to be offering; if it's there in some way to illuminate
people's lives, to stimulate thought, progress, whatever it may

be. Then, the choice of plays in one sense is limited. I'm fortunate in my festival that it happens to be Shakespeare. There can be no other author who has covered more widely the whole range of human behaviour. One is pretty likely to find a play that will work for each year. I think to find a *season* of plays that will work for each year is pretty unlikely, and you are bound to have to choose some plays that are just being done again and you hope the entertainment value will be enough to justify their choice. But at least one play a season will have something specific to say to that audience that year.

RB You've just had a very successful season, both critically and in the popular esteem. Going entirely on the reviews, one would perhaps suggest that your most successful production has been *Measure for Measure*. Would you agree with this? And could you tell us why? What is there in this play, and your production especially, which has got across, here and now, to the audience that you encounter?

RP First of all, we have to admit that we're fortunate in having a play that isn't seen all that often. That's a help. It's also a play that possibly has been out of favour for a while, or not seemed important enough to warrant a revival. It is possible to explore the essential sexual core of the play now. Clearly there have been periods since it was written when this would not have been possible. And here we are at the time when people are prepared to accept it; a play that pivots on that central theme is permissible in 1975, for a start. I think also that the other themes of power, corruption in power, sexual blackmail in power, are interesting. I suppose a thousand plays can relate in some sense to Watergate; but corruption, whether or not Watergate had any sexual motives at its core, is neither here nor there. The fact that we've had a major scandal at that level allows one to explore a play with that as plot. And consequently one is prepared to delve into the reasons – not the ones that we've explored in our newspapers, but totally different. I also think of all Shakespeare's plays, it's the most ambiguous. He leaves so many questions unanswered. And one senses that ambiguity is something that is allowed; we are prepared to accept more, theatrically, in unanswered questions and to answer them for ourselves. This play is not resolved, and I think we can find excitement and theatricality in its lack of resolution.

Measure for Measure is also a very strong play for the misuse, or the rights of, women. By that I don't mean that I think it's a Women's Lib play. But there are questions posed that suggest these problems that are very much on our minds. It's International Women's Year, the year we do our play. And certainly the central female figure has many of those questions posed but not answered, centuries before they're being asked again – questions in the forefront of our minds, the front pages of our newspapers. There aren't many Shakespeare plays that have that. Then there's the requestioning in the play of who's right, who's wrong. It's a good time to say to oneself, but the man is called Angelo and presumably Shakespeare knew what he was doing when he called him that. Lucio (Light) perhaps isn't just low-life, therefore to do with corruption and degrading qualities, but perhaps is able from that sort of background to produce truth. I think we're prepared to accept now that honesty and nobility don't necessarily spring from the upper classes but can be found in the lower orders. In previous productions and writings on the play the Duke, because he's the Head of State, has appeared the one who must be in the right. Perhaps we're prepared to change the structure now and say that maybe it's the one at the top who's in error. The man at the bottom may be the one with the seed of humanity, the seed of truth. And somewhere in between people get trapped. I think the times are right for that revaluation.

RB I take your central points about the sexuality and the ambiguity of *Measure for Measure*, and I think it's absolutely so that they correspond to profound movements of our times, especially with regard to the questions raised concerning the position of women. And also the questions concerning the whole authority-subordinate relationship. On both these issues we're inclined to view things very differently from even a few years ago, let alone a generation ago, and this must modify considerably any production of *Measure for Measure* today. Could we think more specifically of the metaphoric vehicle for your production? I'm thinking of the fact that you locate it in the Vienna of 1912. Now what considerations guided you to that year?

RP Basically, a sense of repression and that could have taken one into a reasonable range of Victorian/early Edwardian periods. Things hinted at but not talked about – things pious outside, but a sense of stronger sexuality produced by the fact that it isn't talked about. The specific period came about because of *Duke* and because of *Vienna*, and trying to find a period when Duke as Head of State could fit quite easily into one's mind without one saying, 'But shouldn't he be a King, or Prime Minister, or whatever?' Just the acceptance that that title and Head of State could go together. There's also, I guess, a fascination with the fact that Isabella seems to me struggling to become a nun; she's none too sure that the order she's entering is going to be strict enough. I was fascinated by an order founded by (I can't remember her name) about this time, where the nun's habits were made by the equivalent of a Dior and it was a select little group that she got together. They lived with their own code of behaviour and beliefs, but nevertheless they had the extravagance of Worth stitching up their habits.

Clearly the play has venereal disease problems lurking as a foundation for the sexual repression. It was necessary to look for a period that contains that too, matching the period that Shakespeare wrote for. I don't, strangely enough, find the play Elizabethan. There are some plays that I do strongly see as Elizabethan; certainly at the moment, the only way in which they should be presented is as Elizabethan. I don't feel that with this piece. It's very hard to tell: there's something about the tightness of the language, the imagery; it isn't as abundant, as rich as in many of the plays. It's tighter in its phraseology. Shakespeare of course is nearly always precise, but not in the same unrelenting vein that he is in this play and that I think is going towards the military, the high dresses that went from the neck to the ankle with nothing showing.

RB Could you elaborate on some of the costuming for the main characters which embodied your concept?

RP Well, first of all it was bureaucracy. Everything to do with the Duke and Angelo was frock-coated, stiff, starched, pristine collars and cuffs, a sense of well-scrubbed fingernails. We actually saw Angelo's desk being polished by a bevy of servants, every detail of it gleaming, no dust, no filth. No naked light, for instance, but flames and oil-lamps surrounded by smoky domes – the fact that it's *naked* is immediately not permissible. Isabella's dress, following through the order that is in the script, basically a white-dressed order, was made in an incredibly soft jersey, so that although she was buttoned from neck to ankle the movement of the material constantly showed the female form beneath. That's another thing that drives me to another period for the play. There was a time when it was a boy playing the part, so that the body could not be part of the performance in one sense. Now we have actresses who can do things with their bodies. Part of the interpretation is how the body moves, how the body responds. And I think that to ignore the fact that we now have the enormous advantage of the female body playing a female role is to ignore our time. The awareness of breasts, however beautifully covered – there is no mistaking that it's the genuine article and not a fourteen-year-old boy padded up to play the role. A sense constantly of military very close to the high-ranking officials – Prime Minister, leader, Duke, Head of State, whatever it may be. Also a strange relationship between the Duke and Friar Peter, whereby one assumes from the brief snatch of conversation that is picked up midway that the Friar has assumed he's come there for some reason of the heart and it's OK for him to come for that motive, although the Duke quickly tells him why he's come there. I think it's important to smell Vienna. I've seen the play many times when I've enjoyed the society, but it could have been set anywhere: *Vienna* is important. The specifics of the locations where Shakespeare sets his plays are always remarkably accurate.

RB Can I question you about that, since I'm not quite sure what you mean? It's obvious that to us Vienna is, let's say, still the capital of the Austro-Hungarian Empire. We associate with it a certain *gemütlich* style of life, a certain array of good things to eat, a certain atmosphere and gaiety of the entire community, and so on. I agree about the specifics of a Shakespeare setting, but I wonder if Shakespeare's Vienna has any kind of connection with what we think of as Vienna? Isn't Shakespeare's 'Vienna' a codeword for a society, which he has imagined in every detail, but which cannot be illustrated from our knowledge of the place called 'Vienna' by us?

RP I think you're absolutely right that his Vienna doesn't have to be the 'Vienna' as we know it today. Nevertheless Shakespeare does establish very clearly, even if it's by some strange prophetic talent, a low-life gaiety and freedom that isn't far from, or doesn't take much imagination to see it fitting into, the Vienna that we know about, together with an extremely sophisticated, knowledgeable, principled upper stratum. I think the interesting one is the political position of the state. That is essential, it's the big one in a strangely positioned group of principalities. It isn't a major power – the Duke would be busier, one feels, if it were! Shakespeare's set it where it isn't a major power, therefore there is time for more intrigue, for a principal of state to take time off and become a friar, and just lurk around his country. One can't envisage that in the America of today. I could envisage it possibly in a Switzerland of today, a smaller pivotal state but not a major power. There's also the question of time and where he's going and how long he's going to be away, those sorts of things, which geographically make reasonable sense.

It can't be by accident that somewhere around that part of Europe we eventually find Freud. I'm not sure that I can accept that Freud might have happened in Italy. There's a national climate that produces varying forms of greatness. In this extraordinary play there's a quality that one senses, however many centuries before that it was written, that seems to be absolutely right for the place. I would not be surprised to find that Freud or Ibsen were devoted to *Measure for Measure*. I do think that the play has such remarkable, silent, motivating forces that it could have stimulated those minds.

RB I think you've certainly laid your finger, with Freud, on a permanent reality of the play, even though it seems patently unhistorical to say so. Vienna, obviously, is numerous cities. Vienna can stand for us as Schnitzler's city – that clearly doesn't seem to resemble the play very closely. But through a curious chance of history, Vienna is also Freud's city. And that does indeed seem to describe the play that we know very well, precisely because the play is concerned to such an incredible extent with repressed sexuality. Here, one feels, it's possible to pick up the chance of history, to identify a particular Vienna that we – I mean a general cultivated audience – would know, and at the same time say that this Vienna, Freud's Vienna, is an admirable and perhaps ideal physical embodiment of the city Shakespeare described.

RP I absolutely agree with all that. I don't, though, plan productions with the most elaborate, calculating intellectual response. I start with my own basic knowledge and intuition is the first thing that happens. I think it's impossible to remove oneself from that play. Once you start with repressed sexuality, you are bound to think of Freud now; we can't ignore the fact that we know about him. Once that happens, the visual side of the play leaps at you constantly. It's also extraordinary that there are very few references (unlike the other plays) to Elizabethan dress. There's one reference to 'codpiece' which can either be simply removed, or left in. We do still talk about codpieces, we do know about them! There's no reason why 'codpiece' shouldn't be mentioned in a modern play. It could just as easily be set in Berlin, at a certain time. One senses something slightly looser. For a time I toyed with Berlin, in the Thirties, and the possibility that productions like *Cabaret* have given us an insight into the seamy side of life that could work for the low-life of the play. But there's an authoritarian element there that's stronger than the actual text suggests. It is strict, but delicate; it has a fineness, a texture. For instance, you go to the architecture of Vienna in 1912. It has for me a quality that exactly matches the strictness but delicacy of texture of the play's language. That is important, not only what people wear but what they live in. 'Moated grange' is Elizabethan/Jacobean, of course, but also there's a smell of romance hidden in the term. It's the idea of cut-off, repressed, again; but it's the combination of a period that allows you to smell romance, gaiety ('her reputation was disvalued in levity') plus strictness and repression that finally narrows you down until you arrive at where you think it exactly matches the Vienna-structure of the play.

RB I'm fascinated by the untaken possibilities that you've been talking about. I can see very well, for instance, that Isherwood's Berlin would go half the way towards *Measure for Measure*, but not the other half. I don't see how Isabella and Angelo could possibly fit (for most of us) into Isherwood's Berlin, though Pompey and Mistress Overdone would so so superbly. Part of the problem is what people know. For instance, if one were to set *Measure for Measure* in the Renaissance, rather late, and put it into what appears the Restoration: now, what most of us know about the Restoration, rightly or wrongly, is that repression was a non-starter. This may be a total historical solecism; for all we know, people by and large were as repressed in 1670 as 1912. But that is not what we think we know. Consequently, a late-Renaissance production of *Measure for Measure* would fail, because of our knowledge. At least, it would fail if it set out to keep strongly in mind the idea of sexual repression. And we can hardly avoid that.

RP Right. We're hardly likely to find posters telling you how you can find treatment for VD in the period we chose, although it is quite clear from the text that it was very much there. It's treated as a scandalous joke, but not nearly with the abandonment that it was treated in the Restoration. I was struck by someone who said, 'But capital punishment for the crime of getting a woman pregnant' – you have first of all to accept that that couldn't happen in 1912. Once you've accepted that, the period works very well. It is amazing to me that as recently as Queen Victoria, a law banning the practice of homosexual acts *for men* was brought in and when it was repealed recently it was discovered to most people's amazement (to mine, certainly) that there wasn't one for females, because Victoria would not accept that such a thing could happen. It seems to me that if that could be the case in Victorian times, it is just as easy to believe that somebody could say, 'And you will be put to death for such an act.' Nobody apparently waged any great battle to convince the Queen that such acts were possible. Because she was so horrified and said that nobody could do such a thing, it was dropped and there was no law.

RB I must say I've long imagined *Measure for Measure* as being essentially a Victorian play and I imagine a subtitle 'The Other Viennese' for my ideal production. The only other period and society that I know at all that seems to be compatible with the text of the play is that of New England in the early seventeenth century, with those amazing statutes prohibiting adultery and related indiscretions that remained on the books until very recently. I dare say that in some cases they are still technically enforceable in Massachusetts and elsewhere in New England.

RP That's exactly the argument too for *Measure for Measure* in 1912. It's clear that nobody in the play believes that the law is *right* – it's something that's been left on the statutes and just been forgotten. Nobody in the play takes it seriously, they all say it's scandalous and the criticism levelled at the 1912 setting (that we cannot believe this law stood then) is to assume that it was accepted as it stood. The whole point is that the play says that it's monstrous and that it shouldn't stand. In the same way it's taken us until a few years ago to remove Victoria's feeling about homosexuality. It's an absurd law and just as silly, but it takes a great deal of time to get it removed.

RB The play actually identifies the absurdity very subtly. It does so by concentrating on the point that what is evil about the sexual act is that it results in pregnancy. Thus we have the pregnant Juliet who is paraded as an emblem of sin and shame, and is obliged to endure a sermon by the Duke. Thus also we have Isabella who at one point says very significantly to the Duke, 'I had rather my brother die by the law than my son should be unlawfully born.' So in this play morality tends to be defined pragmatically, by its fruits.

RP There's a clear difference too in the treatment of a bawd or a pimp, where presumably there is a reasonable amount of skill going into the act to prevent it from bearing fruit. They're treated in an entirely different way from the ones who actually go through with the whole thing with love, with consideration, but unlawfully bringing forth children. But I think the behaviour to the low-life – to the bawds, pimps and brothels – is entirely different, it's not considered as bad.

RB If I've understood your position correctly, then, you are open on the whole question of costuming a Shakespeare play. You are prepared to set some plays in Renaissance (or mediaeval or Roman, presumably) if you believe it is appropriate for that play. Equally, you are prepared to seek your analogue from any period of history, if this seems right for the play.

RP The most important thing is to get through to the audience. Whatever thought you are trying to share has to happen spontaneously – it must be received with as much spontaneity as it is possible with our cumulative talents to achieve. If that means allowing the actress to use her body as an extra tool, which Shakespeare didn't have at his command, then that we should certainly use. If it's to allow an inexperienced company first of all to know themselves and not to appear as masks or symbols but to be recognisable people with hearts, souls, hands and limbs, that is important. Hence using a modern dress approach for the first two productions of my young company here. I hope what they've discovered about themselves and how to stand on a stage and communicate directly with audiences they will now be able to take into a Renaissance period production, but still remain in contact with their modern audience. They won't suddenly assume a stance or a mask-type attitude to their character, but say 'I still have blood, skin, pores – I can sweat, I can bleed, I can suffer in the same way as the people that I am sharing with.'

I also think that there are some plays where we may not know the period at first hand – I don't know 1912 in that way – but 1912 is connected more directly with my life than centuries before. I've often seen newsreels of living people, I haven't just read it in books or seen paintings or pictures. Somewhere there is a connection that is more tangible. It's amazing how many

Hamlet, Robin Phillips, Stratford
Festival Theatre (Stratford, Ontario),
1976; Marti Maraden as Ophelia,
Richard Monette as Hamlet.

Twelfth Night, Robin Phillips, Stratford
Festival Theatre (Stratford, Ontario),
1988; Nancy Palk as Cesario (*left*),
Kevin Gudahl as Orsino (*right*), Albert
Schultz as Feste (*seated harpsichord
right*).

Giorgio Strehler

King Lear, Giorgio Strehler; Tino Carraro (*right*) as Lear.

Peter Brook

King Lear, Peter Brook, Royal
Shakespeare Theatre, 1962; Paul
Scofield as Lear.

A Midsummer Night's Dream, Peter Brook, Royal Shakespeare Theatre, 1970; Alan Howard as Oberon, Sara Kestelman as Titania, David Waller as Bottom, John Kane as Puck.

Timon of Athens, Peter Brook, Bouffes du Nord (Paris), 1974; Malick Bowens as Apemantus, François Marthoret as Timon.

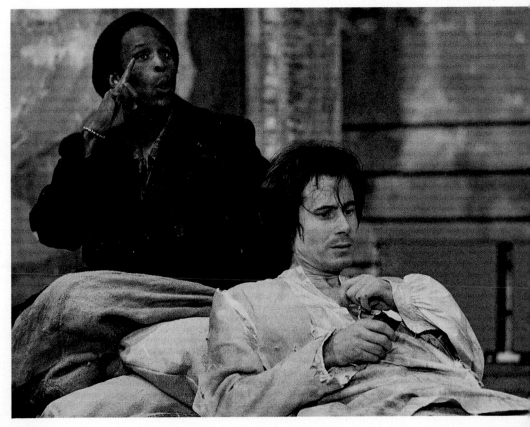

Adrian Noble

As You Like It, Adrian Noble, Barbican Theatre, 1985; Juliet Stevenson as Rosalind, Hilton McRae as Orlando.

Macbeth, Adrian Noble, Barbican Theatre, 1987; Peter Guinness as Macduff, Jonathan Pryce as Macbeth (*stage front*).

The Plantagenets, Adrian Noble, 1988–9

Bill Alexander

Richard III, Bill Alexander, Barbican
Theatre, 1985; Antony Sher as
Richard III.

Model of set for Alexander's 1986 Stratford production of *A Midsummer Night's Dream* by William Dudley . . .

. . . and the production; Gerard Murphy as Oberon, Janet McTeer as Titania.

people said to me that it was in modern dress and I know exactly what they meant. They sensed that they were connected with a period that was to do with their lifetime. Not from history books, not from collections of objects, furniture, photographs, paintings, whatever it may be, but most have a relation, a grandmother or grandfather who was directly connected with the period. There is a much stronger link than if you go back a few centuries, and you can only piece together imaginatively all the documentation and arrive at what you hope it was. But the actuality is there and I think that produces a very special smell for an audience, it hits somewhere quite different.

Then there's the importance of the end of the play, of the dastardly behaviour of the Duke – the omnipotence, the lack of sensitivity towards any other human being, only his own thought, only what he wanted; this, happening in such a ruthless manner in a period where within a very short space of time one would be into a major war, seemed to be another essential quality. History now makes clear to us, I think, that strange things happened to people's morals in those lulls. God forbid that one should appear to be saying 'We need wars' every so often, but if we could look at history and see how our morals decline or the sort of behaviour patterns that finally have produced major wars, we might be able to do something about it before they happen. There is a recurring theme.

RB I suspect that most of us have a deep sense that the most important event in the twentieth century is the 1914–18 War and that the primary episodes that have entered modern consciousness are grouped around that event. To take up modernity from another angle, you were speaking earlier about *Two Gentlemen of Verona* and the extent to which it helped your actors to know certain things about themselves. And this tied in with the fact that in your production you make it explicitly about four young people who are very immature, who are imperfectly aware of their identities. At the end of the play they are very obviously asking questions about themselves and their relationships, and are not at all resting upon any illusory security in the text as we receive it.

RP What I feel most about that play is the infuriating hint at muscle that constantly comes up, the feeling that any moment we might develop into *Twelfth Night* or *As You Like It* – but it never does. The characters are just too young, they don't have the muscles, the development, the competences, the total personality. But then one has to say, 'You can't act that' unless it is part of the given circumstances. It is an unformed person, a person who doesn't yet know himself. He hasn't developed his own muscles; it isn't just an author who hasn't supplied them for him, it's a boy who hasn't yet discovered about the world about him, about anybody else. One feels that a lot of those characters could swap lines. They could just as easily be placed in each other's mouth; they're that undisciplined. And to come to the end of the play with any resolution is a mistake. The play does not resolve, they have not found maturity by the end. Their passions change from day to day, from minute to minute. To say by the end of the play they have now found the first footing and will continue is absurd. There is no suggestion, I think, that they will develop along certain lines. What we tried to say at the end is, 'And that's as far as it goes. But tomorrow we may well be looking in the other direction. We still have not found ourselves.'

RB And all this marries up happily with the pool-side location in Verona, which takes modernity in one direction about as far as it can go. So far we've been talking, broadly, about the general and strategic considerations that a director has to bear in mind. What about the tactical and perhaps unplannable situations? Do you find that in rehearsals certain scenes emerge, certain facts of the first order emerge, which you haven't strictly speaking planned, but have set in motion?

RP Yes. Basically, of course, it's understood that what we are trying to do is to get to the core of the text, to find out what the guy was trying to say, what the motivations were for the characters, what he wanted to share with his audience. To get to the heart of that matter requires trust to go into any territory that may prove fruitful. It may prove otherwise, but there has to be a trust between actor and director that any territory is worth delving into, to see if it produces an essential core that might be hidden.

We had quite an interesting one in the Ophelia mad scenes recently. I've a dread of those pixie Ophelias who rush around with wild flowers looking fey and pathetic, clutching at slightly disarrayed hair and I'm relieved when the scenes are over. I know the text is important and she has something desperately important to say to Gertrude – but first one has to get over the fact that we do have a backlog of knowledge of that play that can get in the way. The most important things she says in the first lines to Gertrude; and therefore we must arrest the audience's attention very quickly or we're going to have lost that. We have an Ophelia who is everything that is described in the text, but I was a little worried by the delicacy of her hands and, for no reason that I can find, tried tying her hands to a lady-in-waiting, to see if that would produce an extra effort of frustration or energy or necessity to communicate harder the text to the Queen, when the hands couldn't get in the way, being mad. It didn't work entirely, it produced a vague effect. I then asked for a stick and we tied her hands as if to a yoke on her shoulders – her hands were tied over the sides. And that had an extraordinary effect on the rest of the company. It produced the possibility that she was dangerous in her lunacy, that unless her hands were in some way restricted she could damage herself, let alone others. It also became a very dangerous weapon, because the ends sticking out (if she turned too sharply) could hit another character in the face. So she became not only the possible danger, because there was obviously some reason why she needed to be restricted, but also there was the physical danger of what she could do with that device to other people. That has now been carried forward into a design that is totally fabricated in the sense of an Elizabethan strait-jacket. It's a very beautiful object, very like a yoke for carrying milk-pails, made of ebony inlaid with silver with finials in silver at the ends, velvet padding where it sits on the neck, immaculate strapping with silver buckles that brace it around the body. But it has nothing to do with historical accuracy, it's a totally imaginative creation that galvanises the scenes into something that allows Ophelia to stay on stage long enough to say all the things that she says and for our attention to be arrested firmly enough for us to want to listen to what she has to say.

I guess that with a lot of my productions I will have 'gimmick' hurled at me, which seems to happen all the time, and it seems to me that a 'gimmick' is something that has no justification and that is lightly conceived. I don't think that I've ever done a production that has been lightly conceived. Nothing, whether it be sitting beside a pool (in *Two Gentlemen*) or this particular gadget for Ophelia, comes without a great deal of consideration. It would have remained just a rehearsal technique and never have got into the production unless it had proved to support or in some way assist the sharing with the audience whatever the given thought is. That's always the hard decision about any idea that comes from the text – yes, they start from there, but you eventually get beyond. How far beyond can you go before you are padding the text rather than supporting it? I don't care what it is, if it produces the direct contact between actor and audience so that they are spontaneously arriving at a scene together, then any trick should stay in a production. Even if it's as anachronistic as a car suddenly driving into the middle of a Renaissance production, I don't care, if it makes you at that point listen to a line of text that you can't achieve in any other way. God forbid that one *should* drive a car into a Renaissance play, of course. But the light-hearted, the cavalier attitude in which a new thought is referred to as a 'gimmick' is very alarming; it's pretty obvious when something is a gimmick or a considered, illuminating effect. It may not be necessary for certain scholars to have that part of the text illuminated, or pointed out, or explained. But you don't direct plays for scholars. I direct plays for a fourteen-year-old of either sex who's never been to the theatre before and I want them to understand it, I want them to experience something remarkable for the first time. If I achieve that, the majority of my audience will share a similar experience.

RB There's no reason whatsoever why the text at a given point should not crystallise into a physical embodiment, an icon, of the energies which are generally expressed in that situation. And such a happening doesn't deserve to be called a 'gimmick'. It's clear, for instance, that the situation of madness and needed restraint in which Ophelia finds herself can logically be realised in the piece of apparatus which you've created for her. I would judge this to be far more effective with audiences than the setpiece, recital-type mad scene of Ophelia – which, let's admit it, is more or less a cliché of *Hamlet* productions and which I also on many occasions have found extremely unmoving. Now this is a subjective fact and I suspect that this is a collective fact for others too.

RP There's the other one, that is marvellously performed, where you are so in awe of the remarkable talent that has produced this detailed and realistic creation of madness that you are only admiring the acting. There are some scenes where the text is full enough for the point to be made, but when wretched Ophelia comes on and in the first few lines says – it's the only occasion in the play when anyone says it – those incredible lines to Gertrude, 'How should I your true love know/From another one?' Will I know him by his clothes, or will I know him by an unnatural grave? – it must alarm Gertrude no end. How will I know your first husband from your second husband? By his dress, or by a grave that suggests some unnatural death? She says that at the beginning of the scene. It's the most important thing she says in the scene, the only time that Gertrude is given an inkling of what's happened before the play begins. And if you're not careful, it's gone and over in either a fascination with the technique of the actress, or, as you say, thinking, 'O God here's that dreary scene where the girl skips around and looks pathetic.' If we can arrive at a point when the first image is so alarming that that arrests our attention, by the time she starts the first dialogue we are absolutely with her. Then we've got a fighting chance. That's the important thing about the scene, to get that first line over. It's a great help that she has to sing!

RB With that image – I've long had a theory that what's important in drama is what the audience remembers, after it's forgotten everything else. I find that I can usually remember, years after, just one or two major moments. But these images that I retain are always significant and they always seem retroactively to govern the production in my mind. And I'm sure that this can be said of the image of the poor Ophelia tied to this gilded yoke, which even as you describe it is to me immensely pathetic and moving. How much more must it seem to the audience in the theatre?

RP I agree about images – if the image exactly matches the text, as with the instance in *Measure for Measure*. After the big duologue between Angelo and Isabella, in our production Isabella is left with this incredible proposition. Martha Henry, heaving partly from fright, partly possibly from an unsuspected excitement, but in what is usually an ice-cold scene, dipped her hands into a water-jug that is on the desk and splashed cold water on to her forehead and we knew she was hot. And it seems to me that to be left with the image that this glacial, white-dressed, pure virgin is *hot* is a crystallisation of what the scene is about. And if that is what is remembered, in fact people are also remembering the text, because every ounce of the text leads you to that action. The almost unbearable bewilderment at the end is that of decision. She does not, as we are told by many essayists, marry the Duke. She may, after the play, but she doesn't in Shakespeare's play. She neither accepts nor rejects him. From the text, we assume that she doesn't accept him, because he repeats the offer. But she doesn't say anything, so we are left to make up our own minds. The pivoting figure of Isabella in our production, as she slowly turned, removing her glasses and then her nun's headdress, and finally the back of the hand just resting on the forehead, but at the same time the body never stopping to turn, but just spinning before our eyes, seems to me to be exactly what that silence is saying. If Shakespeare wanted to say that she accepts the Duke, he would have said it. If he wanted to say that she rejects him, he would have said it. But she says nothing. We are left with a bewilderment, with an ambiguity, with a woman who has not yet decided one way or the other. And it seems to me that if that is the image that is left, it is also the embodiment of what the text (or the lack of text for her) is saying. If it's the right image, it will also be finally the text that you're remembering.

RB The search, then, is for the necessary image that accords with the most scrupulous fidelity to the text and communicates this remembered text to the audience.

May I ask you, now, what Shakespeare play you would like to direct? It's clear from the tenor of our conversation that this isn't a throwaway question, it's the logical extension of everything that we've been talking about.

RP I want to direct *A Winter's Tale*. I'd like to direct *The Tempest* that I think Shakespeare wanted to write, which isn't the same as saying I'd like to direct *The Tempest*. I am in fact at the moment directing *The Tempest*, but I have a terrible feeling that it isn't quite the play he wanted to write; I think he gets caught up with the fashion of his own time and gets trapped in the middle of perhaps his most remarkable freedom with Elizabethan masque-work, at just the moment when he appears about to break beyond the bounds of even his genius. But I think that most of all at the moment I want to direct *A Winter's Tale*. I don't know when I will. I'm pleased to be doing the ones I am doing and I think that the ones I'm doing at the moment have something new to say, something new to experience. And I hope and pray that I won't have very often to direct the ones that just come around again because it's time they came round again.

RB And that leads me to my final question: what are your ambitions for the Stratford Shakespearian Festival?

RP I would like Stratford to see its position in the graph of a theatre nationally. I would like other theatres in Canada to see their position in that graph as related to Stratford. I would like Stratford eventually to know its audience.

1976

Giorgio Strehler

Giorgio Strehler is the most distinguished Italian director of the day and has for years been a leader of Continental theatre. He is especially associated with theatre in Paris, Milan and Salzburg, and his productions of King Lear *and* The Tempest *have a European renown.*

Ralph Berry I'd like to begin by asking you about Shakespeare and Italy. If we exclude England – and Shakespeare sets his plays in England only when he is virtually compelled to – the country that he most frequently selects is Italy. It is a fact that Shakespeare sets many of his plays in Italy, of his own choice. Now this must be significant. It is not simply a matter of Italy being an exciting, exotic, interesting background. It's clear that Shakespeare has a great feeling for locale in his plays. So I put it, then: the Italian element is important in Shakespeare. And I ask, how do you respond to the Italian element?

    Giorgio Strehler The question is important and difficult to resolve. The problem of locality in Shakespeare, whether in the Roman plays or in the other tragedies or comedies set in Italy, is critical. One has to search for Shakespeare's reasons in choosing to set so many plays in Italy. Much has been written on this: obviously, I don't have a complete answer, for it's one of the fundamental issues with Shakespeare. For instance, there's the primary problem of knowing what were the direct relations between Shakespeare and Italy. If Shakespeare was a butcher's son, it's certain that he never knew Italy directly, that he had never seen a town in Italy. And perhaps one wonders if it is possible that the William Shakespeare whom tradition describes to us could ever have known Italy (directly or indirectly) through the available cultural sources. Now, I would say quite simply of the mysteries in this phenomenon of Shakespeare that one knows what it is necessary to know, that is to say, one knows what he wrote. And the fact is that he gave, miraculously, a different accent to a play unfolding in one country rather than another.

That is not a question of poetic intuition, you understand; one can intuitively comprehend the general character of England, or if you like the general character of an Italian or Frenchman. It's rather broad, but not too difficult to grasp. I can talk about America with you, but except for a month I've never been there. All the same, I have some insight into what America is. I am not absolutely convinced, though, that I understand the difference between someone living in Tennessee and in Alabama. That would be an affair not of culture but of poetic intuition. One needs poetic intuition to be able to write a play like *Romeo and Juliet*, which takes place in Verona, and create an impression of the events, the characters, and the townsfolk generally, which have a terrible exactitude and reality; and all this in a small part of one town in a country of forty-five million inhabitants (of course, there were many fewer then). It's something I've often thought about, the character of a nation or of a town like Verona. There's a character-type that is found in this part of Italy, which has a tendency to extreme violence and to behaviour just like that of the Capulets and Montagues, the two houses continually at odds. These people are excitable, hot-blooded. It's a regional characteristic, though I don't say that all the inhabitants of Verona are like that. But if one takes up the story of Romeo and Juliet, and sets it in Italy, in Verona, that is certainly more appropriate than placing it in Turin, or Milan, or Venice. The precision of Shakespeare's poetic intuition is inexplicable. We know well enough that *Romeo and Juliet* was taken from a novel – I don't recall its name – a tale of the period when this town had two leading houses. But this inner acquaintance with the character of a small town, that is something that one can only have if one has lived there with its people, truly knows the place. If one has merely met two or three people from Italy, that is insufficient. So that's the problem and it's a large one.

RB I think I phrased the original question rather badly, because strictly speaking Shakespeare does not write about Italy at all. He writes about Venice, Verona, Milan, particular locations with a particular character. Shakespeare is always trying to create a local society, a society which explains and accounts for the events that go on. As you say, the events that make up *Romeo and Juliet* could only have occurred in Verona. They could not have occurred in Venice, because the Venetians are not hot-blooded.

GS That reveals the artist. The tragic events in Shakespeare are of such magnitude that it cannot be said that a play like *Romeo and Juliet* could not happen in Venice. That is possible – certainly, there were families and characters who could have been close enough to that. But the grandeur of Shakespeare cannot be restricted in this way. It's impossible, for instance, to think that Prospero should not be Duke of Milan in the romance, if Prospero is Duke of Turin. It's the same thing. Again, *Othello* could have been set in Naples, shall we say.

Othello is a particularly clear issue, illuminated by the consti-tution of Venetian society. A tragedy like *Coriolanus* (or *Julius Caesar*) is based on Roman history, but there are things in it that could have happened anywhere. Now this is not the case with *Macbeth*, which takes place in a certain era in a certain part of Britain; it's necessary to place the tragedy in an ambience nearest to what the drama seeks to signify. That is to say, when Shake-speare sets *King Lear* in a country and an era which is not precisely indicated, it is exactly because these matters must be left vague. It's understood that *King Lear* is set in a distant epoch. It's a kind of biblical tragedy, shall we say an archetype of tragedy, more so than *Hamlet*, which takes place in Elsinore. Now it's exactly right for *Hamlet* to take place in Elsinore.

RB How, as a director, do you seek to realise the society, the national background or ambience? For instance, in *King Lear*, as you say, the place and time are vague, distant. How did you devise sets and costumes for *King Lear*?

GS When Shakespeare provides the ambience of one country or another, he has good reason for doing so. He always finds the exact context, of geographical and national character, for the drama that he is going to write. And for the historical era, too.

So one question is place and the other is time. I think that the Roman plays are Roman plays, even if the general character of Shakespeare's work is Elizabethan. There is always a partial vision of a certain moment in history. Now, you ask about the realisation of Shakespeare's plays: nowadays a director must preoccupy himself with historical reality. If, to represent this problem, one takes all the plays about kings, which are obviously the most historically defined – *Richard II, Henry V, Henry VI* and so on – one calls these plays 'The Kings' because they make up a part of English history. But I ask myself if it is necessary to set *Richard II* in the time of Richard II. It is idiotic to dress the Scots in kilts, for instance, though I have always seen it done. The plays of Shakespeare should be staged always in the *type* in which they should be displayed. One solution is to dress the *dramatis personae* in Elizabethan costume. Now, I think it an error to present *Julius Caesar* in Roman costume, just as it is an error to put *Richard II* in English costume, to make the face of Richard II resemble somewhat the historical Richard who is buried in Westminster. There are two poles: it's an error to choose Elizabethan costume and it's an error to stage *Hamlet* or *Julius Caesar* in contemporary costume. Julius Caesar has been presented as Mussolini, for instance, and I recall Alec Guinness as a contemporary Hamlet and Orson Welles' *Julius Caesar* at the Guild Theater in America. The question, then, relates to the twin problems of setting and critical interpretation. Today we have progressed further in actualising and historicising Shakespeare. An orientation must be found for each play that is not solely one of costume: an ambience, a setting which corresponds to the profundity of the piece.

RB Could you illustrate this from your work?

GS Well, I've staged eight, ten plays of Shakespeare – I really don't remember. For twenty-five years it's been a path to knowledge with Shakespeare. The point is that it doesn't correspond with what I think today. The record of my productions is simply a process of learning.

RB Very well, your latest production, then. Tell me about that.

GS When I produced *Julius Caesar* I created a setting which was passionately historical, with Roman costumes. That is gone today. I would not have done anything else, you understand. I did it because at that moment, I saw no other possibility of doing it differently. To take another instance, I produced *Richard III* in Elizabethan costume, but today I would no longer choose a setting which resembled a reconstruction of the Elizabethan theatre. When I did *Richard II*, I created an abstract setting, a symbolic, poetic abstract of the Elizabethan stage. Because at that moment, five years ago, we were obsessed by the Elizabethan stage. Today I would not do it. I set *King Lear* in an empty stage, where one could think of a kind of metaphysical circus, with a cyclorama. One entered into a stage of plastic material. And there were very few words for decorative purposes. The stage for *Lear* was based on Eliot's *The Waste Land* – the ambience of the production was that of the poem. It was an empty plain which could be the terrestrial planet, or a cosmic circus, where this event, at once very ancient and close to us, took place. The actors were clad in the manner of the Italian Renaissance, but all in black leather. In my imagination they were personages of Shakespeare's time, but transposed with people who could have been motor-cyclists of today. The kings, Lear and the others, were dressed in long theatrical robes, with crowns of paper.

RB Paper crowns?

GS Crowns made of gold paper. The style is eclectic. Eclecticism, be it understood, has positive or negative possibilities. Now, I see Shakespeare as a poet who surpasses the age in which he is enclosed, but at the same time bound to it. He is at once national, English, Elizabethan and universal. That is the central fact that one has to interpret. It's too easy to make Hamlet come on dressed as a young man of today, or the Ghost dressed in something military with a mask. It's just as easy to do that as it is to mount *Hamlet* in Elizabethan costume. Given that the play is set in Elsinore, in Denmark, should Hamlet have blond hair (because he's a 'Dane') and be dressed in black? We've moved beyond those things, which are no more than a kind of heritage of Romanticism and a species of naturalism applied to Shakespeare. Shakespeare breaks out of this schema; and for each of his works one must find the precise ambience which is contained not in the stage directions, but in the lexicon of the piece itself.

RB You spoke of the historic moment in Shakespeare, and you obviously have a very acute sense of time and place in Shakespeare. Can we go beyond that and consider history itself in Shakespeare? I'm thinking particularly of the eight plays of English history, which run in order of composition from *Henry VI* to *Henry V*. You have been concerned a great deal with Shakespeare's history plays and I'd like to ask: do you consider that a certain view of history emerges from these plays?

GS Yes. It's an enormous problem. Shakespeare is a continent: there are the problems of history, of man with himself, of man in love ... One must try to attain a broad vision of Shakespeare. But history is a specific issue. One has to ask, 'What is happening?' of all the plays in the canon; because the sense of history is not, as I think, confined to the King-plays, or those plays which are classified as 'histories'. History is present in all his plays. But what do we derive from this sense of history? Very well, there's a vision of history, of a certain pessimistic cast. Pessimistic, but not despairing, because Shakespeare is always *active*. The pessimism of Shakespeare's tragic vision is never absolutely negative. He's not a Beckett. There is, however, a kind of conviction of the corruption latent in power.

RB I'm fascinated by your remark about the pessimistic vision of Shakespeare. I was thinking of the curious fact that he begins writing his history plays with *Henry VI*, which tells of a social and national disaster, and then he goes on to *Henry V*, the last in the sequence, which tells of a brilliant success. But in the chronology of English history, the reign of Henry V comes before Henry VI.

GS Immediately before.

RB Immediately before, so therefore what emerges is a kind of cycle, a cycle that goes from the disaster of Henry VI to the triumph of Henry V. But we know that the triumph will again be followed by disaster.

GS Yes, I think that's understood.

RB So does this suggest a cyclic view of history?

GS Cyclic, yes. It's a circle of history. But when I spoke of a pessimistic vision, I wanted to say also a dialectical vision. It's not a pessimistic vision which offers no possibility of issue. Shakespeare finds himself, I think, in a situation when Henry V could be a glorification of a king whom Shakespeare as an Englishman loved well, or who was at that moment necessary for a glorification of his country. At which point Henry is as virtuous as Richard II is a monster. Perhaps all the plays of Shakespeare are to be seen as a grand allegory of history in which all those with power are kings, who kill each other for power, the power which corrupts. It's a process from which the people are absent. Apart from *Hamlet*, the only revolt on stage in Shakespeare is Jack Cade's rebellion, is it not? But all these forces are seeking a power which corrupts and hates and at the same time may close the bloody circle of history. Now Shakespeare could not fail to perceive this enduring element of human history. The question is whether Shakespeare's vision perceived a point of exit and that is hard. My view is that Shakespeare had a pessimistic vision of history, but not a pessimistic vision of man.

RB But you spoke a moment ago of the dialectic of history. Are not the implications of dialectic basically positive, optimistic if you like?

GS Myself, I'm a socialist, with a materialistic view of history: I'm a Marxist; so I believe personally in developing the dialectic in a positive sense. But the dialectic itself is neither positive nor negative. Dialectic is dialectic, it's thesis and antithesis, that which is balanced in the movement of history. I happen to believe in a positive development in the movement of human thought. He did not, surely, believe in a blind movement of history, a process where one murder succeeded another. I think that Shakespeare always let it be understood in his tragedies that man himself had his rights even against history, or in dialectic with history. All the great personages of Shakespeare are in dialectic with history, with fetishes of power. What is

Macbeth but the inner dialectic of Macbeth in the fifth act, 'Tomorrow and tomorrow and tomorrow . . .'?

RB I'm going to suggest that Shakespeare's last history play was *The Tempest*. I don't know if you'd agree with that; but if you do, I'd like to ask you, what is the verdict that comes at the end of *The Tempest?*

GS It's undoubtedly Shakespeare's last play, in the sense that he terminates a certain poetic course. I would suggest that *The Tempest* is indeed, a resumé of his entire work. In *The Tempest* one finds as in the memory a repetition of all the dramatic situations which run, if you like, from *Romeo and Juliet* to *Macbeth*. But what conclusion is one to infer from this?

RB I had in mind this particular difficulty: *The Tempest* is very much concerned with the problems of power, of how people are governed. But the play ends with a kind of open-ended question. Prospero knows how to govern, but he is going to die. What will happen? Will Ferdinand and Miranda, those nice children, be able to govern and succeed? Or will Sebastian and Antonio, who are still there, be able to take over? Then there's the question of Caliban at the end.

GS Prospero gives Ariel his liberty. But what does he do with Caliban? It's a question that has always given me intense perplexity.

RB So the real question is what will happen when Prospero dies? What will happen to history?

GS It's certain that Prospero abandons power. But not only power: he abandons all the powers of his being, even the power of enchantment, which is to say the power of becoming a poet. He has broken his staff and Ariel will not come back. It's a pessimistic position, which makes this statement: Now I will retire and I have ended my power. It's yours, to go forward. Prospero has not only set aside power, he has decided to think only of his death.

RB '. . . where/Every third thought shall be my grave.'

GS He's a man who says, no more writing, no more making poems. Now, one must consider the people who are going to live. Shakespeare, I am certain, always had an enormous confidence in the coming generation. At the last, Shakespeare breaks his magic wand and permits the young people to depart, one of them the thing most dear to him – his daughter – and the other, a young prince. They are most like the couple from Pamino in *The Magic Flute*, the pairing of Adam and Eve to renew the world. You ask if they will be capable of that renewal. Prospero says, 'Are you capable of carrying on before history and against these forces and these limits?' But he, who could command and see truly, will not be present. That is an agonising question, concerning Shakespeare's vision at that moment in his life. What did he think? Evidently, he no longer had the strength to fight against the destiny of man. He had already done what he could.

RB So Prospero's final appeal to the audience is a statement that the future is over to you, the future is with you. You must decide.

GS That's exactly what I think. He says, 'Over to you now.'

RB That's not really pessimistic, neither is it optimistic. It's a simple statement that you must make society work.

GS Precisely. That's to say, to the pessimistic vision Shakespeare gives always a point of optimism, a point of possibility. There is a universe, let's say Beckett's – I don't want to set up a Beckett/Shakespeare opposition – which is clearly restricted to oneself, it's finished. Shakespeare always leaves the possibility of the decision with the coming generation and the society which is going to make itself. It's always projected to the future. The circle is never absolutely closed in itself.

RB If I have understood you rightly, then, you regard the work of Shakespeare as a statement of human possibilities?

GS Yes, yes.

RB Can I ask you, finally, what is Shakespeare for you today?

GS In all the panorama of dramatic poetry in the world, there's a choice which is personal, one of taste. It has to do with the personality of each director. Myself, I have staged the work of Chekhov, Goldoni, Molière and so on. Amongst the phenomena of world drama, Shakespeare holds a special place. Why? Because Shakespeare, of all the great dramatic poets, had the largest, most universal vision. Naturally, there are some problems which present themselves to humanity which are not reflected in Shakespeare's work. But one finds always the possibility of speaking to contemporary audiences of problems which pierce us today through something that Shakespeare has written. What I find in Shakespeare is contemporaneity. I produce Shakespeare because he is my contemporary.

1974

Peter Brook

Peter Brook has been responsible for some of the most celebrated Shakespeare productions of the post-war era, including Love's Labour's Lost *(1946),* Measure for Measure *(1950),* Titus Andronicus *(1955),* King Lear *(1962) and* A Midsummer Night's Dream *(1970). Now based in Paris, he has been co-director of the Royal Shakespeare Company since 1962 and director of CIRT (International Centre for Theatre Research) since 1971.*

Ralph Berry In *The Empty Space* you wrote, 'In the second half of the twentieth century in England ... we are faced with the infuriating fact that Shakespeare is still our model.' I wonder if you would like to modify now either the general proposition, or perhaps the word 'infuriating'?

Peter Brook No, it is infuriating and infuriating in a very good way, because it would be nice to feel that we could do as well. Everything after all is a product of its times to a large degree – not totally, but to a large degree, and everything that is produced at any moment reflects the quality and understanding of life at that moment; and it's quite clear that to find a richer model than the model we can produce ourselves we're forced to look backwards. I think the thing that is infuriating about this is that each generation needs to find its new way and not refer constantly to given models. Never has that been truer than today, when the whole need is to break out of one set of forms and find new ones. And there's no doubt that today there is a barrier in accepting something, however valid, however truth-containing, if its outside form reflects the past. And that's why one puts the real accent on the word 'infuriating'. There are thousands of people for whom a playhouse, in which the imagery is to do with kings and queens and goddesses, is virtually intolerable. Now I don't think we have to discuss the rights and wrongs of this – it may be childish, it may be ridiculous, but it's certainly one of the factors that makes the meaning and the potential life-giving qualities of the performances of Shakespeare's works handicapped, compared with the lesser qualities that come through in an electronic, science-fiction, crash-helmeted idiom.

RB So, the fact remains – though for reasons on the one hand of a genetic accident, the birth of Shakespeare, and on the other hand the immense cultural convulsions that we're going through – he remains the one playwright that one has to face up to, who is alone in his league.

PB Of all time.

RB It seems to me that the most immediate way in which Shakespeare impresses himself upon us generally, and upon you as director particularly, is in the choice of his plays for performance. I know that this isn't always true. Someone who's directing a summer season, a festival season, let's say, will have to have a pretty good reason for not producing *Twelfth Night* or some such crowd-puller. But a man in your position is able to select only the Shakespeare play that he wishes, at that moment in history, to produce. Now could you enlarge on some of the reasons that lead you to select, of this large canon, one play at a given moment when presumably you feel that this is the moment, this is the right play for now?

PB That's a vast and in a way absolutely marvellous question, because through this question (I don't think there's any other) everything is brought into relief. I think that through it one can see perhaps the great misunderstanding that hangs over Shakespearian works, but I'd be very interested to try to answer it. To begin with, I don't think I can face the question without dwelling for a moment on what Shakespeare is. As you said very rightly a moment ago, he is alone in his league. And I think that one of the things that is very little understood about Shakespeare is that he is not only of a different quality, he is also different in kind. And this is very little understood. So long as one thinks that Shakespeare is just Ionesco but better, Beckett but richer, Brecht but more human, Chekhov with crowds and so on, one is not touching what it's all about. If you can talk about cats and a bull, one sees that these are different species. In modern scientific analysis you would beware of the dangers of mixing categories, and talking about a person in category A as though he really belonged to category B. I think that this is what happens with Shakespeare in relation to other playwrights and so I'd like to dwell for a moment on what this particular phenomenon is.

To me, this phenomenon is very simple. It is that authorship as we understand it in almost all other fields – in the way that one talks about the authorship of a book or poem, and today the authorship of a film when directors are called authors of their films and so on – almost invariably means 'personal expression'. And therefore the finished work bears the marks of the author's own way of seeing life. It's a cliché of criticism that one comes across very often, 'his world', 'the world of this author'. Now it's not for nothing that scholars who have tried so hard to find autobiographical traces in Shakespeare have had so little success. It doesn't matter in fact who wrote the plays and what bio-graphical traces there are. The fact is that there is singularly little of the author's point of view – and his personality seems to be very hard to seize – throughout thirty-seven or thirty-eight plays. Now if one takes those thirty-seven plays with all the radar lines of the different viewpoints of the different characters, one comes out with a field of incredible density and complexity; and eventually one goes a step further and one finds that what hap-pened, what passed through this man called Shakespeare and came into existence on sheets of paper, is something quite differ-ent from any other author's work. It's not Shakespeare's view of the world, it's something which actually resembles reality. A sign of this is that any single word, line, character or event has not only a large number of interpretations, but an unlimited number. Which is the characteristic of reality. I could say that is the characteristic of any action in the real world – say, the action that you're doing now at this moment, as we are talking together, of putting your hand against your head. An artist may try to capture and reflect your action, but actually he interprets it – so that a naturalistic painting, a Picasso painting, a photograph, are all interpretations. But in itself, the action of one man touching his head is open to unlimited understanding and interpretation. In reality, that is. What Shakespeare wrote carries that characteristic. What he wrote is not interpretation: it is the thing itself.

And if we're very bold and think not in very constricting verbal terms, 'He's an author, he wrote plays, the plays have scenes' and so on, but think much more broadly and say 'This creator created an enormous skein of interrelated words,' and if we think of a chain of several hundred thousand words unfolding in a certain order, the whole making an extraordinary fabric, I think that then one begins to see the essential point. And that is that this fabric reaches us today, not as a series of messages, which is what authorship almost always produces – it is a series of impulses that can produce many understandings. This is something quite different. It is like tealeaves in a cup. Think of the chance arrangement of tealeaves in a cup – the act of interpretation is a reflection of what is brought to the cup by the person looking at it. The whole act of interpreting tealeaves – of interpreting the fall of a sparrow, for that matter – is the unique meeting, at one point in time, between an event and the perceiver of the event.

I think that two things come out of it. On the one hand, it is obvious that every interpretation of this material is a subjective act – how else could it be? – and that each person, whether it's a scholar writing, an actor acting, a director directing or a designer designing, brings to it and always has and always will, his subjectivity. Which means that even if he tries to bridge the ages and says, 'I leave myself and my century behind, and I'm looking at it with the eyes of its own period,' one knows that this is nonsense and nothing bears this out more vividly than the history of stage costume, which shows more than anything else two periods at once. The designer tries to interpret one period and is not aware of the elements of his own moment that he's also bringing – so he produces a double image. We look at Granville-Barker's productions – or we look at any production anywhere – and the double image is always there. This is an unavoidable human fact, each person brings what he is; there's no man walking around this world that's somehow dropped his ego. How you use your ego is the question. You can wilfully and blindly give your ego free rein, or you can put your ego into play in a way that can help the truth to appear. For instance, the history of leading acting. The actor who's the crude, bombastic, self-inflated type seizes on Shakespeare's plays because he sees, in their million facets, the facets which are food for his 'me'. He certainly gets a powerful energy out of what he finds and the demonstration may be dazzling. But the play has gone and the finer content, and many other levels of meaning are steam-rollered out of existence. Of course, the theatre artist's relations with his material are basically affective, they come out of a love for and affinity with what he's doing. Doing a play as a duty, even on the highest level of duty, won't work. The mysterious and essential creative channels will not be opened and so he will only be able to call on his reason, he won't actually be able to bring out the fullest and richest possibilities. So obviously for a director as for an actor there is a moment that is purely instinctive and affective that makes the decision to do a certain play. And this is something that must be respected. In the same way, you don't beyond a point force an actor to play a part that he doesn't want to do; you don't coax people into working in a play that they have an antipathy for and so on. On the other hand, the danger that also has to be watched is when any of the artists or scholars dealing with a play of Shakespeare allow their love and excitement and enthusiasm to blind them to the fact that their interpretation can never be complete. There's an enormous danger that takes very precise form; and if that's forgotten, one gets into a form of acting that one's seen over many years, a form of directing, a form of designing, which proudly presents very subjective versions of the play without a glimmer of awareness that this might be diminishing the play – on the contrary, a vain belief that this is the play and more – not only Shakespeare's play, but Shakespeare's play as made into sense by such-and-such an individual. And that's where the virtue of having a feeling of love and enthusiasm has to be tempered by a cool sense that anybody's personal view of the play is bound to be less than the play itself.

I saw the other day an interview on French television with Orson Welles, on Shakespeare, where he started by saying something like 'We all betray Shakespeare.' The history of the plays shows them constantly being reinterpreted and reinterpreted, and yet remaining untouched and intact. Therefore they are always more than the last interpretation trying to say the last word on something on which the last word can't be said.

So to come back to your essential question: all the plays of Shakespeare that I've done, I've done for no other reason than that I've wanted to, very strongly. On the other hand, over the years my own view of what I'm doing and why has changed enormously. The very first production of Shakespeare that I did was *Love's Labour's Lost*, I think, and at that point I felt and believed the work of a director was to have a vision of a play and to 'express' it. I thought that's what a director was for. That was how I understood directing at that time – I was nineteen or twenty. I had always wanted to direct films and in fact I started in films before going into the theatre. A film director shows his pictures to the world and I thought a stage director did the same in another way. Even before I did *Love's Labour's Lost*, when I was up at Oxford I terribly wanted to do *Coriolanus*, and I remember very strongly that the way of wanting to do *Coriolanus* was sitting at a table and drawing pictures. I drew images of *Coriolanus*, which is the film director's way of wanting to bring into life a personal picture one has, a picture of Coriolanus walking away in brilliant sunlight, things like that. When I did *Love's Labour's Lost* I had a set of images in mind, which I wanted to bring to life just like making a film. So *Love's Labour's Lost* was a very visual, very romantic set of stage pictures which I then did in a Watteau-costume, eighteenth-century Romantic manner. And I remember that from then all the way through to *Measure for Measure* my conviction was that the director's job, having found an affinity between himself and the play, was to find the images that he believed in and through them make the play live for a contemporary audience. In this sense he was always a man of his time, in an image-conscious time. I believed designing and directing to be inseparable. A good designer – in any field – has to sense just how the shapes are for a particular moment, and therefore produces the right car body and so on. In exactly the same way I understood that a director studies deeply, is as in tune with the play as he can be, but that his work is the making of a new set of images for it. Since then, this view has changed, evolved, through a growing awareness that the total overall image was so much less than the play itself. And eventually, as I worked more and more outside proscenium theatres and in the forms of theatre where the overall image proved to be less and less necessary and important, it became clear that a play of Shakespeare, and therefore a production of Shakespeare, could go far beyond the unity that one man's image could give, beyond that of the director and designer. And it was only through discovering that there was far more to it than that, that my interest moved from liking the play, and therefore showing my image of the play, to another process, which starts always with the instinctive feeling that this is the play for now.

This is a big change of attitude: without thinking consciously or analytically in these terms, a sense that this play is meaningful in many ways at this moment opens my awareness. It's not only that it's meaningful for me autobiographically at this moment. At certain points in one's life one can identify with and wish to do a youthful play, a bitter play, a tragic play – this is fine, but one can then go beyond to see how a whole area of living experience that seems close to one's own concerns is also close to the concerns of the people in the world around one. When these elements come together, then is the time to do that play and not another.

Fortunately, I've never been in the position of having to do lots of plays systematically. I think it's always destructive, to have to do plays in this way. I started wanting to do certain plays, which I directed, and not being interested by certain others. For years I wanted to do *Lear* and I did it; for years I wanted to do *Antony and Cleopatra* and I haven't. I never wanted to do a *Twelfth Night* – these are purely personal things, I think that every director has them that way, plays he's more drawn to, and every actor has. But I would now say that that's our loss; choosing plays is a Rorschach test by which you can tell the openness and blinkeredness of each individual. Because if I could sympathise and empathise with every one of Shakespeare's plays, and every one of his themes, and every one of his characters, I would be that much the richer and I think that goes for any actor. And if a theatre were to take on the task of doing the entire work of Shakespeare, out of an absolute conviction that this is the greatest school of living that they know, that group would be an astonishing group in human terms, because the mere fact of being able to do that would be an action of pene-tration and understanding. In the very first instance, I think one must be led to a play by certain instincts which at the same time reflect something of one's times – it's a violent play at a violent moment, or a joyful play at a moment when one needs joy. A fuller attitude begins to shape itself when there is not only a response of the ego, of the personality, to what it likes and dislikes, but when there's a response of the personality to what it can discover through working on the play; and this is a very big step, because as long as one's in the first instinct, 'I like this, I want to do it,' one is most likely within the closed circle of wishing to illustrate what one likes. 'I like it and I'll show you why I like it.' The next step is, 'I like it, because it parallels all that I need to know about in the world.' If I spend three months on a play, at the end of that time my wish to understand will have taken me further along through its complexity and in the same way will take an audience eventually on the same experi-ence. And thus, from personal expression as an aim, you go to shared discovery.

RB May I take up a couple of points there? First, when you were talking of image-making, I thought of your *Love's Labour's Lost* and I'd like to refer to the great theatrical moment in the play, in the entrance of Mercade. Could you elaborate on the way this was staged?

PB If I remember rightly, I was struck by what seemed to me to be self-evident, but which at the time seemed to be unheard of: which was, that from the moment Mercade came on, the whole play changed its tone entirely, because he came into an artificial world to announce a piece of news that was real. He came on bringing death. And as I felt intuitively that the image of the Watteau world was very close to this, I began to see that the reason that the Watteau 'Age of Gold' is so particularly moving is that although it's a picture of springtime, it's an autumn springtime, because every one of Watteau's pictures has an incredible melancholy. And if one looks, one sees that there is somewhere in it the presence of death, until one even sees that in Watteau (unlike the imitators of the period, where it's all sweetness and prettiness) there is usually a dark figure some-where, standing with his back to you, and some people say that he is Watteau himself. But there's no doubt that the dark touch gives the dimension to the whole piece. And it was through this that I brought Mercade over the rise at the back of the stage – it was evening, the lights were going down and suddenly over it came a man in black. And the man in black on a very pretty, summery stage, with everybody in pale pastel Watteau and Lancret costumes and golden light dying, and suddenly this figure coming over the skyline in black was very disturbing and at once something in the whole audience was felt.

RB This presence embodies a reality which has gradually been making itself felt in very complex ways throughout the play, a reality assuming mass and direction in the later stages which finally materialises in this.

Could I also go back to what you were saying about the wholeness of the canon? It seems to me that one of the great difficulties of interpretation is that when we look at the apparent objects before us, that is to say a text of Shakespeare, our view is going to change if we take it in relation to other plays around it in the canon. For instance, if we come to *Twelfth Night* chrono-logically, via *Much Ado* and *As You Like It*, it will appear to us in a certain way. If we come to it backwards, via *Troilus and Cressida* and *All's Well*, it assumes a different reality – the play of lights and shadows falls from a different angle.

PB Which is what Peter Hall brought out by playing the

histories in the order of the canon. I think that's absolutely true, but I think that what you're putting your finger on there is still another way of seeing the endlessly moving, endlessly changing, unique nature of this material. The plays in themselves seem, falsely, to be static things because you see them on a shelf – a real naïveté of vision! One says, 'If that book's on a shelf, I'll go out of the room, I'll come back and it will still be there,' and it's still there – therefore one believes it's static. It isn't. I've just been reading Tarzan to my little son, and when Tarzan first discovered a book he saw little squiggles on a page and he felt they were little bugs. And he looked at them: 'What are these little bugs?' and he came back and there were more little bugs. It's marvellously right, because I think that Shakespeare's plays, deceptively in hard covers, are big bugs within which there are smaller and smaller bugs. And when the grown-ups go to bed, they move.

I'll give you two examples. I've been working in France on a translation of *Timon of Athens*, for the French, because they think in schematic terms always and because they know very little about Shakespeare; they – most of the French – have only seen four or five plays of Shakespeare. They've seen *Coriolanus* and therefore they conclude that Shakespeare is a fascist. He's a great writer, they say, but he's a fascist. I know that when they go to see *Timon* it's going to be very disturbing, because suddenly this same author, who's proved to them that he only likes generals who despise the crowd, has now written a play in which you see that the only sympathetic people are the honest servants, without money. This is just another version of the very thing that you're talking about, which is that you can build a season and make any patchwork of plays, and a whole new set of bells starts ringing.

This comes out even further working on a translation. I'm working with a very imaginative, and free, and intelligent French writer called Jean-Claude Carrière and constantly we come to a phrase and he says, 'What does this mean? What exactly does this word mean?' He knows English very well, he brings out a dictionary: does it mean this, or this? And I say: both. And so in explaining lines to him, we find we work on a page a day.

Because in the explanation, the word begins to take on more and more dimensions, until he now says, 'Ah, now I understand: the structure of writing proceeds from *des mots rayonnants*.' I thought this was very interesting, because that was how he suddenly understood the different sort of syntax he was trying to translate, finding what words in the very un-*rayonnant* nature of French language matched the original. When you have a word that has these senses, you can see how from it you can draw a line to the third word or you can draw a line to the fifth word, or another line to the fifteenth word and once again you get into infinite combinations. When I started work in Shakespeare, I did believe to a limited extent in the possibility of a classical word music, that each verse had a sound that was correct, with only moderate variations; and through direct experience I found that this was absolutely and totally untrue. The more musical the approach you bring to Shakespeare, which means the more sensitive you are to music, the more you find that there is no way, except by sheer pedantry, that can fix this line's correct music. It just can't exist. And the more you get into this, the more you see that an actor who tries to fix his performance is doing something anti-life. He has to keep certain consistencies in what he's doing, or it's just a chaotic performance – within the central nature of the music each single line as you come back to it another time reopens itself to a new music, made round these radiating points.

RB '*Des mots rayonnants*' is excellent. I think of 'vibrating' as a way of describing so many words in Shakespeare, in that they cannot be and should not be restricted to a certain meaning. For instance, when Cleopatra says of Antony, 'the soldier's pole is fallen', well, what do we see? A tentpole, or a Maypole, or the pole star? Do we see it as phallic in its implications? There are other possibilities and I don't even think that we need to establish the priorities there. It's sufficient to think of the term's vibrations.

PB I think this is very important, because the great harm done by scholarship is to try to make choices, and even make quarrels over who's right and who's wrong, which is what the whole world of footnotes has been. Rather, you want endlessly to come back to meeting this vibration in all its fullness and with all the ambiguity of something that does change through the ages.

RB It may go even further than this. In the instance I quoted, there is unarguably one word – the textual scholars are happy with 'pole' as the original word, therefore we need only discuss meanings. But so often what textual scholars are discussing is the word itself. And here, I sometimes suspect, we are in the wake of something approximating to a pun with Shakespeare. When, for instance, in *Macbeth* he speaks of the 'temple-haunting martlet' (if it is 'martlet') and then talks (in the Folio) of 'loved Mansonry,' how does one emend it?

PB In California today, you'd get great shouts of delight on 'Mansonry'!

RB Anyway, most editors like 'mansionry'. Pope and others prefer 'masonry'. And I think we can see the word as hovering between 'mansionry' and 'masonry'.

PB I think this is absolutely true. And it's very necessary to see the harm that's done when a fixed meaning is established, which is what so much scholarship has done. This is the true scholarship, what you're speaking of. I was talking the other day of doing what I think would be a marvellous thing, a Shakespeare production with captions on a screen giving a running commentary on every single word. It would be the most hilarious thing, to show the difference between living expression and all this terrible interpretation. Because the harm in the quibble is the implication that Shakespeare was communicating intentions, and therefore we are trying to discover once and for all what the man meant. And the further you go down that road, the nearer madness lies. If on the other hand, you go on the principle of the vibrating word, you then depersonalise in a sense the author. You see Shakespeare not as a communicator but as a creator, you see him creating marvellous objects, like a potter, like sets of earth figures. Now even the most pedantic collector of pre-Columbian art doesn't look at some Mayan figure and try to pin down what the maker of the figure was trying to say. On the contrary, he's up against something where the name and the personality of the maker and what he was trying to say doesn't come into it, although there was a maker. But the figure itself is something that is vibrating with many layers of meaning – everybody dealing with primitive art recognises this. If then one can see that this is a higher level of creation than the 'I communicate my message to you' level, then one perceives that Shakespeare, alone in all playwriting, made plays like those sorts of figures and that each word is like a little figurine, vibrating with all these layers of meaning. So one comes towards these elements, whether as an actor or director, with a quite different attitude, quite different relationship. The vibration cannot take life unless it comes once again into a human organism. So it has to vibrate through an actor; an actor is not meant to be an empty vessel. He and the material enter into a momentary fusion. That's perhaps the great change in our time also, to recognise that an actor is not just a glove, the actor is *all*. He's partly a channel but he's partly all that he has lived through, all that he has developed in himself – and the same goes for the director.

And so one isn't 'serving' Shakespeare. Ever since I started working with Shakespeare, I've resented one of the idiot clichés that are always coming up, which is talking about 'serving the author' and 'serving the play'. My instinct of resentment against this cult of personality is such that however much I love Shakespeare, the moment I'm told that I'm serving Shakespeare, there's another instinct that says, 'Fuck Shakespeare – why him more than anyone else?' No one in our time actually, specifically wants to go and serve the Duke of Edinburgh, the Queen, Shakespeare . . . Now one has to recognise that there is only one service, which is to the reality which Shakespeare is serving. Then you're serving something very valid, you're serving the bringing into our unreal life the elements of reality. And you've got the greatest channel to it, through the greatest creator in this form, who is Shakespeare.

RB In fact, of course, the phrase that you take exception to is a formula for somebody's version of Shakespeare.

PB You know, for instance, it was very interesting that with

A Midsummer Night's Dream, however well it was received in America, nonetheless it caused a resentment because of something that was very unimportant in England. In England, there was resentment about the sexual side. That was small but strong – I used to get so many letters a week about the phallus, regular as clockwork. In America, with the same big middle-class audience, nothing: because America is much more attuned, has been attuned for years to nudity, and cocks, so that nobody, even the matinée ladies, noticed it. Not one letter, not a postcard. But what the Americans had to swallow was something that hadn't occurred to the English – Americans complained that the Company didn't 'look nice'. And where in England it was considered a vivid young Company, nice young people, working with zest and enjoyment and not too old for their parts – in America they were considered a scruffy lot. Even in the papers, people were saying things like, 'What a pity they're not better-looking,' which is always a mean thing to say about actors, particularly as they're a sexy lot of people who consider themselves appealing. And then we understood what it was all about. In America Shakespeare has become such a middle-class, middle-aged, matinée ladies' entertainment, so closely bound to images of gracious living, that a lover in Shakespeare and his girl are assumed to be like the President's son-in-law and daughter. Therefore the whole class of people who go to Shakespeare, not knowing what it's all about but feeling somehow that Shakespeare is a part of gracious living, expect to see the sort of person that you would hope to see marrying your President's daughter up there, otherwise he can't be acceptably the son of a duke in the play. And that was something that certainly hadn't occurred to us.

RB It's something that brings us up against the fact that Shakespeare is a codeword that in each country designates a certain set of values and expectations. And finding a way through this barrier to the reality that was originally discerned by Shakespeare is always hard.

PB I think that on the one hand the material is so rich that one can say that if you take even a corner of it you're doing pretty well. So one can well understand how in Poland, Brazil, anywhere – where anybody looking at these plays is bound to get ninety per cent of them all wrong because of the translations they've got, not knowing what they're really about – someone will suddenly say, 'Ah, we could do *Much Ado* as a comment on what's happening in Chile at this moment.' And they do it. Well, good luck to it, every interpretation if it works in its place and its moment has some life. But I think that into that totally permissive view, everything is possible, one can introduce a certain scale of values. One can ask whether the act of interpretation takes the smallest or the widest view of what the play contains. For instance, if in Poland today you see in *Macbeth* something extremely close to the Polish situation and in doing this interpretation you impose it so firmly that, however much it works, you rob the play of all its ambiguities, you may be doing a successful performance, but you are cutting off your own nose and tying your hands behind your back, because you are at the same time diminishing the play unnecessarily. If you can do the double process, which is to say, 'My interest in this play today is clearly political, but that doesn't blind me to the fact that the play is also anti-political and contradictory and metaphysical. Therefore I won't, because I'm not interested in other aspects of the play, pretend they don't exist' – then most likely I'll discover something and the group will discover something and the audience will discover something. But if I *use* the play, the permissive attitude is at its worst. Because the play is then no longer a vehicle for a re-exploration of truth, it becomes a vehicle for exploitation.

RB Can I take up the word you used, 'diminishing', and ask you to apply it to the problems of costume, or more broadly the metaphoric vehicle for the production as a whole, like the Watteau *Love's Labour's Lost*? Do you think nowadays that a Renaissance costume – which is able inherently to contain many meanings and which denies very little, I would have thought – is the best, or are you prepared to find your metaphoric vehicle in costume terms in any point of history?

PB There are two stages in that. The first stage, literally, is whether or not you're working in the proscenium theatre. For instance, when we did *A Midsummer Night's Dream*, we did several performances of it outside. There was one performance when we took the whole company from Stratford to London and played in the Roundhouse. And we left everything behind – scenery, costumes – and played in our ordinary working clothes. And what was appropriate in one would not have been appropriate in the other. But when you're on anything resembling a proscenium stage, or in that sort of relationship with an audience, when a bank of people are looking at something displayed in front of them, a costume has a quite different meaning from what we've been doing for the last three years, going round Africa and other places. You put down a carpet in the open air and a few hundred people gather round and watch, and whatever you happen to be wearing is a part of life, as in the Elizabethan theatre. It's a quite different thing. So it's a two-stage question. I think the aim, the necessity is that anything visual in a Shakespearian production should not confine the audience to a single attitude and a single interpretation. That's why I think any complete and consistent set of historical costumes is a fantastic imposition, and forces the play in certain directions. Nothing brought this out more strongly than all the work we did on *Lear*. It's quite obvious that all periods are inappropriate – but equally the Elizabethan. I've seen an Elizabethan/Renaissance costume *Lear*; it isn't natural. Take as a yardstick the uninformed audience – and we want the very bright but uninformed audience, with no prejudices, as the yardstick – who's interested if it's interesting and not otherwise. If it comes and sees a lot of Renaissance people, that's a fantastically specific statement that's being made. And if your aim is to make a reality re-emerge, then you don't make a sort of comment in parenthesis, this was written in a certain period; it's irrelevant. While you're watching the play you want to be in connection with the living element that's unfolding and you don't want to be reminded of anything that's extraneous to this. There have been many attempts made by political groups – they do this in the German theatre quite a lot – which is to say that the proper Marxist way to look at a play is constantly to be kept aware of the play as something emerging from a certain date in history, a certain time and to keep all these factors before us, trying to force you to keep that sort of alienation. I saw recently a play directed in this manner, so that for two and a half hours you were always conscious of the play as an example of writing at such-and-such a moment of history. Of course, it's intolerable. You cannot enter into a play if part of you is squashed into that footnoting attitude, you cannot enter into the experience. Now, I think that in a very different way any set of costumes that is self-consistent will have this effect. That's why I think that it's an endless question. I don't know the answer, except that each production will try to come back to it and reopen it. But I think that a mixture of any sort is already a better solution than one that is consistent. And the moment anything is all of a piece, then it's putting a straitjacket on to Shakespeare.

The other day, we did something that would interest you very much. We filmed for two days experiments with Shakespeare, for French television, in a ruined theatre. It was an absolute ruin, with no stage, a great pit – it was rather like a dump that we were working in. We did a scene from *Coriolanus*, we did a bit of *Hamlet*, a bit of *The Tempest*, a bit of *Romeo and Juliet*, and it was absolutely thrilling to see people in just their ordinary working clothes sitting in a pile of dust and paving stones, broken stones and rubble, doing the first scene of *Coriolanus*, their imaginations totally released by this. It was very visual, highly evocative. But the visual elements were making provocations to the imagination, not set statements. To put it very simply: the trap is to make statements and to make illustrations. And this is close to thinking that Shakespeare himself was making statements and making illustrations. If we recognise the danger of both and that he wasn't doing that, we can then discern the other world of vibrations, provocations and radiating points.

RB The trap may be convention in the widest sense. I'm thinking of the fact that I've several times seen eclectically costumed productions of comedies, which have worked very well – I think of William Gaskill's *A Chaste Maid in Cheapside* at the Royal Court some years back. But I've never seen a tragedy played eclectically. Perhaps there is an inner expectation that tragedy, or serious drama, ought to be consistently costumed.

PB But you saw the *Lear*, in the theatre?

RB Yes.

PB Because in the theatre, there was no consistency, although there appeared to be, because there the eclecticism was not in different styles, but in the fact that we mixed together complete and sketchy costumes. So most of the characters had almost neutral costumes, but key characters had specific and detailed ones. This was a psychological trick that gave an impression of a single world, but in fact being in a way completely eclectic.

RB My recollection is of a complete stylistic unity.

PB Yes, but that was an impression, because in fact we stripped almost everything inessential. One has to be undistracted; a wide eclecticism is distracting, it's busy. You constantly note it in a comedy, you notice all those things, you can't not notice them. And the tragic form of that needs to be as free, but much more invisible, so that you don't notice it.

RB Yes. It's the underlying assumption of jest, of making fantasy about a comedy that permits one the licence to go for the provocations that you speak of.

PB But you know, an example of this is that I've found many times that if today you want an actor in either a tragedy or a comedy to look natural – natural in the sense that you accept him – you just watch him, and look at his face and his hands, and you listen to what he's saying and yet you don't want him to look contemporary – almost always you find that the best way of clothing him is to put him in some form of trousers. And you'll find that in many, many productions designers and costume makers instinctively do something which in photographs fifty years from now will stand out as being so ridiculously characteristic of our time. But for us, men's legs in stockings and breeches have a desperately period flavour. There are many ways of cheating in period costumes, like for instance Lear's servants. If we dressed Lear's servants in any of those horrendous primitive little skirts and thongs around their legs, you would never have looked at anything else and you could never have believed in their reality. Actually, the actor wouldn't have been able to believe in it himself. We put him in something that looked like a simple garment, but was actually a sort of painter's smock and trousers and boots. The trick is that nobody analyses this and thinks, what are they doing in trousers? Trousers are as natural and invisible today as in Arab countries a robe would be. Tomorrow, we must think again – but the truth of any given production is only for the people who are actually witnessing it.

RB To move on to another aspect of the matter: what are your views about cutting nowadays? Let's say, the text that you receive that you begin to work on.

PB Well, again I think that in a way we're getting the same answer on every single point. It is with a double attitude, and that is respect on the one hand and disrespect on the other. And the dialectic between the two is what it's all about. If you go solely on one or the other way, you lose the possibility of capturing the truth. I think that the plays are not written with the same degree of finish, it's not in their nature. And some plays are looser and some plays are tighter. In the *Midsummer Night's Dream* I didn't have the least wish to cut a word, to cut or transpose anything, for the simple reason that it seemed to me an absolutely perfect play. In giving oneself the respect for it as something you don't pull around, you then have a much greater chance of getting into its depths, setting yourself the absolute conviction that each word is there because it has to be. Otherwise, to go back to your word 'vibrations', certain vibrations won't take place; but by total belief in the text you find its rightness. Alan Howard played over two or three years with an ever-greater sense of secret meanings he found for himself. In the play, on many levels, endlessly discovered and rediscovered, meanings came from him that made vibrations pass through Theseus into Oberon and back again across the whole play. And the play was at its best when the whole cast was at a point of high attunement, so that within the performance those vibrations went across it. It's like those sculptures made out of tight wires making a complex pattern, where if the wires aren't tight you don't get the pattern. So that with the *Dream* – although I can well imagine being very entertained by somebody taking a totally iconoclastic view and turning it upside down – I'm certain that in enjoying and laughing at and going along with such a production, I would find it less than, a diminishing of, the play itself, where I don't think you can move a word. I think that in other plays you can move words and scenes, but you have to do it in full recognition of how dangerous it is. And I think that this is really something for which there are no rules except the rules of sensitivity, that what in one line doesn't really matter in another line matters like hell.

RB I think we've come back to a redefinition of the word that you quoted Orson Welles as saying, that we 'betray' Shakespeare, and I wondered about that word, because it seemed to me that it stated by implication an ideal or ethic of loyalty, to which we ought to adhere and which alas we are not observing. And I wondered how this could be formulated. But in talking as you do about sensitivity and respect, one is perhaps getting as near to the ideal of 'loyalty', if that is the word that one wants to choose, that describes one's feelings for Shakespeare. So could I ask you finally now, how you'd like to state your relationship to what we call 'Shakespeare'?

PB Yes, very simply. I don't have any sense of or interest in history as a reality. History is to me a way of looking at things and not one that interests me very much. What I'm much more interested in is that, in the present, and I mean each person's present, wherever he is and whenever it takes place, he and we are constantly betraying reality, which we don't succeed in perceiving, grasping and living, and we're continually diminishing and reducing it. This is the way that we live through our lives and live in our present, because however we live the present it's always a highly diminished view of the present moment as it might be. It's always been broadly recognised that what's been considered as the artist's vision is never a vision turned on the past or the future, but is a greater possibility of seeing what is actually happening than the duller vision with which we live through our everyday lives. This function has been partly taken over by drugs and drugs have to a degree once again shown the present in a different light from the everyday, which is why they have such enormous appeal. But my interest in any form of art is nothing to do with culture; that doesn't mean anything to me, either. What interests me is that there are channels through which we can come into contact for a limited time with a more intense reality, with heightened perceptions. Therefore Shakespeare to me doesn't belong to the past. If his material is real, it is real now.

To me, it's like coal. One knows, if one wants to go into it, the whole process of the primaeval forest and how it goes down into the ground, and one can trace the history of coal; but the meaningfulness of a piece of coal to us today, or anywhere, starts and finishes with it in combustion, giving out the light and heat that we want. And that to me is Shakespeare. Shakespeare is a piece of coal that is inert. I can write books and give public lectures about where this coal comes from – but I'm really interested in coal on a cold evening, when I need to be warm and I put it on the fire, and it becomes itself. Then it relives its virtue.

Now take this one step further: I think that today the understanding of what perception is is beginning to change very greatly and one's beginning to recognise that the human faculty of apprehension is not static, but is a second-for-second redefining of what it sees. Look at those visual conundrums where you don't know if something is upside down – you know, black and white squares that seem to be jumping inside out. You can actually see how the mind copes with something which it is trying to reunderstand, trying to verify whether it's upside down or not. The mind is constantly trying to remake a coherent world out of such provocations. Now to me the total works of Shakespeare are like a very, very complete set of codes and these codes, cipher for cipher, set off in us, stir in us, vibrations and impulses which we immediately try to make coherent and understandable. If we enter wholeheartedly into this relation, then all the steps of understanding and reincarnating are steps towards making a world in the present tense, in the present moment, whose only virtues are the standards of meaningfulness, significance, coherence, depth and one could say reality, truth, as perceived: and that nothing else comes into it. Now within that, because of the completeness of the picture, it can't be simplified in many ways, so that there are archaic elements that are part of it. There are many complex, archaic things that I look at as coming not from history but as something which stirs up in me at this moment my own corner of responses to archaism, which is a very different thing. And so I have to take account of it. What I'm interested to see is not the historical sense but the actual, what makes a meaning for me. And it was through that channel that we eventually, for instance in the *Dream*, came to say: what does magic, what does fairy magic actually mean as a reality within the two hours that you're in the theatre? Not as a convention, but as something which still has a reality. Maybe with completely different outer forms. The word 'fairy' suggests a lot of things; it suggests dead associations. Far behind, it also suggests very living values. If I can touch them, then the coal is burning now.

1974

Robin Phillips (II)

Ralph Berry You've directed something like half the Shakespeare canon and I know that in the last few years you've revisited three or four plays. I can think of *Antony and Cleopatra*, *Twelfth Night*, *As You Like It*, the *Dream* that you've returned to. Is there something in the process of revisiting Shakespeare that you find especially beneficial?

Robin Phillips Although to direct seems to become more difficult each year, it is certainly easier to be simple – to do things more simply when you come back to the plays. One needs less visual aid the second time around. Of course, that may also mean that I have become a little more mature and have learned to trust the text more.

I have learned to trust the text in a special way. One becomes aware of the enormity of truth *beyond* the text, and that truth becomes more and more clear as one revisits the plays. It becomes much more obvious to you how the evening's communication is not, *in truth*, the text; in *fact*, but not in truth. The text is the means to the end. The end is a spontaneous communication of whatever lies beyond the text, beyond the subtext, the cumulative effect of thought and feeling. That's much more apparent when you revisit the play, because why else is it different? Why does it mean something different this time, why does the play appear to be saying something different? How can it be saying something entirely different when the text is exactly the same? We refer to a play as 'speaking' to us and so believe that the communication (or perhaps the communicator) is the text, the voice. But then we are aware that the play 'says something different to me tonight'. How is that possible? It is possible because we sense a truth beyond the accumulation of fact that is clearly presented by the text. We are aware of an elemental truth and yet can only sense it, feel it, experience it. The feelings of the moment seem to link backwards and forwards in time, recalling past emotions and pointing towards an enlightenment still to come.

RB You're talking about something that goes far beyond a mere restaging. Can you give me an instance or two of a play that you've redirected that seems to throw up a substantially different meaning?

RP I was certainly most fearful of attempting a new production of *As You Like It*, having done it twice before.

The first production was with Maggie Smith as Rosalind and Jack Wetherall as Orlando. It was alarming to come back to a play when, rarely for me, it was one of the productions of mine that I happened to like. But it proved not to be so very difficult. It was very interesting to see what had so clearly, *textually* appeared to be a wise and more mature Rosalind leading a less experienced Orlando towards love, teaching him, guiding him towards experience and understanding. It was a divine performance by Maggie Smith of aching beauty and wisdom, totally supported by the text. How could a new performance differ radically from this original?

In the new production an entirely different relationship emerged, from exactly the same text and imagery with a Rosalind (in the Nancy Palk version) who discovered freedom in disguise, personal freedom. This was not so much in her relationship with Orlando, but you saw a girl who, disguised as a man, stepped into her own enlightenment and self-discovery.

As we moved into the new production of *Twelfth Night*, we made new discoveries, prompted by the proximity of the two plays. Now Nancy's Viola was in disguise for her life. I hadn't noticed this as clearly the first time round because with Patricia Conolly it was an older Viola. It was because this (later) Viola and this Rosalind happened to be in the same season with the same company, the same actress, that one saw very clearly the suffocating covering that disguise created for Viola and the pain she experienced of having love held in and controlled by Cesario. She is unable to express herself as she would wish.

That was a different, a new experience because of the new actress. In both circumstances, the experience was totally supported by the text. And although both actresses were precise in their exploration of the text they couldn't have been more different in what they were communicating to us. The remarkable thing about Shakespeare is that his texts (his maps, his signposts) are so complex and varied that although you may intellectually follow the clues and piece them together along similar scholastic lines, they will lead you towards different emotional conclusions by which you arrive at totally unexpected human truths.

RB It's a set of issues stemming from the question: how old is the actor playing this part? It seems to me that while Shakespeare is sometimes specific (Hamlet is twenty-eight to thirty, Iago is twenty-eight), much more often he gives a set of impressions of what we believe to be the age of the part. At the same time it is possible to cast this part in such a way that there is a range of options. For example, in *Twelfth Night*, I remember you had a mature Olivia (Pat Galloway) in your production a few years back. She was able to give a special resonance to lines like 'For youth is bought more oft than begg'd or borrow'd.' But on the other hand it's easy to see Olivia as very young, twentyish perhaps, and you had a young Olivia second time. These old-young possibilities seem to be contained within the same lines of the same part.

RP Yes, isn't it fascinating? It also changes dramatically with the balance of the boy-girl and girl-boy components. There are times when the specifics of any given year – the society, the community in which the play is to speak – will change the attitude towards the girl-boy disguise. Depending on the attitude of the present, girl-being-boy-being-girl may be able to show her femininity through her disguise or her masculinity. The balance constantly changes back and forth, and it is through this shift too that we get entirely different relationships. One is used to seeing Viola and Orsino get so close to discovering their relationship that by half-way through the play it is almost unbear-able. One longs for the end of the play when they may reveal to each other that love is permissible. It is usual to see the Olivia/Ces-ario/Viola relationship kept at a slightly more giddy level. But there is also the possibility of a deeply serious sexual pull between Olivia and Cesario that is a hundred per cent there in the text, of course it's there in the text. The sexual ambiguity is there in equal measure both in its seriousness and in its comedic possib-ilities, but our values change. The audience participation, assist-ance ('*J'assiste à une pièce*,' the French say – it's better, isn't it?) not only permits the play to ring with a resonance that is heady in its sexual implications, but allows it to vibrate with emotional layers of confusing contradiction of pain and pleasure. But, you say, 'This would have been a *boy* playing the girl playing the boy . . .' Then which scenes would have taken on the serious overtones? Let Olivia rehearse with a young man playing Cesario, then, 'i'the orchard' let her 'do more *favours* to the Count's servingman' than ever she bestowed on Sir Andrew.

RB I confess that that text seems to me bafflingly open and as I read the words I don't know what to make of them. When at the end Orsino says 'Let me see thee in thy woman's weeds' it seems to me (in the abstract) impossible to construct the psy-chology of Orsino at this point. I mean, until we know the casting, we are not in a position to comment.

RP That's right.

RB You're saying, then, that what interests you especially in a Shakespeare text is the sexual underplot, which can only be revealed through casting and through rehearsal, and that a very considerable part of your work is to uncover what this sexual underplot is?

RP Yes, I think that's absolutely right. We are told that we live in the age of the image maker; I believe we always have. I think that at all levels of society, whether we're choosing our political leaders or where we are going to bank, or where we are going to buy our groceries, there is constantly sex appeal and/or a sensual relationship in our daily lives. As our societies change and we make hopefully a little progress in our understanding of

Shakespeare's observation of the human condition, the common denomination of these plays and what we have to communicate to an audience is always a tiny fraction of the only worthwhile topic for all our studies: *human truth.* We have to start with animal instincts and animal desires, and how these basic qualities of the human animal change, first because of language and then education and the society that we produce. But we must begin with instinct.

RB Of the two ways this can go, the animal and the sexual, you're not, I take it, thinking of 'animal' in the sense of that story that's told of Alan Badel, that he found visiting the zoo useful for the Fool in *King Lear?*

RP No. I'm not talking about that. I think, of course, that there is some value in such observation, but that's just a minor part of the actor's craft. It is important to understand what links the Greeks to the eighteenth century, to the Edwardians, to now. There are links of human behaviour and needs that change with different societies, different cultural environments, all of which have to be understood. You can't understand the changes unless you get back to the basic things and then see how they have been shaped and adapted by society.

RB The cultural links that you speak of come, in your own work, from the larger nineteenth century, from something like – you might care to adjust the dates – the 1830s or 1840s to the First World War. I know that you like to go as far as the Edwardian era. And with you, clearly, this is not simply a device but a preferred mode of discourse within which you develop your statements. Can you say something about the nineteenth century and why you find it so appealing?

RP The most important thing for me is the birth of photography, and the major role it has played culturally, socially and in education. Consequently I come back time and again to a period that includes photography. There are many other reasons. But it seems there is a total change in the perception of history from that invention on.

It's like the invention of the rules of perspective. Once these were in existence they allowed us to have a better understanding of the period that preceded that development. Cave drawings are much better understood once our minds are able to accept the rules of perspective. Understanding photography, and the enormous changes that photography has brought about, makes for a richer understanding of ancient Greek or Egyptian art for example. It is more tangible, it is understood in a three-dimensional way since the birth of photography. Photography changed our way of seeing things and continues to do so.

RB But life is always specific, highly specific. What I always find in your productions, especially with this time frame, is a very dense sense of social relations and the history of the period, and what effect this has on the words of the play. For example, in your *Timon of Athens*, Timon is a wealthy Edwardian – you might say late Victorian – who has endured the indignity of the *crash*. The *crash* seems a more loaded and emotive word in the Galsworthy/*Man of Property* era than before or since. The *crash* is very terrible and your Edwardian setting locates that sense.

RP I hope nevertheless that through its specific details it illuminates both what has gone before and points to what is yet to come. The precise moment where, beyond the text, the human, emotional response to a situation can be explicitly understood, where your responses are both spontaneous and specific, where you can comprehend with all your senses what happened in Shakespeare's own time or what may have happened to the Greeks or Romans or Egyptians. We can't truly comprehend a special moment in history unless our emotions are spontaneously dealt with as well. Therefore one chooses a time where the emotions are spontaneously provoked.

RB The specifics give us what I think we need, which is some kind of explanation. Take, for example, your *King Lear*, set in the mid-nineteenth century, in which we learn early of Gloucester's bastard son Edmund. It occurs to me that Gloucester is a Regency buck who grew up in an era when this kind of libertinage was much easier, socially easier, than later. He had learned to be ashamed of his own son. Now there is an explanation which your production does not insist on or elaborate, it is simply an easy recess of the dating of the production. Which I found helpful, as a member of the audience.

Can we talk about the text itself? You have, I think, certain reservations about the limitations of the word alone.

RP I'm sure that the text is purely a series of signposts. It's the map that will lead us to the truth that is to be communicated. Because it is a very well-defined and accurate map, drawn by an experienced craftsman, we must follow it with immense care. It's a complicated and tricky one, and like all maps there will be many pitfalls if you veer from the prescribed route. Nevertheless, if you follow the route, the text, it leads you to the hidden truth. Truth, that reaches beyond the intellect to the heart, to the emotions, feelings and responses.

It's the same with many writing or language arts. The best journalism is about giving you facts in a straightforward sequence as honestly as is possible, but usually because the journalist believes the more clearly they are placed the more they will reveal behind the accumulation of facts a truth that is of greater importance than the sum of the facts themselves. That's why editorials used to be called 'leaders': it was to guide us towards this truth, this knowledge, this understanding, that should not be put into words because it would diminish its scope and its size, and its personal acceptance for each reader. It led us there and left us to do the rest of the work personally.

RB But always for the director choices have to be made. Another example from your work: Arden is, of course, a country of the mind, the absolute rural idyll of our dreams. It's got to be located somewhere, in the text itself perhaps. It might be mid-Warwickshire, with this talk of sheepcotes, forests, woods and so on. In your recent *As You Like It* it was a Mennonite community,* which is something that means a good deal to many people in North America. They have some basis of knowledge, perhaps experience, to relate to your ordering of this idyllic community.

RP Not only is the work you're going to do connected with

---

*A Protestant Christian sect. European in origin, it established several new, rural communities in North America in the nineteenth century.

the artists you work with, the actors and the designers, it's also being presented in a specific place and communicated to a specific group of people. Within that community you have to be prepared to make choices that make the response personalised for them. I was amazed to discover some Mennonite poetry that was so close to the banished Duke's description of where he and the forest lords were living, and what they thought they could achieve in their new community, that it was hard to believe that the author had not read *As You Like It*. Textually, Shakespeare and the Mennonite society matched very well. I will never forget the first public performance of *As You Like It* here, in Stratford. As we went into the first forest-lord scene with Mennonite dress, there was a gasp, a sigh of recognition that was one of the most amazing sounds I've ever heard. The audience knew in a way that mere design could not have revealed to them. It was a combination of text, sound, light, costume, colour and the very rhythm of movement that the actors had acquired. Something was shared that was beyond the sum of all those things put together. That's precisely what Shakespeare expects us to do.

RB What do you do with a play like *Julius Caesar*, which doesn't in any immediate sense seem to relate to its audience in a close way? What can one do with that challenge?

RP Everything that Shakespeare wrote relates to an audience in a close way. In *Julius Caesar*, for example, let's talk about Act III, Scene ii, the Forum: a scene with politicians, heads of state and crowds of citizens. What specific images can we piece together to strike a chord of recognition? Martin Luther King on the steps of the Lincoln Memorial; Pope John Paul II on the Vatican balcony behind a bullet-proof screen and a microphone; President Reagan addressing the United Nations; the inauguration of President Bush; the Prince and Princess of Wales on the balcony of Buckingham Palace; John F. Kennedy addressing the nation on the Cuban missile crisis; the inauguration of President Johnson. (These all have something to offer our scene, if only the sound of a large crowd.)

Consider the 'reverse shot' of the Vatican or Buckingham Palace balcony or the Lincoln Memorial and compare this photographic image with Shakespeare's play. Officials gathered together in an anteroom behind huge doors leading to the open air. The doors swing open and a person steps out into the sunlight. The crowd roars. We see the figure silhouetted against the sky. We hear his first words; the crowd is hushed. But *we* (the audience) remain inside with Brutus and the others. They are silent. We observe them as they listen to every word of Antony's speech. They listen for nuance – for any sign of emotion – they strain to catch the slightest murmur of response from the crowd. They watch each other, they think, they feel, they react but they say nothing. Are they worried? Are they concerned? Do they feel the same things from moment to moment as the speaker continues? Do they perspire? Do they drink? Do they move?

This 'reverse shot' is our link to today. There is nothing in the *text* that says Mark Antony must face the audience. There is nothing in the *text* that says that the conspirators *must* all leave the stage. (Yes, I know the word 'exit' may be present as a stage direction but let us remember that every 'entrance' is an 'exit' from another place and so all 'exits' are also 'entrances' to a place elsewhere.)

Imagine the group of politicians gathered in the Oval office listening to Martin Luther King at the Lincoln Memorial: 'Friends, Romans, countrymen . . . I have a dream . . .'

You don't have to do the production in modern dress. You can show the Roman equivalent of the Oval office and let the characters live their offstage scene in our presence. We have been brought up and educated in the language of film and television technology and this reverse shot will be immediately if subconsciously understood.

There are connecting truths beyond the text and, finally, it is at this level that we communicate spontaneously. It may be eclectic but the chord is struck and the shock of recognition occurs.

1988

Adrian Noble

Adrian Noble has directed many Shakespeare plays for the Royal Shakespeare Company, including Measure for Measure, As You Like It *and, most recently,* The Plantagenets. *He has been Associate Director at the RSC since 1982.*

Ralph Berry Whom do you think of as ancestors, among directors, those people who have influenced you?

Adrian Noble I think one has to look at the formative period in one's life, which was the time – late Sixties, early Seventies – when I was leaving school and going to drama school, going to theatre and if you like looking for heroes. The heroes that one looked up to, the shows one saw that were seminal, were Ariane Mnouchkine's *1789*, Peter Brook's *A Midsummer Night's Dream*, several different pieces at the Open Space Theatre, very experimental stagings. I have earlier memories than that, having been brought up in Chichester – memories of early National Theatre work, *The Royal Hunt of the Sun*, pieces like that. Star actors, strong ensemble playing, exciting pieces of work. I was a child of the Sixties in production terms. If I go back further, the route I probably have to trace is my drama school, which was founded by people with a strong European tradition, people – Saint-Denis, Devine – who had worked at the Vic school.

RB Are there any figures from the remoter past, with whom you have no direct connection, but upon whom you look as having meaning for you? If I could give one instance, when I saw your *Comedy of Errors* a few years ago it seemed to me very much in the spirit of the Komisarjevsky *Comedy of Errors*, that first appeared here in Stratford in 1938. Do you recognise Komisarjevsky as an influence?

AN That's really the only one of his productions, apart from the Chekhovs, that I know much about. To a degree, yes, but not in particular. I suppose the person to whom most directors owe most, this century, is Tyrone Guthrie, who created the idea of staging as we have received that idea and as we now challenge that idea. He was a man who rewrote the agenda for most theatre directors of this country. After him, of course, came Brook and he adjusted the agenda. For most English directors nowadays I would imagine that we look more to Europe for influence than to our contemporaries – to Patrice Chéreau, to Giorgio Strehler, to Peter Stein – for excitement in the theatre these days.

RB This may seem too simplifying a question, but what is your sense of the agenda – the agenda as you receive it now?

AN I think Tyrone Guthrie stepped into the shoes that used to be worn by the leading actor of the company. In other words, he would set the time and place of the production; he would give relative value, production value, to different characters and scenes. He would actually, by doing these things, create an interpretation above and beyond – probably in sympathy with, but certainly above and beyond – that of just the leading actors. That was massively important in the twentieth century. It has roots of course in the nineteenth century, in the Meiningen company. That agenda has been rewritten since the Second World War, by Brook in the first instance, possibly by others like Devine, whereby the director as circus master was revalued and the director became more of a collaborator with a group of people, including the designer. And you would get situations whereby in the Sixties someone like Brook would go into rehearsals without a concept, without possibly a design, sometimes without even a script, and would make theatre. That's the particular branch of that inheritance that I've picked up most of all, those productions at the end of the Sixties.

RB May I take up what you were saying about the design and the concept. Isn't there a hard, practical point here? Is it possible for the director of Shakespeare to go into rehearsal without a concept? I mean, that design itself may involve a commission, may involve a great deal of practical work to be done, which has a timetable that extends back from the actual first night. And that it may therefore be impossible for the director not to have a design, and a concept, before rehearsals begin.

AN That's true, particularly of the modern theatre, whereby sets, costumes, props are very expensive, and the earlier they are designed, the cheaper they become. You get more for your money. This is a serious problem for modern theatre – for any theatre, ancient or modern. Actors find this very limiting. This is a modern problem, though, because for centuries actors turned up and received last year's costumes; it was perfectly normal. Directors find this a great limitation on their exploration. One hears this sometimes in the rehearsal room, with an actor looking at his costume and saying, 'Ah, that's my character, is it?' Every production requires a different approach, and different approaches occur according to where one is in one's life and one's career, what relationships one has with one's leading actors. For example, when I did *Macbeth*, I worked for eight months with Jonathan Pryce, before we started rehearsals, and for the first four months the designer wasn't even appointed, let alone involved in that process of discussion and debate. When I did *As You Like It*, we had not designed that production on the first day of rehearsals. We designed it during rehearsals. And that wasn't a totally successful concept.

RB It was a fascinating concept, though. What I and I'm sure everyone remembers is that billowing dust sheet that first swathed the furniture, and then became some kind of emblem for Arden.

AN It also became a mantrap. Not only was it extremely slippery, which meant that you would find yourself physically in danger, but it became a bit of a worry for everyone. The very point of it became its problem. We wanted something that was genuinely plastic, that would change shape according to what the actors did, according to the moment in the play, because the Forest of Arden in *As You Like It* changes shape, dimension, character, according to the perception of each person. At one point it's a friendly place with bunny rabbits, at another point it's a dangerous place with lions. And we thought we had the solution. The problem was that while physically it was a bit dangerous, the actors would never know what it was going to do next, which meant that you would walk into the wings during that production and continually see the actors anxiously peering on to the stage to see how they were going to make their entrance. Not how they were going to do that scene or what their character was feeling like, but physically how they were going to get downstage, which is the kind of worry you don't want.

On the most recent production I've done, *The Plantagenets*, we went into rehearsal with not a stick of furniture, not a design idea in our heads, and that turned out very successful in terms of concept and design. And that was worked out on the rehearsal floor.

RB Which you consider to be the ideal way, if it can be done?

AN It's the ideal way if it can be done, yes. It does require time and it's a high-risk business. It's not necessarily the right solution for all productions. I was very happy with the way I approached *Macbeth* whereby we created a world in which those rehearsals could take place. I think it was on the whole the right world; it didn't put anything in the actor's way and it gave a framework within which we could create symbol, meaning, claustrophobia, all the things we were looking to explore.

RB In your productions one is constantly encountering exciting and vivid theatrical moments, which you have found for the characters and the world of the characters. I'm thinking, for example, of the lances in *Macbeth* that penetrate the walls in the last act and threaten Macbeth so dramatically. Is that what you are consciously working for, much of the time, this eliciting of metaphors and vivid theatrical images?

AN That's the easy bit of directing. I find it very stimulating to create exciting pictures on the stage. I can do that. The real grind of rehearsals takes place with the actors trying to make a text 400 years old alive with meaning, now, that it should have the right rate, the right phrasing, that it should penetrate our dull ears. That's the real work, not thinking up pictures of King Lear twelve feet in the air, or spears coming through walls. That's easy. I can do that.

RB So this 'world', then. Do you think of the world also as a society? In other words, a particular period of human progress, which we can relate to a nation, an era, where there is a reasonable homogeneity of costume style?

AN What's exciting for me about theatre is that each event creates its own rules. No two theatrical events will be the same. I believe that happens for many reasons, but one in particular, which is that our national playwright, one of the prime creators of our consciousness, is William Shakespeare, who worked in a theatre and explored an aesthetic in which each play created its own imaginative world, its own cosmology, if you like, its own earth, heaven and hell. Which are different from play to play. And which indeed are sometimes different within the plays themselves. For example, you will go on a journey in a Shakespeare play and you may well *en route* visit paradise, briefly. You may well visit Dante's purgatory. The world changes in the course of the evening and has its own rules.

It's so for most of the Elizabethan and Jacobean dramatists. Take Webster, in *The Duchess of Malfi*. When the Duchess goes into prison, in the fourth act, he creates a purgatory on stage for her, through the imagery of the language, through the way in which he makes the audience's imagination work. He takes us into the very heart of despair.

RB But he does this through a particular image, does he not, which is specifically social and early seventeenth century. I mean, here is the Duchess of Malfi, a very great lady, in her court, sitting on what is probably, on stage, the only chair, and she is present at a levée of madmen. It is a caricature of court order, but it is the court order of – all right, an Italian, but you could also say an English, society of the seventeenth century. Specifically that.

AN Yes, I think that's true. When I did *The Duchess of Malfi*, I did it in period. But I don't think the deduction from what you say is that 'period' is the only way of doing it. The point is not so much to do with the social order that Webster is evoking, it is the imaginative world he creates in the audience's mind, in the whole of that section of the play. One's job, when directing, is to create a world that is logical for that event. A play, under certain circumstances of production, will have a different logic for different events.

RB How about the problem of *King Lear*? Most of the text seems to invoke a barbarous and primitive society, or world. In the past, of course, it's often been evoked by Stonehenge images. But at the same time there's a strain in the text that seems to point to a courtly, sophisticated, quite advanced society. In the past few years, as you know, some first-class productions have been located in the nineteenth century. To put it crudely: Stonehenge v. the nineteenth century, those are possibilities. Do you feel, as a director, that there is a moment when you have to throw the override switch and declare for one or the other?

AN I don't tend to work that way myself. I very rarely set a play in period. I did it with *Measure for Measure*, which I set in the eighteenth century. There were anachronistic elements in my *Measure for Measure*, though. I'm not arguing for some kind of fantasy, mystical, mythical world. And some plays demand different things. *Measure for Measure* demands a specific world in which to operate; and so, in my view, does *Much Ado* and *The Merry Wives of Windsor*. I don't think this applies to *Macbeth*, *King Lear* and certain other plays. In *King Lear* Shakespeare assumed a theatrical dimension to our reception of his plays. There was never any issue, for Shakespeare, that we were in a theatre. He would not have understood the idea of modern naturalism; it wouldn't have meant anything to him, I think. To impose naturalistic or realistic disciplines on Shakespeare is not, I think, necessary. Likewise, I think that Shakespeare made certain assumptions about theatre and its parameters, the way it worked upon the people in the audience, that we have to study and think about. That seems to be our main business.

RB Does this mean that you openly embrace eclecticism as the style for your Shakespeare productions?

AN No, not at all. I really believe in horses for courses! I believe that it is the business of a director to create a world in which it is logical for those events to take place. Later on this year, I will be doing a piece of theatre in which people sing, and dance, and speak verse, at different times. I have to create a world in which it is logical to do all those things.

RB The plays of course are different. Robin Phillips said that in the text of *Measure for Measure* he could find find nothing that pointed to the Elizabethan period bar a reference to codpieces. In other words, the text seemed consciously designed to be open to the production style of the director, the imaginative idea of the director. There was absolutely nothing against it in the text, which was a kind of massive *nihil obstat* if you like.

AN One could argue about the stews stuff as pointing to a particular time and place. But certainly, the recent productions here, such as Nick Hytner's, have related the play to the modern world, because that's what he saw the play was talking about, that element of sexuality and the use of government power.

RB Or, as Jonathan Miller discerned, the play is very considerably about sexual repression, which means that it can be set in Freud's Vienna and whole areas of the text leap into life.

AN Yes. This brings us to another interesting topic, the nature of the public debate within Shakespeare's plays. We have a tendency nowadays to closet Shakespeare, because since Shakespeare wrote one or two other gentlemen have written: Strindberg, Ibsen, Freud, people who have examined human behaviour. The greatness of Shakespeare lies I believe in this, that that he allows us to examine behaviour in a private and a public context. There's a danger for us directors in being over-attracted to one element of the play, and thereby, through the lack of water, allowing another element of the play to wither and die. *Measure for Measure* does seemingly ricochet between public and private, and that's part of its dynamic. The nature of drama is that people behave in a certain way in private and a different way in public. One has to make a very full attempt to make the public debate in the play as alive as possible. Oddly enough, since Jonathan Miller did that, directors have tended to go towards the public debate in the play, rather than the private psychology of the characters. For example, when I first saw *Measure for Measure*, here in Stratford, in 1970 – John Barton's production – the leading character was Angelo, without doubt.

Nowadays the leading character is either Isabella or the Duke – probably the Duke.

RB I would say the Duke always, these days.

AN That's to do with the shift in our interest from Angelo. Jonathan Miller's production was the pinnacle of interest in Angelo and subversive sexuality, which I think doesn't interest people so much these days.

RB I think you're raising by implication a large question about casting. Nowadays the centre of interest in the play is so much the casting. This takes us a good deal beyond the old days, when the casting was obvious: 'I am the actor-manager and I'm going to play Hamlet; when I get a little older, I will play Claudius.' Or it might come to something a little more subtle than that, when Beerbohm Tree decided that Antony would be better for him than Brutus in *Julius Caesar*. But nowadays the dynamic centre of the play seems to open out from, one oughtn't to say the most interesting actor, but from the one who is able to create the most possibilities.

AN Sometimes directors look for actors who will be willing to explore their ideas. I don't think that particular attitude is dead yet. You have to have an actor who, you believe, is capable of or willing to address the agenda of the play. And that agenda changes from age to age.

RB My proposition would be that the agenda changes because the public changes, the world changes. To take the enormously important point you made a moment ago: if it is true – and I think it is true – that Angelo used to be the key casting in *Measure for Measure*, and today the Duke is the key casting, then that must tell us something important not only about *Measure for Measure* but the world we live in.

AN And about how our age is coming to understand what Shakespeare's political wisdom was. I believe *Measure for Measure* deals with central political issues, for the state and for individuals. As Shakespeare directors we have to understand what his way is. With *Measure for Measure* he tackles the subject of government. He creates models of change. He deals with the choice: how does one, as governor, choose different options?

The Merry Wives of Windsor, Bill Alexander, Barbican Theatre, 1986; Francine Morgan as Anne Page, Lindsay Duncan as Alice Ford.

The Merchant of Venice, Bill Alexander, Barbican Theatre, 1988; Antony Sher as Shylock, John Carlisle as Antonio.

Declan Donnellan

The Tempest, Cheek by Jowl, 1988; Michael Jenn as Trinculo, Duncan Duff as Caliban, Keith Bartlett as Stephano.

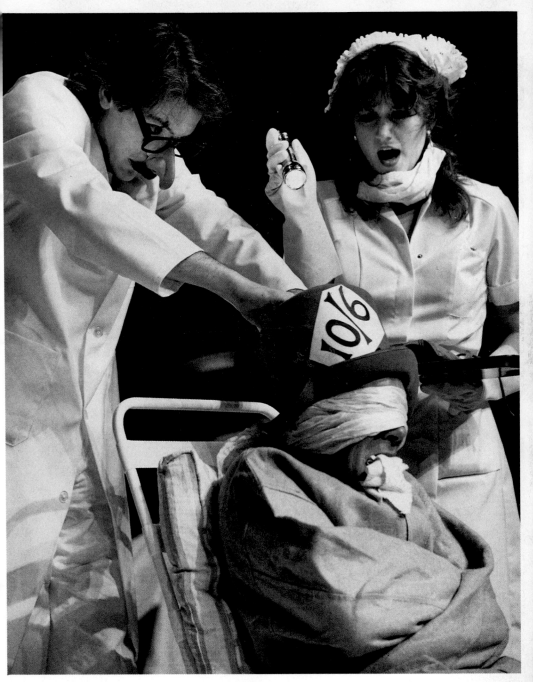

Twelfth Night, Cheek by Jowl, 1986; Steven Simms as Feste, Melinda McGraw as Maria, Hugh Ross as Malvolio,

Cymbeline, Peter Hall, National Theatre, 1988; Geraldine James as Innogen, Tim Pigott-Smith as Iachimo.

Cymbeline, Peter Hall, National Theatre, 1988; Peter Woodward as Posthumus.

Sir Peter Hall

The Winter's Tale, Peter Hall, National Theatre, 1988; Ken Stott as
Autolycus.

The Tempest, Peter Hall, National Theatre, 1988

Michael Bryant as Prospero

Steven Mackintosh as Arie

'This is a most majestic vision, and / Harmonious charmingly.' (Ferd., IV.i.119–20);
Steven Mackintosh as Ceres, Sally Dexter as Juno, Jenny Galloway as Iris.

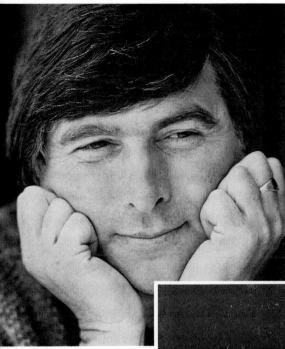

Michael Bogdanov

The Wars of The Roses,
English Shakespeare
Company, 1988; Francesca
~an as Doll Tearsheet, Barry
Stanton as Falstaff.

The Wars of The Roses, English Shakespeare Company, 1988; Andrew Jarvis as Richard III.

The Wars of The Roses, English Shakespeare Company, 1988: Jack Cade's rebellion (*Henry VI: House of York*).

How does one govern one's self? How does the state actually mature, learn to govern itself better? I always think it very interesting that the last scene in *Measure for Measure* takes place outside the gates of the city. And I believe they would stay outside those gates until they'd cracked the problems that are in the play. They sit there, or stand there, until they sort out all the problems. When they're fit and ready they will re-enter the city. I'm not making a case for the city as Jerusalem when the Duke comes back. They are all fallible mortals and vulnerable.

RB The basic programming of *Measure for Measure* is that we move from the closet or the inmost sanctum of government in Scene One, to – what is the usual scene location? – 'a public place near the city gate', which is the whole of the last act. There must be some deep directional statement in this movement from the closet to the open place.

AN The Duke says that Angelo and the others are to meet him at the gates, and not inside the city. It's how, symbolically, you re-enter that the last act is about and the pain you have to go through, the self-discovery, the use of artifice in government, all these things have to be gone through before everyone is fit and ready to go in. That play is a great public-political examination. Shakespeare doesn't teach you how to become the great Marxist state. That's not his business. The business is change; how do you change? How do you take responsibility? These are the essential questions, whatever form of government you go in for.

RB You are saying, then, that *Measure for Measure* is about government, rather than, to simplify, the sexual hang-ups of Angelo. And that, in the last scene, the question is should Angelo be fired from the Cabinet because of a sexual scandal?

AN No, that's one of fifty questions. Equally important is what should happen to Lucio. That's as important as what happens to Angelo. Equally important is whether the Duke should ask a woman to marry him. Equally important is whether Isabella should decide to be a nun or not. I think your question implies that Angelo is the most important thing, which I think he is not.

This idea of change, and how Shakespeare examines change, and why therefore he is a contemporary writer as much as one of his own time: you can look at *As You Like It*. There, at the end, they're getting ready not just for matrimony but to return to the state, to town. They've been through something and they've learned something. That's one of the great production decisions you have to make: how do you end it, what sort of world are they going back to? So what I am suggesting to you is a development of the old Sixties/RSC idea of a character going on a journey. That's true, but I would also argue that there is a political journey that people go on. There was a marvellous statement in *The Independent* at the end of the year, by Enoch Powell, talking about Shakespeare's history plays. He said, 'I'm a government minister and I've been in politics all my life. It's uncanny how Shakespeare is so accurate – he might have been at all those meetings.' A wonderful comment.

RB Could we turn to *The Plantagenets*, which is manifestly about government – there'd be no difficulty about that, I suppose. Do you discern prime issues, or even lessons, that Shakespeare is imparting within the framework of the Wars of the Roses – the brutal changes of government then shown?

AN I think Shakespeare's reputation as a maker of history plays has been rather cursed by the seemingly brilliant discovery that he's nothing more than a Tudor propagandist. A nasty old reactionary who is really a pedlar of right-wing ideas. This is a major twentieth-century discovery which is of course tosh. We have to understand the political context in which Shakespeare was writing and we have also to understand that Shakespeare was a moralist. He's not a materialist. He clearly believes that moral lessons are to be drawn from history. To that end he created history. I don't believe for a moment that Shakespeare thought he was creating the objective truth about the rise of the Tudor dynasty., I don't think that was his interest at all. It would not have struck him as a particularly crucial moral issue, whether or not he was telling the truth. He'd have thought about that but not seen it as a central issue. He saw history as providing him with opportunities whereby first and foremost central moral lessons could be drawn; and secondly, very complex and often paradoxical situations could be explored. An obvious example of the first is the famous scene in the Third Part of *Henry VI* – 'Enter a Son *that has killed his Father*' – '*Enter a* Father *that has killed his Son.*' You can regard it as a lesson for Brecht, how to use drama in a didactic fashion. You come away feeling that war is fundamentally wrong.

RB And especially civil war.

AN But of course it's much more complex than that. While making those obvious statements, he will create a tapestry that is extremely complicated, that in no way suggests that the Tudor inheritance is the great cure for all leaders. If you look at the second tetralogy (which I worked on a bit, because I did *Henry V*), you will experience almost completely contradictory feelings. You will feel, if it's done reasonably well, great jingoistic pride, that kind of awful hot feeling that politicians and warmongers try to encourage in you, to give you the courage to kill your fellow man. You will experience those feelings when Henry V inspires you to war. You will also feel completely sickened by the whole business. You will feel at one stage that Henry V is the perfect king. If I was going to be led by anyone, I'd like to be led by him, because he's clear-headed, he's compassionate, he's robust, he's approachable. You will also hear him confessing privately that his father was wrong to steal the throne. You will hear the son saying, 'I have no right to this throne.' And so there's a marvellous paradox there. Shakespeare isn't just saying that it's bad to kill kings, bad to steal thrones; he doesn't say that at all. The great highlight of English history was stage-managed by a man who shouldn't have been there, who had no right to be there at all, who was a usurper. That's complex, that's not just Shakespeare saying, 'Good old Henry V, he was a good fellow.'

RB That's complex, as you say, but it's also simple, in the sense that Henry V is a very effective king because he tries harder. He tries harder knowing that there is considerable doubt about his claim. Richard II is a total failure, but is absolutely legitimate. He inherits a legitimate throne, which he believes to be his total right, his total moral and divine right to inherit and use as he thinks fit. And this is part of what makes him inefficient. He simply doesn't try in the way that Henry V does.

AN I don't know that Shakespeare would agree with what you're saying, if you're saying that the difference between Henry and Richard is one of the work ethic!

RB I'm saying that success or failure is, obviously, the total mesh of circumstances and character, but also there's the starting point, what one is given, and the psychology with which one reacts to what is the given.

AN I wouldn't argue with that. And therefore what?

RB I think, that in the end Richard II and Henry V are case histories, no more, no less. Here is a failure: why is he a failure? Here is a success: why is he a success (at least, up to a point)? But we note that the very end of *Henry V* is the Chorus's admission of defeat and failure, and we know that in the grand cycle of history Henry V is followed by Henry VI, about whom Shakespeare has already written, who is a predetermined, pre-programmed disaster, that disaster is cyclically attached to success.

AN Yes, I'd agree with that.

RB So is there a more pointed conclusion that you have derived from *The Plantagenets*, from working so closely with the first tetralogy of Shakespeare's histories? Does a conclusion emerge for you from those four plays?

AN There isn't really one conclusion. It's too huge an issue.

RB So in that case, technically, what aspects of the drama most engaged you as director? What did you find formally most interesting or difficult?

AN Formally, the most interesting things were the ways that each section of the narrative created its own world, its own rules. The first half of my first part found its own style during the rehearsals, which is different from what you feel after the interval. After the interval, the style is similar to that in what we call *Edward IV*. After the interval of *Edward IV*, the style changes again. The extraordinary thing about that is that the style – in the writing, in the presentation – changes again, when a new king comes to the throne. It's quite extraordinary. Of course, Henry VI is there at the beginning of *Henry VI*, though he's hardly present. It's really when Margaret arrives in England at the beginning of the second half that a whole new authority and style of writing emerges. The first half is quite emblematic, strongly charactered, almost caricatured but not so, with a very strong flavour of episodic, heavy past. After the interval, when we return to England, it becomes more intimate, more complex (verse-wise), more politically complicated. We found, which is always thrilling in rehearsals, that we were developing style. As the day wore on a different style was developing, a different way of relating to the audience and creating character. One actor I spoke to a couple of days ago – he has a lot to do in Part One, not much to do in the first half of Part Two and a lot to do in the second half of Part Two – said, 'When I go back after that gap, even though it's only an hour and a half, I feel that the world's changed. I feel I have to catch up somehow!' It's a bit like being asleep for ten years. Which is most extraordinary. There's a different landscape, which is obviously leading up to the second half of *Richard III*, when the third king comes to the throne, when there's a whole new landscape which is the bleakest.

RB I think Shakespeare always shows us a world which takes on some at least of the characteristics of the ruler. In *Henry IV* we start with a divided land and therefore, one might say, with a sick ruler. Edward IV is sexually active and everything that seems to flow from him moves through scenes that encompass Edward's easy sexuality. And that colours everything. The sex, like everything else, changes with Richard III and the play changes accordingly.

RB Finally, to take up again your term the 'agenda', for a Shakespearian director the agenda always comprises the next play. Can I ask you in what direction you are looking?

AN I really don't know the answer. The next piece I'm going to do, as I hope, is an Ibsen play, a mature Ibsen. After that I don't know. I might not do any Shakespeare for a bit.

RB Perhaps I oughtn't to press you, but I will. In the area of unfinished business, whether you think of it as comic or historic or tragical-comical-pastoral, do you have any leanings, or an inclination, that this is perhaps a text that a few years down the road is waiting for you?

AN I think *Henry IV, Part Two*, I'd like to do. I'm not one of those people who has a list of pieces they'd like to do. It really changes from year to year, according to how things go. I don't have a checklist after which I will retire!

RB Everybody denies the existence of a checklist, by the way.

AN I'm sure they do. Obviously, I've thought about *Henry IV, Part Two*, because I've done *Henry V*. You have to reflect upon the earlier play, to do what you did. It's not possible to plan that play without a Falstaff, though; so I don't know.

RB So, your final statement of your position with Shakespeare, what Shakespeare holds for you?

AN He is the ruler against which we measure ourselves. He is the challenge we have to meet, that we want to meet. He demands more of you than any other writer. So the experience of working with him, though it can be arduous and frustrating, particularly in a big house, is expansive. He tackles areas of experience that aren't dealt with by many writers: sickness in the ruler, ill health in the state. He deals with pain, with the difficulties of growing up, and he does so in a compassionate way. It's very nourishing.

RB I like your word 'ruler'. So, 'Shakespeare is the measure of man'?

AN Surely.

1988

Bill Alexander

Bill Alexander is Associate Director of the Royal Shakespeare Company. His productions there have included the acclaimed Anthony Sher Richard III, The Merry Wives of Windsor *and* The Merchant of Venice.

Ralph Berry I'd like to ask you first about your choice of plays for production. In the last few years, you've directed four comedies, a romance and a history. That obviously reflects your areas of interest in the canon. Would you like to say something about your sense of the canon, your choice of those plays and what perhaps the absence of a tragedy implies?

Bill Alexander That's very interesting, because already in the question you've defined certain things. Whereas I wouldn't necessarily disagree with them, I think they are an interesting topic of conversation. As you know, *Richard III* is in the Folio called *The Tragedy of Richard the Third*, though we might well define it as a history. The term 'romance' is applicable to a group of genre plays within the canon. So is the term 'comedy'. What attracts me to these plays is not the fact that they might be considered as a tragedy or comedy or history, but how the elements are mixed in them. For instance, in the history or tragedy of *Richard III*, I approached it in a way that was very much to do with its relationship to the old mediaeval view of theatre. I wanted it to be a morality play, but a morality play of the new psychological renaissance of the Elizabethan theatre, which I think it is. *Richard III* stands as a massively important stepping point between the moral analysis of the world by the mediaeval mentality, and by the more realistic and humanistic Renaissance mentality. But what that involves, like the old moralities, is a large ingredient of comedy to make it work. One of the things that's brilliant about the play is the way it moves from a quasi-comic ambience towards a tragic one, all contained within the vehicle of history. The most obvious things in this respect are Richard's relationship to the old vice of the morality plays. On one level he represents the total essence of evil. And yet Shakespeare manipulates the character, first of all to be with us totally through his soliloquies and have us behind him in his actions, and laughing at his deceits and his successes. Then he gradually withdraws him from us by way of the absence of soliloquies and his increasing isolation, and our own increasing fear of what that character means. Now with that character you have ingredients of comedy and tragedy, as well as good and evil. I was drawn to that play because I believed I could explore these complexities with a particular actor, Tony Sher, whom I had worked with a lot before.

The whole point of getting *Twelfth Night* right is to find out how it is not totally comedy, not only to accept the fact that on a superficial reading there seem to be some scenes which are very funny and other scenes which are rather serious, not to say melancholy, but how in *every* scene all those elements are mixed. No production of *Twelfth Night* can work – and I'm not very happy with my own production in that respect – unless it reveals the pathos to the comedy in the scenes between Orsino and Viola as well as the heart-breaking elements in the comedic scenes between Sir Andrew and Malvolio and Sir Toby. It's one of the most perfectly mixed plays in that respect.

You can say the same thing about the *Dream* and the same but in different terms about *The Merchant of Venice*. I think *The Merchant of Venice* is even harder to put into a category than either of the plays we've been talking about so far. That is a production in which I've tried ferociously hard to find the balance of good and evil in all the characters, to find out what drives Shylock to do what he does, what are the groundrules of behaviour in the society, what are the abuses and humiliations that lead towards the unleashing of that terrible potential action towards the end of the play, and how the society that Shakespeare is describing contains the elements of Old Testament justice and the New Testament morality of forgiveness, and the themes of legality, justice, revenge and mercy. That play is a *drama*. I think to a certain extent that is true of all Shakespeare's plays; they are all dramas and any attempt to call them histories, tragedies, or comedies is not helpful to theatre practitioners – a director and a group of actors. I think it's perfectly helpful as a way of separating them for purposes of analysis and putting them in volumes of plays.

It may seem from the Shakespeares that I've chosen to do that I'm more drawn to comedy than tragedy, but that really is not the case. Were I able to launch into a major tragedy next week, say *King Lear* or *Hamlet*, I would really be trying to find out in what sense it could be described as a comedy.

There is also, it needs to be said, something a little accidental about the choice of plays if you are an RSC director, because you negotiate what plays you're going to do with a group of other directors and indeed with outside directors coming in. One cannot always do the play one is most driven to do. One some- times does the play that most needs to be done. He only wrote thirty- seven plays, the great tragedies come around every four years and you get through the cycle pretty quickly.

RB What interests you then is not, let us say, the absolute categories of comedy and tragedy, if indeed they can be con- sidered absolutes, but rather the generic complexities of each play. Can I pick out the word you used of *The Merchant of Venice*, 'society', which is clearly something you've thought about very deeply? The instance that I'd like to put before you is your production of *The Merry Wives of Windsor*, which you set in the late 1950s. What I found striking about the production was not only that it worked extremely well and was extremely funny, but that the period metaphor seemed a complete container, a complete envelope for the personages in the play. They were all able to identify themselves as belonging to Macmillan's England, from the wives with their Harrods shopping bags to Mine Host of the Garter with his blazer and so on. Could you speak of the way in which that production as a society came together?

BA First of all, as a run-in to that: to tackle the question of how and why one does a Shakespeare play in a particular way, why one should choose an analogical modern context rather than setting the play in its own context, in which it was written. One can very loosely say that there are three ways of approaching it as a director. You can either set it in the Elizabethan period, when it was written. You can transpose it to some other period and try to create a complete social context to unleash the play. Or you can attempt some form of eclectic version of the play, which may be fairly neutral or very abstract and amazing and adventurous, but is essentially a world of the stage rather than the world of a society. All those categories are sub-divisible, but there is a basic trinity of approaches.

For me, it all boils down to this: how best can I reveal this play, how best can I release my own perception of the play, my own feeling of what it's about, and what it says and why he wrote it? It seems to me there's a rule to do with unleashing and limiting. If you take a play like *King Lear*, which is a great play because of its monumental universality, it seems to me – though I might change my mind if I were about to do a production of *King Lear* – that that is the perfect candidate for a fairly neutral approach. To be very specific about the setting could limit its universality, its message. You cannot say the same thing about *The Merry Wives of Windsor*, which is essentially a comedy of social and sexual manners, which I believe needs the specific containment of a society. You have to perceive the way people interact with each other, their little habits, their manner of walking, their manner of speech, the places where they live, the things they do, the kind of society they had, in order to make that play work. It's hopeless to conceive of some vaguely universal version of *The Merry Wives*, because it doesn't contain on that level those kinds of thematic challenges. Specifically, in the case of *The Merry Wives*, I sat down and, having decided not to do it in the Elizabethan England (I must confess for the very elementary reason that the last two RSC productions of the play had been set in Elizabethan England), I went through decade by decade all the possible ones between then and now. And it wasn't until I came to the England of the 1950s, and particularly the late 1950s, that I thought I was close to the balance of society that is in the play, a time before life became international. That's very important, looking at the onwards limits of where one might have gone, beyond 1959 – before life was international, before the post-war consensus had disappeared in a haze of liberalisms and drug culture and Americanisms. I don't think that has any place in the world of the play. But the 1950s, a time of economic growth within a particular social class, the lower-bourgeois milieu, was a time when the image of the penniless aristocrat in decline was also present in our society. It's there in the character Ian Carmichael plays in *I'm All Right, Jack*, for instance. So that the idea of that man encountering those women and being so out of touch with the way the world has moved, that he's convinced they will be an easy lay, because their mothers or grandmothers might have been to a man of his type, and finding that far from it, there is no greater insult those women could have been paid . . .

RB That's completely Shakespearian, it's there in the text. Falstaff thinks they're an easy lay and that is what most offends them. 'What doth he think of us?'

BA If you take a character like Ford, he completely exemplifies the insecurity of the *nouveau bourgeois* with regard to an aristocrat. He doesn't realise that concepts like fidelity and security and strength are now accruing to his particular branch of society, as opposed to the old world. And it's through that that Shakespeare explores the notion of jealousy in the play. He does it in different ways in *The Winter's Tale* and *Othello*. But in *The Merry Wives* it's related to class and money. You could say that my treatment of the Merry Wives themselves is harsher in the context of the 1950s than if you set it in the 1600s. In 1600 you could portray them as jolly and warm-hearted, whereas I've portrayed them as spiky and rather tasteless, quite cruel in their judgment. But then I think there's a strong element of cruelty in the play. It's a cruel pay, a play of quite unnecessary revenge. They could quite easily have written back to Falstaff, 'We're deeply offended, please don't come round here again.' But they decide to punish him. Bit by bit all the characters began to fit in to the confident, late-Fifties world, a world that was putting the

war and austerity behind it. It's a world not unlike the Elizabethan: the Armada was a thing of the past when Shakespeare
wrote the play, the bourgeoisie was rich and confident. It's the
only play he wrote in which the central characters are middle
class. Everything fitted perfectly and I knew I could say more
about the play by doing it that way than any other way. It became the world of Giles – the vicar, Hugh Evans, the ex-RAF bar-
man, the little boys and the crocodile on the way to school . . .

RB And the spivs!

BA That's right, the spivs, the people who hang around with
Falstaff, of a different class . . . Falstaff's hanging out in some
suburban inn, because he's lost credit in the nightclubs of the
capital. But I think it's quite rare that one finds such strong
reasons for moving a play out of its historical context. In the
1950s after the coronation of Elizabeth II, you often saw adver-
tisements for cigarettes, electric fires etc – a society referring to
itself as 'The New Elizabethans'.

RB As I take it, you're a pragmatist about eclectism. You
would say that certain plays accommodate or even invite an
eclectic approach to costuming, to identification of social context
and that other plays (the *Merry Wives* is one, I absolutely agree)
welcome a strict container. I found the *Merry Wives* striking in
this respect too: it seemed to me archaeologically accurate. This
is a notion that we've tended rather to despise since it lost its
hold on the minds of the Edwardians, who always prided themselves on getting history right. But it seemed to me that you got
the detail right down to the last bottle on the shelves of the bar of
the Garter.

BA Yes, the designer, Bill Dudley, and I researched the period
very carefully, and we knew from the word go that detail was
absolutely necessary – the hairdryers, the Morris Minor, the way
they smoked their cigarettes and poured their gins – that's all
part of it.

RB You said that you looked for a context that could reveal
the idea of the play. In your production of *A Midsummer Night's
Dream*, you found the 1930s as the envelope for the ideas. As I
remember the production, what came over immediately, in the

first scene, was the clash between the values of Theseus and Hippolyta – Theseus representing a certain kind of male supremacy that was not going to be possible for very much longer. 'Either to die the death, or to abjure/Forever the society of – men!'

BA I'd be interested to know whether you saw the production in Stratford or London.

RB Stratford. When there was still the double of Titania and Hippolyta.

BA The production changed a great deal on its way from Stratford to London. I was very unhappy with the production in Stratford, I felt there were many things wrong about it, and would be quite prepared to give a detailed analysis of what I got wrong and what I got right the second time round.

But we're talking about social context and doing plays in period. I'd like to compare it with my production of *The Merchant of Venice*, which is set in the Jacobean period, i.e. about thirty years after it was written. It was so for strong reasons. Any successful production of Shakespeare is to do with the director having strong reasons initially for doing what he does, and secondly carrying them through and making them consistent with themselves. I was convinced that *The Merchant of Venice* had to be set in a Jacobean period, because I am convinced that you cannot do that play unless you understand the cruelty of the world, the society in which it was written. All the themes of the play – justice, mercy, the law, revenge, money, love and how they relate to all those things – are thrown off centre if you try to find an analogical social context. And central to that is the notion of justice, and what justice meant to the Elizabethans and Jacobeans, in physical terms. Their direct experience of justice was that if you transgressed you were likely to end up with your head on the Bridge – or, in the case of the Venetian traitor, buried upside down in the pavement with your feet sticking up, or hanged, drawn and quartered. Those were the realities of punishment. We have to believe that all the people involved, at that crucial point of the play, accept it as perfectly likely that Shylock will carve the heart out of Antonio. If you put that in a

Victorian context, or any other twentieth-century context, there is a suspension of credibility. Apart from which, the casual cruelty of the world we have to see is partly what motivates Shylock's desire for revenge, the world in which he is treated with a casual humiliation, the hypocrisy of the role of the Jews in seventeenth-century Venice. They were there in order to lend money to the Christians, because the law forbade Christians to lend money to each other. And therefore, they couldn't finance their capital ventures any other way than by having people prepared to lend money. The whole of the social context is vital to unleashing the themes in the play. Anything else would obscure it. I know that sounds dogmatic, but I'm convinced that's right and I think anyone who sees the production will accept that point of view.

I did not have the same strong reasons for setting *A Midsummer Night's Dream* in the 1930s as I had for setting *The Merry Wives* in the 1950s, or *The Merchant of Venice* in the 1620s. And that's one of the reasons why I believe the production was not successful. Certain elements in it were successful but not others. My hope was that the conundrums of the lovers would find a home in the emergent sexual liberalism of the 1930s, in the new world of social habits and personal sexual freedoms that were being investigated in the post-World War I period. But I think Shakespeare is writing about a far more humanly endemic and timeless state of love than that particular social idea can really help. Although I think that had I followed it through in a different way I might have made it more applicable than I did. Most important though is that I believe the aesthetic of that production (in Stratford) did nothing to help the play, was in fact highly detrimental to it. This was not the designer's fault; this was my fault. We worked very closely on it and what ended up on stage was our joint responsibility. I don't believe you can do *A Midsummer Night's Dream* if you have a beautiful and exotic shop window of a set, that is also making a statement about size. If you remember, it was a set that contained a giant cobweb and vast leaves, in which people were very small. That is wrong, for two reasons. It is wrong, first, because it immediately defines what happens in those forest scenes as being a dream, whereas I believe now that the whole ironic point of the title is that it is not a dream. Second, it is almost impossible to relate to the beauty of the verbal scene-painting if you have a trivialised aesthetic in front of you. How can you really respond to Oberon's 'I know a bank where the wild thyme grows' if you are looking at a twenty-foot cobweb and wondering when the spider that lives there is going to arrive? I found the whole of what I put on stage a massive distraction from the text and I bitterly regret it. That's why what arrived in London, apart from many other changes that I made, was a much simplified, pared-down version of the production.

RB If I may say so, I think you're rather hard on your production, because the memories that I for one have are of some appealing sets. I can see now the art deco court scenes . . .

BA They were retained in London.

RB . . . and I remember that when the gauze curtain went up on the Arthur Rackham wood, there was a round of applause from the audience. Surely applause is not to be taken lightly?

BA I think it's a bad sign! We're getting into a contentious issue, but I think a round of applause for a set is a bad omen.

RB It was so unusual. And I noted it down at the time as something that was unfamiliar to me in recent years.

BA I also think that the doubling of Hippolyta and Titania was a mistake. If you're going to double them, then Oberon and Theseus must be doubled as well. I now think that you either double both pairs, or you have four actors. I don't think it's worth going into my rather perverse reasons for wanting to do it in the first place. But basically, I think I got the beginning and end of it right, and I don't think I got the middle right. I love what I did with the mechanicals; I thought that idea of the misguided 1930s avant-garde group of artisans, trying to put in proto-Brechtian ideas of alienation, is absolutely there in the text. They're talking about 'You can't bring in a wall – you have to *be* a wall.' 'We have a man coming in who represents Moonshine.' Having them in black tights and berets for the performance of

Pyramus and Thisbe, and being part of the avant-garde scene of the 1930s, was good and really worked.

That kind of silly-young-thing element of the 1930s *could* have worked for the lovers. I think it worked much better in London, where the setting was more realistic. In London the forest set was black, and they were picked out only by shafts of light that moved with them and by the silhouette of the woods in the background. It was much simplified, and focused the attention on what was being said and what was going on far better.

RB I thought that the actors brought out very well the emotional distance between Hippolyta and Theseus in the opening scene, and this seemed perfectly to fit with the 1930s as one of the last eras in which a woman might pay an outrageous emotional price for a social position.

BA Yes, absolutely. The distance between them did work well in that sense. The most important thing about Theseus and Hippolyta, though, is the cultural difference between them, the fact that he comes from a highly rational, organised, profoundly realistic and slightly unspiritual society in Athens, while she's an Amazonian, she comes from a mystical, 'backward' culture. Their marriage is going to supply the blend of reason and emotion that Shakespeare is always looking for. Aren't we all?

RB Indeed. How about your concept of *Twelfth Night* as being set on a Greek island?

BA I decided, rather shockingly, to set the play in Illyria! *Twelfth Night* must have been done in every way under the sun, but I've never actually seen it set in Illyria. There really was a country called Illyria and it was the northern Greek coastline, what is now northern Greece and a bit of Yugoslavia. It was a perfectly real place and you could go there just as much as you could go to Venice. Therefore, I decided it was Greece and should respond to our ideas of what Greece is – timeless, whitewashed buildings, costumes that are Elizabethan but are Greek-Elizabethan, they're traditional Yugoslav-Adriatic costumes, and I thought that was a good way of realistically setting the play because on some level it's a very realistic play. All Shakespeare is realistic; but that is one of the most remarkable things about

him, the balance between realism and surrealism, between inventiveness and the observation of the way people really are.
Particularly with *Twelfth Night*, something about the flow of the
dialogue, the subtlety of the way the characters express themselves, the painful conundrums of speech and behaviour that
they get into, I wanted to explore realistically. I wanted the fell
and flavour, the texture of the language to flow out in a very
naturalistic way. So I had to have a naturalistic context,
rather than some more emblematic or eclectic context that
might have done better in addressing the broader issues of the
play – but then I think the broad issues can only be approached
through the individuals in it. Love, madness – are not the two
the same thing? Through the convolutions and conventions of a
contrived comedic structure, it puts incredibly real emotions in
the middle of it.

RB What about Sir Toby and Sir Andrew, though? As
their names indicate, they're very English. How did you see
them – as being beachcombers, or vacationers in Greece, or
whatever? How did they fit in to the social context?

BA You're right, the manners of the play are very English. It's
set in Illyria, but the people are English. That's one of the first
problems with the play. We decided that they were second-
generation English, i.e. a combination of Mediterranean mentality and Englishness. So maybe Sir Toby hasn't been there
quite as long as the others, maybe he's come over from England
because the estate's collapsed at home and he's leeching off his
niece in Illyria. They're a kind of displaced group of English
people in Illyria, but they've picked up certain of the habits, like
pasta and falling in love at first sight, which doesn't seem to me
a particularly English characteristic.

RB Well, things happen in the Mediterranean.

BA That's right, in the heat. I thought a lot about this thing
of mad dogs and Englishmen, who go out in the midday sun.
The heat for me was very important, in the relationship between
madness and love in the play. I thought it might well affect a
group of people who were English in their blood. What does
Olivia say about Malvolio? 'I am as mad as he,/If sad and merry

madness be.' Madness must be the common image in the play. The English are, notoriously, driven a bit barmy by the heat of the sun, so I tried to account for their behaviour partly in that way. I lit it very hotly, the white walls reflecting the heat. It was more extreme in Stratford; we took the walls down a little bit for London, made them a little less strident than in Stratford. I don't know if you remember Malvolio standing there after he's appeared in his yellow stockings, and saying, 'Why, everything adheres together, that no dram of a scruple, no scruple of a scruple . . .' You can see he shouldn't be out in the heat! So I bring up the cicadas and they're mixing in his brain with the intoxication of persuading himself that everything adds up. She does love me! There can be no doubt of it! And yet you want to get the feeling at the same time that something terrible is being repressed, some awful, latent knowledge is being repressed by his appalling painful desire and ambition to achieve what another part of his consciousness knows is impossible. That's why when he returns to some kind of rationality in the madhouse and has to persuade other people that he's sane, in order to get out, you're profoundly moved by the man, the man you have laughed at till then.

RB In all your productions the design concept has been central. How do you see the relationship between yourself as the director and the designer, whom of course you choose?

BA I think that any director who decides to do a Shakespeare play, and then goes to a designer and says, 'Look, how shall we do this, come up with some ideas,' is wrong. That's a crude way of putting it – but simply wrong. I couldn't approach a Shakespeare play that way. I have to know how I want to set it and what I want the set to say. And as I see it, the relationship is that I go to the designer and say, 'OK, help! Help realise this: use your art and your talent to realise this.' And then we work together on how best to achieve this, technically, aesthetically, effectively and without clumsiness.

RB Now with *Cymbeline*, no single social context is going to work, because there are four different countries of the mind in that text. So how did you approach *Cymbeline*?

BA You've analysed the problem straightaway. How does one contain the variety, not only of social context, but also the variety of realistic and non-realistic elements within the play? How does one reconcile a play that is very realistic about sexual jealousy, with one in which the ancient gods appear to sort things out? How does one reconcile the world of pre-Christian Britain with that of Renaissance Italy? The approach I decided on was through storytelling and that's why I wanted to set it at The Other Place in an even more intimate way than you normally get at the theatre. To bring the audience on to the stage – it's hard to describe, but you know The Other Place is a small theatre; the audience was arranged in a horseshoe shape on a variety of chairs in the middle of the stage, leaving a very small acting area, but also leaving scope for the actors to pass behind the audience and to play instruments behind the audience. The actors mingled with the audience at the beginning, welcoming them into the theatre, asking them if they'd been to *Cymbeline* before, wearing clothes that were a gesture towards period dress, having been picked out of costumes that no one wanted to hire – Renaissance doublets, the odd bit of toga, the odd cloak, but a modern shirt and trousers underneath. Talking to the audience – have you seen *Cymbeline* before? Have you seen this production before? We had a lot of people coming for the second and third time, chatting about how it went last time. This was to build a relationship with the audience from the word go, saying, 'We are people who are now going to tell you a story.' For me, that became the containing context, rather than a social context, of a court world of the 1930s or a suburban world of the 1950s. It became about a group of people gathering together and sharing a story that is very powerful because it moves from the painful reality of the human experience of separation, sexual infidelity, jealousy and revenge, through to a religious perspective as a way of reconciliation via a mythical, romantic, almost utopian story of princes living in caves and thereby preserving an innate nobility that the corrupt, civilised court would otherwise have contaminated. I think we achieved that, to a certain extent. The spatial limitations made it not possible to achieve the grander things in the play – the war, the physical presence of Jupiter. Those are things that I would like to explore in the production by transferring it to a larger space. That element of spectacle could be very important in revealing the play.

RB How does one retain the element of intimacy, which is organic to your production, on a larger stage?

BA First of all, you have to design it right. That is a matter of detail: how do you lift that stage back towards the main house audience and how do you back it, and all the rest of it. Once the actors have got so far into their characters, the lifting of that to the level of the main house should not be too difficult a job. I would like to preserve the relationship with the audience in the sense that the actors would still be there at the beginning and would be on view all the time and would talk to the audience, and would be seen to be doing things other than what is necessary for their characters, i.e. rattling oil drums or shaking mobiles or scraping piano wires. All that could still be observed. But one would be able to broaden the scope of the play by being able to express the grandeur of war and religious visitation in the latter stages. You can actually be quite intimate on that stage, if you are really inside what you're doing.

Take for example the scene in which Iachimo first challenges Posthumus to the test of Imogen's sexual fidelity. You could really enhance that scene, having got the psychological realism of it, by adding to the numbers there and making that Roman room a more decadent place and focusing more people's attention on what is going on between Iachimo and Posthumus – by bringing in the Dutchman and the Spaniard and the Italian who are mysteriously there in the text as witnesses to this challenge. By making it a far more public and therefore more dangerous scene, one could lift an extra something out of that.

It is very important to me, particularly with these difficult plays, these not so popular plays, these slightly lost plays in the canon, that one explores them thoroughly in a theatre like The Other Place and then develops that work on to a new level so that more people can experience it. The plays can be shown to bigger audiences and revealed as the great plays they are (which I think *Cymbeline* is), and this extends the diet beyond *Hamlet* and *As You Like It*.

RB It's clear that the next play you want to direct is *Cymbeline* in a somewhat different mode. Can I ask you finally if you have a shortlist of plays that you would like to direct in the next few years, if circumstances favour you?

BA Top of the list is *The White Devil*, which I am passionate to do in the Swan Theatre. As far as the Shakespeare canon goes, I am eager to do *Romeo and Juliet* and *Coriolanus*, and a little part of me would like to do the *Dream* again, in order to get it right.

1988

Declan Donnellan

Declan Donnellan is co-director of Cheek by Jowl, *a company whose work in Shakespeare, notably* A Midsummer Night's Dream, Twelfth Night *and* The Tempest, *has attracted great interest and a large following in recent years.*

Ralph Berry I'd like to ask you first about Cheek by Jowl. Could you tell me something about the structures and ideals of your company?

Declan Donnellan The reason that Nick Ormerod and I started Cheek by Jowl was that we wanted to work in the theatre. That's how we wanted to express ourselves. It's both him and me; the distinction between me as director and him as designer is very much blurred. He will do all the casting with me and so on. I think we both – I'll speak for myself from now on, but you'll understand that I include Nick – very much enjoy entertaining people. I'm at my happiest when I'm entertaining people. It's become almost exclusively through the theatre that I do that and for me theatre is entertaining people on a profound level. That's basically what's behind Cheek by Jowl. In order to entertain people, we use classical texts, but I don't acknowledge any commitment to the tradition of Shakespearian production. My only commitment is to entertain the audience in the best way possible. And I can be the only judge; it has to come back to my responsibility.

To entertain them well with an old play, I have to unleash the spirit of that play. It will differ according to the actors, who happen for one reason or another to be with the company at that time. The most important thing to remember about Shakespeare is that he's dead and we're alive. It's an odd thing to perform something written 380 years ago; I always start with that.

RB You've made clear your freedom from Shakespeare, the fact that you're not subject to the shade of Shakespeare. That said, you still choose to play Shakespeare. What makes you select his plays?

DD We don't select them because they're old, but because they're the best possible scripts we can lay our hands on. They are the best and most satisfying way we can share with people. Theatre is an act of union with a lot of people; we like to be together.

RB You stress the word 'entertainment'. Does this mean you are especially drawn towards the comedies of Shakespeare, which may have an actual entertainment in them, as is the case with *The Tempest* for example?

DD No. I'm sure that the Crucifixion was entertaining. I'm sure the crowd found it interesting or stimulating or entertaining to watch someone being tortured for a day. It can obviously be a bad thing; it can also be a very serious thing. The liturgy is a form of entertainment. I'm only interested in a very broad view of entertainment. Lear's sufferings are entertaining, because they involve us and we have union with him at a very deep level.

RB Yes, I see that. I wondered if there were a significance, for example, in the fact that you've directed *Twelfth Night* in the last year or so, which as you know is an occasional play and very probably was devised as a court entertainment – that is the occasion of the play.

DD Yes. So many of Shakespeare's plays face both ways. It may have been written for a marital celebration, but a play that celebrates matrimony less it would be hard to imagine. You have three extraordinarily mismatched couples at the end of the play, whose marriages are so grotesque that (a) they show many signs of surviving and (b) they are just like the marriages of all our friends. That's what I think is wonderful about the end of *Twelfth Night*; we're being entertained with something that isn't a diversion from real life, it is something about ourselves.

RB Is that what attracted you to *Twelfth Night*, the idea that it is a story of mismatches?

DD It's more than that. Shakespeare investigates love in all its political aspects. He is extraordinarily wide-ranging in political and love relationships. He doesn't have a narrow or limited focus. He talks about relationships at a very deep level; he talks about the dissolving ego and people's fantasies.

RB Given this view of *Twelfth Night*, how did you set about putting it into practice?

DD *Twelfth Night* was quite interesting, because like *The Tempest* which we're now working on, we went into rehearsal with a *tabula rasa*, without a single idea. Of course, we knew the scripts very well and we'd worked on them over the years so that we knew our way round the scripts in terms of geographical coordinates. We knew the terrain, we went in with the actors and sorted out a way of doing it.

RB Did a certain theme, or mode of operation, emerge from your rehearsals?

DD Yes. We knew certain things about *Twelfth Night* before we went in. The play is obsessed with madness, like Lope de Vega's *The Lunatics of Valencia*, which is about the idea of love as madness. We decided not to do *The Lunatics of Valencia*, because the play is rather linear and Lope de Vega says in a whole play what Shakespeare says in a few lines. Shakespeare also explores the theme of *nothing*, which is a theme that goes through into *King Lear*. 'Nothing will come of nothing' is the great theme of zero and the most terrible thing in the canon. Feste has echoes of it in 'Nothing that is so, is so' and 'What is love? 'Tis not hereafter.' There is the abyss, there is hell.

On a more practical level, we started with character improvisations, to give the actors the first requirement of creativity: confidence. They improvised with great warmth and humour the nightmares and fantasies about their characters. One teabreak I discovered the company killing themselves with laughter because the line 'I am a great eater of beef' sounded hilarious in a Texan drawl. But we suddenly realised that the clichéd Texan oil millionaire hopelessly impressed by European aristocracy was a near-perfect modern equivalent for Andrew and we had decided *for* an anecdotal modern-dress production. Aguecheek starts the play as a clichéd stock character from Renaissance literature, the gull from the country, and develops, with lines like 'I was adored once too', into a fully rounded person one can love, or hate, or both. That's one of the brilliant things about Shakespeare; not only do characters develop but so does the form of the play. Farce turns tragic, two dimensions acquire a third. Shakespeare subverts the form. In delivering 'a Shakespeare' to the audience, you often have to direct more than one play.

RB To come back to the main figures in that play, you make it sound as though the end of *Twelfth Night* is a half-way staging point between coming together and parting. We can all feel that there is something, shall I say, distressingly volatile in the coming-together of Olivia and Sebastian, and there are observations we could all make on the likely prospects of Orsino and Viola. Did you, in the staging of the ending, bring out these reservations, which we could easily feed from our knowledge of life, into the relationships there?

DD Yes. In the play it's quite clear that Orsino has fallen in love with a boy, which is very inconvenient for Viola who is in love with him and that is the comedy. It's similar to the comedy in *As You Like It*, when Orlando falls in love with a boy, who is in fact a girl who's in love with him. The comedy is very hard, but it's a situation we all recognise. At the end of *Twelfth Night*, Orsino had to come to terms with the fact that he'd fallen in love with a boy. As he went off, Viola made him feel her breast. Viola made Orsino acknowledge the fact that she was a woman.

RB So marriage is going to be some sort of therapy for him, which may or may not work?

DD Possibly. I think it very unlikely that Orsino is converted to clear-cut, complication-free heterosexuality in the space of a short speech. The audience should be left to make up its own mind as much as possible. But it is a grotesque imposition by an actor or a director to *exclude* Orsino's sexual confusion. However, no play speaks for itself. Every production is an imposition. Casting a tall Olivia excludes the possibility that she may be short.

RB It's fascinating that at the end Orsino says that he would love to see Cesario dress up in her woman's weeds.

DD He says that in public!

RB You regard it as perhaps an impulsive admission on his part?

DD The wonderful thing about Shakespeare is that we have an objective point of view from the characters, and a really good production opens space between the actors and the audience, so that the audience can walk around the character and make its own moral judgments. What can destroy the audience's independence is the actor or director's sentimentalism. Nearly always this sentimentalism is unconscious and consequently extremely dangerous. The audience can have no real relationship with the characters or situation if they are sentimentalised, just as the best way to destroy a friendship is to sentimentalise the friend. Sentimentality is not a part of love, it is love's opposite. There are countless subtle ways of sentimentalising in life and so in the theatre, and continually in rehearsal we find that we have taken little short cuts through the character or situation, instead of having pierced to the heart. I do feel that no one is nice, but everyone is good, no one is pretty, but everyone is beautiful. Often our beauty lies in our ugliness. Shakespeare has enough confidence in human nature to celebrate marriage in all its uncertainty and pain. He doesn't degrade his characters into a trivialised 'happy ending'. He sends them off to the future in the hope of re-creation.

RB You'd agree, I imagine, that the marker in the play is Malvolio, who illustrates vividly what you're saying about liking people, since in the first half we're invited to dislike him. The second half starts making a case for him and we are, I think, manoeuvred into modifying our view of Malvolio.

DD I think, if I may say so, that that is an interpretation. It happens to be mine. But that is for you and me in the audience. I'm staging the play and I have to give the audience the freedom to come to the conclusion you've arrived at.

RB May I press you on this? In the case of Malvolio, surely there's clear evidence that Shakespeare is setting up a number of lines which are obviously calculated to glean a certain reaction. The opening lines of Malvolio, for example, present him as a pompous ass. Now there are many lines later in the play that don't support that view. Can we not at least put on the table the idea that Shakespeare is manipulating the audience into a certain view of the character, early on, which he then changes?

DD If that is true, and it may be true, I don't think it's Shakespeare at his greatest. Shakespeare at his greatest allows you to walk around the character. I think I agree with you here though. As a director, I try to unleash the spirit of the play as it is now for an audience of the later 1980s. Which may be different from the author's intentions; playwrights find it difficult to swallow the fact that the spirit of the play may be different from their intentions, but indeed it may.

RB How did your Malvolio come across at the end? What was the final situation?

DD He was absorbed back into society, which I think is very important. He laughed, everyone laughed with him. He enjoyed the joke on him. He started to laugh and forgave everyone on stage. It's very unsettling for the audience to see Malvolio warm-heartedly forgiving Feste and everyone else! We froze the stage and he came up in a blackout with the final line, 'I'll be revenged on the whole pack of you.' It was quite chilling, because you felt he was biding his time.

RB So this was a public submission, but privately he retained his deep sense of grievance and hurt?

DD Yes, absolutely.

RB I don't know if I have, as it were, a place in what you're saying here, but may I raise my voice in favour of the fellow who just likes to get some sleep in during the small hours and would prefer the noisy party to go somewhere else?

DD I know, I know. We just had a lady in Sicily (where the company was playing *The Tempest*) who did exactly that to us. We'd just opened the show there and we were having a drink on the terrace in the hotel. It was very late, and this English lady stormed out and made this wonderful speech. It was pure kitchen scene. 'You have made me ashamed to be British.' And we'd only been talking, we hadn't been actually carousing and singing 'Tilly-vally, Lady!' The second thing was, 'I have heard from the hotel people that you are theatricals. If so, so much the worse for you!' It was very salutary for us. Now I know what it's like to be the sort of English person that people are ashamed of abroad. She was silhouetted in the moonlight, too, it was as in a romantic production of *Twelfth Night*. She almost came on with a gold chain round her shoulders.

RB Could we move on to *The Tempest*, while keeping your sense of walking round the character? Everything in *The Tempest* comes down to and starts with Prospero. How did you confront this issue?

DD We had a very fine young actor, Timothy Walker; we wanted him to play Prospero, basically because he's a wonderful actor with piercing intelligence and an ever-growing range. The more we looked at the play, the less we believed in the traditional serene image. It had a very noisy title. Prospero we saw as a magician who can transform himself and other people's perceptions of the world. He is obsessed by his power, his rough magic and his art. The narrative line of the play is often crushed under Prospero's erratic creative energy, as, for example, when he aborts the masque. We felt it would be a withering imposition to strangle the play with a narrative control, e.g. by setting it in a specific period, on a specific island. We had to find a way to match Shakespeare's outrageous inventiveness and breathtaking disregard for any theatrical tradition (never mind the three unities!). Trinculo and Stephano come from another *play*;so, more disturbingly, do forgiveness and redemption.

The play explodes with the irrational, creative unconscious. The play lurches from one wonderful revelation to the next, rather as in a novel by Dostoevsky – the spiritual lurks around the most unexpected corners. Epiphanies tend to be as unexpected as they are shattering. The violence of the play's jolting, shuddering form is reflected in the inner violence of the characters; fratricide, rape, assassination are all plotted soon after the shipwreck.

We hit upon the idea of presenting the play as an improvisation, originally organised by the actor playing Prospero, who would gradually, more or less, lose control. The art would be theatrical, the magic would certainly be rough, the lines would be spontaneous instead of just coming up book titles and above all the audience could share in that peculiarly theatrical unpredictability, in exhilarating emotional danger. We wanted to reinvent the play each evening with the audience. We felt this was a good way to liberate the play's spirit. We felt that to tie the play down with a historic narrative control would be the greater imposition.

RB How did you impart the idea that the play is being invented?

DD We began it with a rehearsal for a play. The stage is littered with the débris you find in the theatre, like fire buckets, property skips, bits of wire and curtains. And strange old costumes, terrible prop crowns that you might find in the wardrobe. We brought a dressing table on to the stage and a side table with things on it, like a wig stand. The actor playing Prospero presents an improvised play in it. He doesn't know how to begin it, and he sees a sailor's hat and decides to call one of them 'Bosun'. And then the Bosun starts the play. We haven't changed any of the words. The actor playing Prospero dismantles and destroys the set creating a storm, and that's the end of the play Prospero wants to improvise. Then one of the actresses comes forward and makes up the line, 'If by your art, my dearest father', and so turns him into her father and begins a whole new line of story. The most important thing is that we feel an arbitrariness in the happenings on the island and destroy that sense of liturgy that one has sometimes in *The Tempest*, which is dangerous with that play. I think it is important that theatre is both sacred and vulgar. That is its strength; theatre is an animal that draws its sustenance from both extremities. Once you dry out one of those sources, it withers and dies. *The Tempest* is one of those plays that can become too sacred, can lose the elements of vulgarity and arbitrariness.

RB Doesn't Peter Brook say that the situation is always saved by 'rough' theatre?

DD I'd concur. One must always remember that theatre is rubbish, but rubbish in a way that makes it fantastically important to us. We live in a world where we have to have theatre, because we tell lies to each other all the time. We can't express ourselves because our verbal communications are totally inadequate. The more important something is, the harder it is to express: if I say something like 'I love you', then what I'm saying is so inaccurate as a description of my feelings that it is tantamount to a lie. Theatre was invented in order to express things better that we can't otherwise express. In the theatre we use illusion to tell the truth. It is probably the best means we have of telling the truth to each other; it's a religious function.

RB You take the 'holy' and 'rough', or in your terms 'vulgar', as the twin essences of theatre, which it is your business to bring together on stage.

DD Yes. And Nick and I only choose those plays, and actors, and everything in the theatre, that has that range. I love wide range; I love being exhausted when I go to the theatre. It is my job to make sure that the audience's world vision isn't seen through two degrees but 360 degrees.

RB So what was the story of Prospero, as you finally arrived at it?

DD Prospero's improvised play climaxed and ended with the storm. He couldn't go any further. He fell apart and attacked the other actors with a big stick; it was a breakdown, the storm was in him. To save the day, a young actress decided to throw him a lifeline. She started to create him as a cruel father. Somebody cruel, but somebody to love and be loved by. Miraculously, he went along with the story. It was a good context to provide for the play, because thereafter, everything was very emotional and very dangerous. Every now and then he would fly off the rails, as when he destroyed the masque. From that first moment he started to create out of immediate terror and the glimmer of hope that love would happen.

Prospero invents the plot, he invents the wicked brother, he invents the Queen of Naples, he invents the extraordinary people on the island: Ferdinand, Caliban, a very articulate Caliban and different from the one Prospero describes. He sets up the improvisation by describing all the people who are to come to the island; and then they work out and rebel against him, as actors. They make a story happen, somehow, mystically, magically, in a way that it would be wrong to explain even if we could. It includes this strange creature Ariel, who is subhuman because he cannot love. It's a great danger to think of Ariel as a further evolution of humanity, someone who doesn't need to love.

RB I seem to remember, when I saw your rehearsal, the inflection with which your Ariel said, 'Do you love me, master? No?', as a reproach. Or do I misremember?

DD That was a rehearsal, so he could have done anything! What we arrived at was this: 'Do you love me, master?', Ariel has been on stage examining all these strange things that humans indulge in – politics, love and so on. Rather like a zoo. Prospero is almost as subhuman as Ariel. Prospero wants to remove himself from the moist world of feeling. It occurs to Ariel just before the masque that Prospero might be in love with him. So Ariel said the line with the inflection, 'Do you feel this strange thing for me?' and Prospero covered up, because a problem for Prospero may be that he's in love with a fantasy of sexless, feelingless, loveless intellectualism. At the end he loses his dependence on that fantasy.

RB Or perhaps the simple expectation of a master, that his servant in some way reciprocates his feelings.

DD Yes – that's a more political way of looking at it. 'You served me so long I hope you don't do it just for the pay cheque at the end of the week.'

RB Exactly. The idea that 'We've spent years together and I hope that now our relationship is on a deeper level than mere economic utility.' But one social historian of twentieth-century Britain remarks that as soon as people had a choice, they left the servant occupation which at the start of the century came (I think) after agricultural worker, the largest occupation group. It's now of course tiny. People didn't want to be servants, full stop. I think the social history of our times tells us something permanent about human nature, which Shakespeare knew and coded into *The Tempest*.

DD We try to walk a tightrope, presenting things in such a way that the audience is stretched into understanding the enormous range of Shakespeare. You can have references to contemporary politics as well as prayers for redemption and salvation. We also try not to interpret for them; there are spaces around the characters and situations, but not arrows, not directions.

RB Where does Caliban come into all this?

DD I think Caliban is a wonderful creature, who suffers from a surfeit of love. He's full of love. 'When thou cam'st first,/Thou strok'st me, and made much of me . . . And then I love'd thee . . .' I think it's very important to realise that Caliban is very attractive and consequently very dangerous! He will destroy you. I am overjoyed with Duncan's Caliban, by the way. The scenes between Caliban and Stephano/Trinculo are not people from different worlds, they come from different plays. Caliban speaks the most beautiful poetry of anybody in the play, certainly more beautiful than most of what Prospero says. Miranda has her moments and Ferdinand has a couple. But Caliban, with the most beautiful verse, is thrown on stage with two prose-speaking, dirty-joke-cracking comedians. If we designed the scene so that they all come from the same world, we'd do a disservice to Shakespeare. What he wants to do is to explore the wonderful anarchy, to see what happens if you have two awful vaudeville comedians meet somebody from a different play. That's what we try to do and it can only be done by taking a liberty with it. So our mechanicals (Stephano and Trinculo) are the terrible music-hall act of this century, who get visited upon a more poetical Caliban. This is one way to release the spirit of Shakespeare's intentions; otherwise you're not being true to the essential vulgarity of that meeting.

RB What do you make of the idea that Caliban is Third World and a victim of colonial oppression?

DD I think it's true, but it's more than that; the play explores things that are deeper than colonialism. We are invited to question the reasons why we want to have power over others and why we want to have control over ourselves. Even Ferdinand cheats Miranda at chess. The play's thematic intensity is breathtaking. Gonzalo asks, by what right do we govern? What does authority mean? What is freedom?

RB Your production does nothing to evoke the idea of colonialism.

DD No, but I hope it does evoke some idea of why we get people to be our servants. I think that tackles colonialism en route; you don't need to go abroad to capture the essence of colonialism!

RB I agree that the master-servant theme is the substratum, on which the ideas of colonialism and domination are raised.

DD The play is obsessed with people being tied up. Prospero is endlessly tying people up. Which a lot of us do, metaphorically speaking. There's that wonderful line in the song, 'Thought is free.' Whether freedom is good or not isn't the point; it certainly disturbs some people, who spend a lot of time curtailing the freedom of others.

RB So what does your Prospero do as he contemplates 'retiring' – not in our sense – to 'my Milan'?

DD The play isn't a preparation for death. Prospero has done what he has done in order to turn himself into a human being; the end of *The Tempest* is the start of the rest of his life. Instead of facing a happy retirement, he's equipped himself now to act as Duke for the rest of his life. We all need to equip ourselves and take responsibility, rather than indulge in the strange fantasies of the type that Prospero does.

RB Yes, but 'Every third thought shall be my grave.'

DD That can actually refer as well to the dynastic arrangement he's brought about, that when he dies Miranda is going to inherit the Dukedom of Naples. Poetically, 'Every third thought shall be my grave' doesn't mean that his life is running out of steam. It is a triumph to outface one's own mortality.

RB The next Shakespeare play for you: what will it be?

DD I don't know. I'd like to do *Hamlet*. But one of the things about not having much money is that we don't have enough time to rehearse it. We had six weeks for *The Tempest*, which wasn't long enough and we're still working on it. *The Tempest* is half as long as *Hamlet* and you just need a lot of time to do *Hamlet*. It's too expensive for us to do.

For us, the central moment of theatre is when the audience's imagination and the actors' imagination are perfectly joined, and something is born between them. It's not like a pornographic vaudeville in which something unobtainable is displayed.

What I love to see is the actor's imagination making various events and words inevitable. And a lot of our work, particularly our selection of Shakespeare's plays, has been to explore this theme of the imagination. In *Pericles*, the imagination is central. Very unlikely events are staged in that they can only take place with the connivance of the audience's imagination. Time belts forward, places are changed, impossible scenes are staged and so on. There's a tour de force that's not at all naïve; it's exploitation of the fact that on stage you can make the audience believe anything if they want to. If they don't want to, you can't make them believe anything at all.

RB In *Pericles* you made extensive use of doubling.

DD We did that because of sheer chutzpah to mirror the theatrical bravura of the writing. If the audience is with you, they will suspend their disbelief. The significant thing about the *Pericles* doubling was that people were just dressed in blue pyjama suits. They had no costume additions at all to change characters. As the characters kept coming and going, we had to rely on the fact that the audience had invested enough memory in what they were doing to follow things. It was rather wonderful at the end, when all thirty different characters say goodbye and we had only seven people on the stage to say their farewells to the audience. The audience did actually fully understand who the different people were. It's all about recognition and reconciliation, the prototype of the later romances.

The imagination was crucial in our *Midsummer Night's Dream*, where the fairies didn't exist. The fairies were a possession in the imagination. The comedy of *A Midsummer Night's Dream* starts off, at least, as in large part a social comedy, about people who are real. Hippolyta, Theseus and the mechanicals were very modern English people. The mechanicals came from a modern English, suburban, Amateur Dramatic Society. So when these rather sexual, id-oriented fairies took possession of them, they did all sorts of things that they didn't normally do in the forest with Mr Bottom, who was a vicar. The imagination was crucial again with the mechanicals' obsession with the difference between a real and an imaginary wall. In our production there was a fight between the members of this drama society who wanted a mimed, Marcel Marceau wall and those who brought in a terrible representational wall. There was also a fight about the blood and the dagger, and whether Pyramus' heart should be real. The play measures the distance between being in love with somebody and imagining you are in love with them. We came to the conclusion at the end, just as with *Twelfth Night*, that maybe there's no difference at all. Perhaps the only thing that's real about these actors is that they have an imagination. 'I imagine, therefore I am.' So the whole play of *A Midsummer Night's Dream*, with its real moons, fake moons, real walls, fake walls, real love, fake love, acquires a sense of dizzying, impossible perspective, as in an illustration by Escher.

RB *Macbeth* is a play that's obviously about the limits of the imagination. As everybody says, Macbeth is highly imaginative. And he gets it wrong.

DD Yes. The imagination is neither good nor bad. People imagine how to bring about good things, how to bring about bad things. It's Macbeth's imagination that enables him to become King of Scotland.

RB Surely the challenge to imagination is not morality, good or bad, but the reality principle? For example, Lady Macbeth clearly sees herself as a supreme hostess, presiding over a marvellous banquet in which everyone defers to her and this vision is paramount until the point where she has to make this fiasco of a dinner party work.

DD The dinner party was crucial in our production. Power is banal. If I may digress for a moment about dinner parties, we were being entertained by a Russian theatre, the Maly Theatre in Leningrad. We were put up at the Astoria Hotel. We were told that Hitler spent much time, during the Siege of Leningrad, planning the dinner party that was going to take place at the Astoria. Everything was planned in great detail, down to the places where everyone was to sit. Imagine besieging Leningrad and just worrying about the dinner party. And then we realised, in a blinding flash, that the reason he had tried to take Leningrad was largely in order to throw that dinner party at the Astoria. That is how banal power is and it is a great mistake to glamorise or sentimentalise some sense of territorial destiny. That's non-sense. It's all about throwing dinner parties, making sure that you're sitting over Vice-Admiral whatever who snubbed you when you were in the ranks.

The banquet is Lady Macbeth's last scene and she threw it like that. When the banquet started to go wrong it was very funny and very frightening. She kept on and on serving prawn cock-tails, or caviar. She spent a long time sorting out the caviar spoons. The fact that she should screw up the dinner party was a terrible thing. It's interesting that the more you introduce el-ements of social comedy, the more frightening and poetic is the release when it comes.

RB And we know from *Hitler's Tabletalk* – it's the book's title, I think – how appalling his dinner-party conversation really was. Banal in the extreme. There are no great thoughts of Hitler, not at his dinner table anyway.

DD It was important to him, talking at table?

RB He had I think half-a-dozen or so people habitually at his dinner table. Talking and being head of the table was un-doubtedly a part of his enjoyment of power.

DD Giving other people food is the essence of hospitality. Hospitality is a nexus in which power becomes very dangerous and very apparent. Macbeth is obsessed with dinner parties and gives two in the play. The great crime is not only regicide, but a crime against hospitality. The fact that it takes place in his own home makes it all the worse.

This is an example of something that I call 'vulgar'. Once you call something a 'dinner party', not a 'banquet', you reduce it. The other day I was listening to a favourite piece of Mozart, to what I always thought was the most elegant and ravishing eighteenth-century music – until I could hear the vulgar showmanship in it. Once you can hear the vulgar showmanship, the sublime side absolutely takes off. The whole becomes enormously richer.

RB What emotions does your *Macbeth* create in the audience at the end?

DD I think we should be frightened. Shakespearian tragedy works partially as a satire. There's a danger in depoliticising Macbeth, because he kills babies, and it must be made clear that this is happening. He commits atrocities, he has 'supp'd full with horrors'. Macbeth stirs terrifying feelings in us. It's as if we are part of Macbeth. We put a Jung quote in the programme: 'None of us stands outside mankind's infernal shadow.' The more you pretend you're not part of that evil, the more you become an instrument to that evil.

We did *Macbeth* four times. It was a success in England, so we revived it. Previously we'd done it in Finland, in Finnish, and that had to be revived as well. I had the most terrible nightmares second time round. We chose the Ostrovsky play as some sort of light firework to lay the ghost of Macbeth. Macbeth isn't a horrible man who takes over power when everyone else is very good and somebody else who is very good, Malcolm, takes over at the end. Macbeth is *permitted* to take power by us all.

RB There is a moment when Macbeth is given the benefit of the doubt. He does to a certain extent respect the conventions of his society. The transference of power can't always be a clear-cut and ethically appropriate affair (Claudius and Fortinbras, for instance). I mean of course not the moment when Macbeth kills the King, but the moment when those close to the seat of power admit that, on the whole, though they have private reservations, they do not feel justified going on a crusade on the basis of those reservations.

DD Yes. I think that's true. To a degree we are all responsible for the running of the country.

RB Would you accept the word 'catharsis' for the emotions created in us by the death of Macbeth?

DD I would. I'm a little worried by the term, because it sounds so grand. It's more than just the fall of a great man. Macbeth has murdered those babies and it's very difficult not to stand back at that moment. It's a terrible production of *Macbeth* that goes soft on child-murder.

RB Yes: but the final emotion. Would you prefer the word 'purgation', which suggests something more religious, or even Christian? And seems closer to Holy Theatre?

DD On all those occasions, *Macbeth* was anything but a holy experience for me. I felt soiled by it. The more we worked on it, the less we felt proud of it. I say that for information and not to make a point. Shakespearian tragedy works in different ways from Greek tragedy.

RB So for you, *Macbeth* is the acting of evil?

DD It's more than that, because the audience does identify with Macbeth. The terrible thing is that with Macbeth you commit those crimes.

RB Do you see the function of theatre as some kind of social therapy for the audience? That is, some kind of coming to terms with the bad in it, and working through it?

DD That's one thing that theatre can do. The first thing that theatre does is to entertain and it entertains by giving you a religious experience, or a frightening experience, or whatever. It always has to go through that nexus. If it tries to give you a religious experience without entertaining you, it fails. Theatre can entertain you by making you politically aware. If it's a piece of Brecht, the awareness comes out of the entertainment. But to entertain people properly, you have to do it in a wide range, you have to entertain the dark and the light, the holy and the vulgar. I like to think that the only way that theatre makes people better, the only social service it does, is to make people bigger. It expands their imaginations, even if that means showing people what it's like to kill babies.

RB How does this relate to your experience of playing Shake-speare abroad?

DD Our experience of working in Shakespeare abroad has been very instructive.

We have worked on scenes in Spanish from *Romeo and Juliet* with actors from the Uruguayan National Theatre, in a real orange grove, with a real balcony. In Sri Lanka we worked on the same play with a Sinhalese Romeo and a Tamil Juliet. In Turkey we had a long session working out a production of *Hamlet* set in the decaying Ottoman Empire, but that was considered too politically dangerous for presentation. Similarly our visit to Chile was scrapped when the authorities realised how explicit we had made the play's explosive qualities. In Delhi we discovered the relevance of the caste system to Malvolio's position in a rich household which became very heated. In Katmandu we did a workshop on the *deus ex machina* in *Pericles*, until we realised that the king's son was among the audience and were solemnly informed that, being a god himself, divine intervention had little shock value. In Warsaw, we couldn't do our Shakespeare workshop when the university photocopier was confiscated, as it constituted an illegal printing press. We improvised instead. And with our old friends of the Finnish National Theatre, we scraped our way through *Macbeth* in a non-Indo-European language with a saintly interpreter.

Certain principles have become abundantly clear to us and perhaps the chief of them is this. In the beginning was not the word. In the beginning was the imagination, which longs to communicate with others. Words are one means of doing this. But no word is ever properly understood unless it has been spontaneously created by the imagination. It is possible to have a good grasp of a scene in a totally alien language if the actors' imaginations are genuinely working. There are small technical spin-offs from this: bad diction is normally caused not by a shaky palate but by a sloppy imagination.

The actor can get an audience to believe anything, but only if the actor is prepared to believe it himself. This is the basis of all our work and we have learnt it among strangers.

1988

Sir Peter Hall

Sir Peter Hall has been the leader of both of the two major State companies. From 1960–68 he was Artistic Director of the Royal Shakespeare Company; from 1974–88 he was Artistic Director of the National Theatre. He has directed most of the Shakespeare canon.

Ralph Berry I've just seen your three late plays at the Cottesloe and the dominant impression these productions leave with me is classicism. By that I mean that, for example, you're always working with the grain of the text; scrupulous attention to verse speaking; costuming that moves no further away from Shakespeare's day than Caroline; socially accurate casting and playing. All this seems to me a statement of classicism – I might almost say, if it were not too provocative, 'purism'. Would you accept 'classicism' as a shorthand description of your directorial approach?

Sir Peter Hall Yes, I would. I think that you should not do Shakespeare in English (in other languages it's another matter) without understanding the verse structure, and the signals that Shakespeare writes into the verse about how it should be spoken and the pace it should be spoken at, even the tone. There is a great deal to be learned from the text in notation, almost as much as in a musical score. And it isn't speculative, it isn't a question of opinion. It is the given fact, and if you don't do that you rewrite the text and warp it. And incidentally you give yourself a terrible raft of problems which are almost never solved. There are rules, which are as strong as how you phrase a Mozart aria, where you breathe, what the dynamic is. When you've realised those rules and seen what Shakespeare is asking for, the means by which you do it as an actor is infinitely variable and is still your individual creative choice.

Now I take that to be classical, in the sense that one of the things (I would say) that is essential to the concept of classicism is the idea of form. Form is not naturalism. Greek drama kept the great moments of horror and anguish off the stage. They happen off stage. In a sense, the Greek stage itself is a mask, and behind the mask happens the blinding of Oedipus and the killing of Agamemnon. That in itself is a form, physically. Blank verse is a form, just as singing is a form. These are all artificial means of shaping naturalistic behaviour and speech, giving them a form which enables us to deal with emotions and attitudes and responses which might be too painful or even ridiculous for us if done naturalistically. It's a truism that if an actor comes on stage sobbing his heart out, the audience will find tears generally repulsive. So form enables you to deal with tears either by wearing a mask, or by singing an aria, or by speaking blank verse. I think that is crucial to classicism and to art of all times. In our own day, Samuel Beckett has a remarkable sense of form. So has Harold Pinter and so has Michael Tippett. You have to understand what the form is and then you can find the emotion that is behind that form.

About the question of costuming. I've only once in my life (and I think I've done about twenty-five Shakespeare productions) done a play in a period that didn't have a Renaissance reference. Unless what's on the stage looks like the language, I simply don't believe it. Ruritanian or modern or eclectic costumes are all very well – I can see why people do that – but if you're speaking Elizabethan English, to me there's always a war between the two. Now, I think that the Elizabethan period itself is extremely difficult for us – ruffs, padded breeches, codpieces. I think what happened to costume around the Caroline time makes it perhaps easier for us to recognise the person behind the costume. So that's why I've done that. But I wouldn't be happy going any later.

'Purist' – well, I don't know. I'm very rigorous about the verse, I'm very rigorous about the text, I'm very rigorous about speaking the decided text. Sloppiness in Shakespeare acting, when the words and the form aren't right, always distresses me.

RB To follow through on form, your current trio of productions concerns plays that you term 'late plays'. As you know, these are plays that have always until recently been called 'comedies' and the current scholarly tendency is to term them 'romances'. What do you see as the essential form within these 'late plays'?

PH I think Shakespeare is working at the top of his bent in terms of plot virtuosity. Particularly in *Cymbeline*, which has probably the most complex plot in drama. The last scene with thirty-five discoveries, *anagnorises*, is a delicate act of virtuosity because he could have done it with much less had he so wanted. But he does want now to live in a heightened world, where a wife can wake up finding the apparent headless corpse of her husband. He does want to go on embracing the idea of long-lost sons, of strange facts of nature and oddities of plot. Plots are not in that sense credible. They are, so to speak, surrealistic pieces of narrative. But I think that goes with the total mastery of eclecticism of the style. *Cymbeline* has every known style that Shakespeare ever practised – prose, verse, rhyme. There are different voices. He uses everything. I think it's a man working at the end of his life, at the top of his bent. His preoccupations are with trying to understand man's place in the universe, and the nature of forgiveness and sin.

Central to that is *The Tempest*. I believe *The Tempest* is a Faust play. It's about a man who's been given the opportunity to play God, to punish his enemies and to order another human being's life. At the end of the play, when Prospero asks for forgiveness, and says he will leave his art and break his staff, he confesses that he has actually resurrected dead people. He has opened graves and brought them forth. He asks for heavenly music and is rewarded with heavenly music, which I think not only heals his enemies but is also a sign of God's forgiveness to him. The play is full of near blasphemies. One of the interesting exercises Shakespeare had to do was to write a play about a man who had the temerity to play God and attempted to be Godlike, was corrupted by power and wants to return to being a man again, because of the pain of that. You can sense all the time that

Shakespeare's moving round the subject, because he can't directly blaspheme.

RB This is a difficult problem for the director. How does one locate blasphemy today?

PH You can't. It's one of the taboos in the theatre that's gone. What you can do is show the neurotic, restless, tortured spirit of Prospero. On the Freudian level he is obsessed with losing his daughter. He is losing his daughter for political reasons as well as personal ones. He wants a union between Naples and Milan, but he is also in a Freudian sense obsessed with her chastity and that she might lose her chastity before marriage. Not once but many times does he speak of that. In the masque he puts on for Ferdinand and Miranda he introduces the subject of chastity yet again, and he punishes his enemies in the crudest physical way. His art is not primarily as a theatre magician, his art is about pushing people around, putting them through purgatory. I think it's a very neurotic, restless play. It's not the popular, customary view of the play. But I've been led to it by a study of the text.

Another aspect of the classicism you speak of is that I cannot bear people who do Shakespeare with 'concepts'. A concept is usually like an extreme article in some learned publication about one tiny aspect of the play. It puts blinkers on the play. It's very easy to do, you say: 'This play is exactly like Germany just before Hitler took over ...' Well, it may be that there are certain parallels, but the play is about much more than that. I think you find the concept by *rehearsing* the play and embracing it through the play.

RB But there is a sense, isn't there, in which the director picks up what is in the air – necessarily, by virtue of being alive and open? I mean, for example, a generation or so ago mellow Prosperos were fairly customary. Nowadays Prosperos aren't mellow, they're irascible (which we saw the other day, when a Prospero broke his foot).

PH I agree with that. And certainly, when I did the big history cycle in Stratford in the Sixties, *The Wars of the Roses*, I was influenced by what was in the air then, by politics. Everyone said, 'You're doing it just like Jan Kott.' In fact, I read Jan Kott after I'd done the production. You could say it was in the air. Of course one's got to be open to the moment, one is a living man talking to the audience, but what you're saying to the audience should be the complexity of the work, not a simple view of it. Fashions change and I'm not saying that anything I do, which I call 'classical', is for all time. It's impossible. It's just for now. But unless you start with a classical base I think you're simplifying Shakespeare.

RB What do you see as the unifying principle of the three plays you chose?

PH They're all about journeys through purgatory, which meets some resolution and forgiveness at the end. Leontes has no right to be reunited with his wife, whom he thinks he has killed; Prospero I believe has no right to be forgiven and return to being an ordinary man; and the union at the end of *Cymbeline* is the return of Britain to the Roman Empire.

RB Surely the right to forgiveness does not exist?

PH No. But they are in that sense purgatorial plays. The central characters go through purgatory, a learning, a journey. They come out older and wiser. And sadder. I believe the resolution and forgiveness and the happy ending are extremely fragile. I don't say it isn't going to go on, but it needs more work. It's not enough to say, 'I forgive you.' There are some things you've got to forget in order to relive.

RB Yes. All your conclusions leave the audience with the sense of the ongoing play, that, for example, Hermione and Leontes still have a great deal to work out. Your ending is highly provisional.

PH That comes out of the text. 'Hastily lead away' – why does he want to go hastily? Why does he, as the king, ask others to lead? Also it's not a rhyming couplet. It is a suspended end.

RB Perhaps like the end of *Measure for Measure*, where the Duke has an extra couplet after he might be thought to have concluded the play.

PH That's right. It's a question mark.

RB I was fascinated, in *Cymbeline*, by the way you did everything you could to solve the range of problems of milieux in the text, four areas – Ancient Britain, Ancient Rome, Renaissance Rome, wild Wales. So far as was possible, you kept them within a costume scheme that did seem to bring people into a relationship with each other. For example, Posthumus keeping his hat on had just a hint of an English bourgeois, almost Puritan, of the era, who is a little awkward and out of place amongst the sophisticates of Renaissance Rome.

PH Absolutely. That was intentional. The play is so varied in its periods that you have to embrace the eclecticism, embrace the varieties. You say: try to make a world in which all these disparate elements can live. I think Alison Chitty's designs succeeded very well in doing that. And that variety is echoed in the play's language. The rapid prose in the Italian scenes is terribly different from Lucius's conference with Cymbeline in Ancient Britain and Iachimo's highly-charged lyric verse in the bedchamber scene. It's very different from the direct, forthright speech of Innogen.

I did the play before, many years ago. Something that struck me very much, on coming back to it, is that Innogen and Posthumus are both ungoverned people. They fall in love and go through a secret marriage. That's no way for a princess of the realm to behave. And she's got a fiery temper, which she knows and constantly tries to check. Posthumus does not know himself. He learns himself. She learns what real love is; I think she's in love with love.

RB Even Cloten does have one speech in which he makes a serious charge against her, that the marriage is socially ill-advised and will lead to trouble. The language of that speech – 'You sin against/Obedience' – demands to be taken seriously. He is not a clown at that point.

PH Agreed. But the only way in which the term 'romance' can be justified is that the story is so baroque and complicated. It's easy to opt out of the reality of the play, by saying that the play is bad. And there's much more to it than that.

RB Yes, that would be a cop-out.

PH I wish very much that in addition to doing the three I could have done *Pericles* as well. Though it is very hard as a text

– it's so problematic and corrupt – I think practically everything you find in the three plays is adumbrated in *Pericles.*

RB Does *Pericles* come under the heading of unfinished business? Or can I phrase it more broadly: you've directed three-quarters of the canon now. Do you feel the wish on the one hand to complete the canon, or on the other hand to revisit certain plays that you've already explored?

PH There are some I haven't done that I very much want to do. I have no ambition to complete the canon. That would be a rather external and mechanical thing. I've never done *As You Like It* and *Measure for Measure.* I've never done *King Lear.* I've done all the histories but I've never done *Much Ado. Pericles*, as I say, I'd like to try. But I suppose if I could have my ambition fulfilled, I would like a small theatre with a vast sum of money so that I could teach and explore Shakespeare by performing him. But you can't do that in the pattern of our institutional theatres. Both the RSC, which I founded, and the National, which I opened and directed for fifteen years, are huge institutions that have to put on large numbers of plays. I can't do a Shakespeare play now unless I have a month's work on the text with the cast before I start directing the play. You can just about do that sometimes at the National Theatre. You can't do that at the RSC because they do so many plays. And you can't do it anywhere else. We rehearsed *Antony and Cleopatra* for twelve weeks. For the first four weeks we didn't do anything, except examine the text, largely because only two people in the cast knew how to speak Shakespeare. That is the present-day crisis. It is because our regional theatre cannot afford to do Shakespeare. Most young actors, even twenty years ago, had been exposed to enough Shakespeare just by ear, just by being in a play, to know its tune. Now they don't. We have some very grave problems.

RB You are currently re-rehearsing plays for the larger stage. Could you say something about the order of problem this involves?

PH I've moved productions from the Cottesloe (the smaller one) to the Olivier many times in the past. The stage of the Cottesloe is very large, though the auditorium is tiny, and there usually isn't much of a problem. So far I've only done *The Winter's Tale*, but I think *The Winter's Tale* is better for the Olivier than the Cottesloe and I suspect the other two will be as well, because they have more space to breathe. They have the energy of a great number of people watching. There is only one disadvantage. The Cottesloe is a marvellous space for Shakespeare, because it is large enough to open your lungs and small enough to speak very quietly if you want to. So the dynamic range in the voices is large. I don't like chamber Shakespeare and I don't think you can mutter Shakespeare in little rooms. For that matter, I don't think you can mutter Shakespeare on television either. It is a rhetorical form to wrap the tongue around; it was meant to be relished.

RB I must say I very much enjoyed your 1974 *Tempest* on the big stage. It's a play that invites the showbiz element.

PH There is that. But I don't think any of them will lose. So far they've gained, largely because the set is more spaced and is more comfortable.

One point I didn't make about the form, particularly the verse. If you observe the rules you can make the plays very much quicker, very much shorter. The audience runs after the play, rather than trudges. It's an interesting but true fact; Hamlet's advice to the players should be scrupulously followed.

RB Looking back, I sense a paradox here. Over twenty years ago, your most celebrated production was the great *Hamlet* with David Warner. It was enormously controversial and enormously successful. It appealed to a great many people and offended some people. Today, your style of Shakespeare seems to be headed in a different direction – or is this a false impression?

PH It's a false impression. The David Warner *Hamlet* was dressed in Jacobean clothes. I was as rigorous then about the verse as I am now. Perhaps not as successful, though I think I was. The whole of the RSC in the Sixties was based on it. The only thing that surprised people about David Warner's Hamlet was that he wasn't as romantic as Hamlets had been lately and he wore a scarf because he was fresh from college. But he was a Jacobean student. I don't know what that production would look like if you saw it now, but I can assure you that it's commentators who say I've become a classicist. I did it exactly the same. I was readier in the 1950s and 60s to cut than I am now. Everyone used to cut Shakespeare. We did not give our audience the credit for wanting to see Shakespeare. I believe they'd sooner spend three hours and see everything he wrote than be there two hours and forty-five minutes and miss fifteen minutes at the end. I also think that there's a tendency in Shakespeare to cut it if you don't understand and can't make it work. But I don't do that to Mozart or Wagner in my operatic life and I don't do it to Shakespeare. If I can't make it work, it's not Shakespeare who is wrong, it's me. I would say that the only thing I've changed in is that I don't cut now. What was considered to be revolutionary then is considered classical now.

It's very interesting: since there has been, in my view, such a decline over the last ten years in observing form in verse speaking, you're labelled a classicist if you follow what Shakespeare writes. In the Sixties, you weren't, because we were all doing it in Stratford.

RB One final question. Where are you headed now, in Shakespeare?

PH I want to go on exploring the things I've been talking about. I don't know how I'm going to do it, because I'm neither going to be at one of the big institutions, nor am I going to be in the commercial theatre in a situation where I can do very much Shakespeare. Maybe one in eighteen months if I'm lucky. So there won't be enough Shakespeare. It's a question that I'm having great anxiety about. I would like to run a Shakespeare studio, training actors in the form and what to look for. And I would like to do productions arising out of that. But that is a small thing, it is not a vast Royal Shakespeare-like enterprise. And in this country no one will give me the money to do that and I think it will never happen; largely, of course, because we subsidise institutions but not individuals.

1988

Michael Bogdanov

Michael Bogdanov has directed Shakespeare for the English Shakespeare Company, with whom he was Joint Artistic Director (1986–89), for the Royal Shakespeare Company, for the Stratford Festival, Ontario, and elsewhere. He was Associate Director at the National Theatre from 1980–84. From 1989 he has been Intendant of the Deutsches Schauspielhaus, Hamburg.

Ralph Berry I'd like to ask you first about the English Shakespeare Company – its structures; and how these bear upon the Shakespeare that you direct.

Michael Bogdanov The Company was founded with the prime intention of taking what we call accessible Shakespeare out to the regions, to a lot of theatres that haven't had much Shakespeare in many years – cities where there's been a collapse of the repertory movement, so that it becomes a luxury to do a large-scale piece at all outside musicals or pantomimes, to keep the box-office coming in. So in response to an Arts Council initiative we formed a company of twenty-five actors, which we launched from Plymouth where, in the five years that the theatre had been open, they had never had a Shakespeare. And we toured to all the large-scale theatres in the country. Because there had been such a dearth of classical work, we were received with open arms in a lot of areas, but for the most part it was a question of reviving some kind of folk memory of an old habit of going to the theatre to see something other than a West End comedy or thriller or musical. In our second year of going out we found that in some instances we doubled our audiences of the first year, due to our word-of-mouth reputation, and the knowledge that what they were going to see was understandable and that they would not be mystified.

The basic premise of the English Shakespeare Company is to take the histories, as we are performing them, to audiences that

(a) have not gone to Shakespeare for a long time and (b) may never have gone to the theatre before and couldn't care less whether Shakespeare lived or died; we want particularly to appeal to young people through the way in which we perform. And that is by stripping the plays down to the bare essentials. We make eclectic use of costume. We go for a very direct piece of storytelling that releases the power of the language and at the same time captures the imagination. We talk of the whole seven-play cycle as a mediaeval soap opera, so that all the time we supply hooks for the story to encourage people to come back and see the next one until they can't resist seeing how it ends. We try to achieve this by using contemporary references, contemporary props, contemporary costumes, but mixing them in with periods of costume that are accessible in terms of audience participation. By that I mean we can go back about a hundred years and people can still understand what costume means. Up till this project I had worked almost exclusively with modern dress, since 1976 when I did a disastrous (for me, anyway) production of *Romeo and Juliet* at the Haymarket Theatre in Leicester. I found I was able to contact the kind of audiences that I wanted to appeal to very much more directly when I removed artificial barriers between them and the language. In other words, they could identify with people who wore suits where they couldn't identify with people who wore doublet and hose and tights. They could not distinguish properly between the various ranks and make the correct assumptions about somebody's social status. It always seemed necessary to over-emphasise a costume in order to point out that a particular character was nouveau riche or had inherited wealth. In moving into modern dress, therefore, I was able to establish that link and identity immediately without having to overwork the language or character.

RB What you say about eclecticism is very interesting. Obviously, you see it in part as the best way of making contact with the audiences you play to. But is this now additionally a central tenet of your work as a director, that you prefer the eclectic approach to costuming?

MB Until I reached this project I had worked exclusively with modern dress. But to me, the language is the most important thing. Understanding the language, releasing the language. I'm frightened that in fifty years' time these plays will be accessible only to those people who have studied them and have the annotated editions to say what the words mean. Over the last four or five years we've lost about 2,000 words, struck out of the Oxford English Dictionary as now obsolete. I aim at giving audiences some kind of folk memory as to what the stories are, so that they can be handed down. There are always points in time where people mark off (if you like) the level they've arrived at in the memory of productions, so we always get references by the critics to past productions as the 'definitive' one. I try to give audiences some kind of yardstick by which to measure the next production that they see in terms of understanding the story. Now when I reached this project, it was clear when I came to *Henry IV Part One* that I couldn't use a metaphor for the fight between Hal and Hotspur. No arm-wrestling or chess match or surreal thing was going to do. If I was going to have a fight at all it couldn't be a knife fight or a shoot-out. It had to be a mediaeval fight. So once I had established this principle in my mind, it was of central importance; because after ten or twelve years to return to something that wasn't my basic tenet (modern dress always) meant that I could then run the gamut from mediaeval to modern without hindrance. It was then a question of selecting periods and ideas for costumes to fit characters and scenes, so that you could broadly develop the eclecticism in conjunction with what was needed by the character of a particular type. Now when I say I think this is the best way, I don't by any means maintain that this is the only way to do a Shakespeare. That would patently be foolish. Other people release Shakespeare in a totally different way. For me, still working out my ideas on how to present Shakespeare in a contemporary sense and make the modern connection with Shakespeare, I've moved from exclusively modern dress to eclecticism, which is suiting some areas of the plays and is not entirely suiting others.

RB I would have thought on general principles that the histories are far more resistant to eclecticism than the comedies, for the most part, since the histories are rooted in mediaeval England in a way in which one can hardly say that *Love's Labour's Lost* is rooted in Renaissance Navarre.

MB Yes. I don't find that a difficulty, strangely enough. It's really a question of resources. If one had the full resources to do these plays as I should wish to do them – in other words, if the budgets were ten times what we have – I think that the eclecticism could be more defined and refined, to the point where you would not notice the join. After all, there's twenty-four hours of Shakespeare. If you get ninety per cent right in production, it's still ten per cent wrong. So there's two and a half hours wrong, even if the plays are all brilliant. If you get seventy-five per cent right, and that's a very good production, that's twenty-five per cent wrong. In twenty-four hours that's six hours that are not very good. And when you start using those equations, it's understandable that some things don't work. Interestingly enough, things I don't think work the audiences love. It is a subjective judgment as to what is right.

RB Can you give me an instance or two of what, in your experience, does work and what is resistant?

MB The *Henry VI* plays are probably the most resistant, because they sprawl and straggle in an extraordinary way. They, more than any of the other five plays, are rooted very much in the mediaeval period and are very early Shakespeare. The language isn't as vibrant and powerful, and the problem then becomes whether the images that you're conjuring up have any substance in relation to what is very simplistic dialogue. It's then that you start to subtract, for you're papering over what is often a thin text with images that you're trying to bring forward, for people to make connections with. The plays themselves are very resistant in certain areas. When the language is good and the writing is powerful, there isn't any problem.

RB The problem, then, is that certain passages in the *Henry VI* plays are rather crudely written, immature by Shakespearian standards?

MB Yes. And the characters are simplistic and one-dimensional, and difficult to deal with, even when you contract them and also bolster them by giving them something with a new dimension. John Barton obviously found this back in the sixties, when he condensed the three parts of *Henry VI* into two parts and rewrote one third of the text in order to give it that kind of substance.

RB A good deal of the *dramatis personae* in *Henry VI* are simply class-based. There are scenes filled with arrogant patricians dismissing other nobles as 'base hinds' and so on. That is their one note, the note of class dismissal. How do you cope with this difficulty, this simple, strident note of the characters?

MB As a class? I trace it back to one of the basic reasons why I started doing this in the first place. It was because there were obvious parallels between the England of Henry Bolingbroke and Margaret Thatcher, the regional problems, the North-South divide, the continuing problems of Wales, Scotland and Ireland. Scotland is now almost totally Labour, Wales much the same. So what you have is Westminster rule imposed on minority cultures. You have other spurious associations, like Agincourt and the war of political expediency as put forward by Bolingbroke on his deathbed, saying, 'Be it thy course to busy giddy minds/With foreign quarrels.' In other words, unite the country in a war of political expediency and deflect attention from problems at home – unemployment, housing and so on. The Falklands did exactly that and put Mrs Thatcher back in power.

RB How did you bring out these parallels?

MB The parallels are fairly obvious, once you link the play's regions, which I tried to do with varying degrees of success. We have some authentic Welshmen, some authentic Scots, some Northumbrians, Yorkshiremen and Lancastrians. Other members of the Company have to affect accents. In other words, I'm trying to broaden the appeal of the plays by giving the characters accents, spuriously sometimes, that indicate where they come from or where their titles were rooted. If you've got a big Lancastrian family like the Nevilles, or Westmorelands, they come from that part of the country. You start by making them regional plays and then you can see what Westminster rule is. Immediately, an audience understands what is happening. The idea that no noblemen ever speaks with a Yorkshire accent is crazy, because even in 1988 there are still Scots, Irish, Cornish peers with broad accents.

RB I agree that the *Henry IV* and *Henry V* plays are obsessed with region, with the sense of the disparate areas of Britain. It's said of Michael Redgrave, by the way, that when he did Hotspur he got the accent right to about half a dozen miles. But it really was Northumberland for Hotspur.

MB When you move into the civil war area, you are still in basically the same territory. The Yorkists in our productions are based in York, therefore you have a power faction based around the region. When we reach *Richard III*, we're back in modern dress. I started *Richard II* with Regency, making some kind of parallel with a flamboyancy and a decadence in Richard's court that allows for costume to become much more formal and flamboyant. The advent of Bolingbroke is greeted by a much more austere vision, with frockcoats coming in, and his Council is much more structured.

RB Can I ask you to refine on what you're saying about eclecticism, in this sense? Many directors like the all-embracing period metaphor, in which everybody in a given production is in a certain society, which gives a cohesion to the *dramatis personae*. Are you saying that you can have a kind of fluid eclecticism, in which one moves scene by scene from one period to another, or do you regard each actor as a one-off who inhabits his own individual world in his own individual costume?

MB The answer is yes, to both. You can have the eclecticism moving scene by scene, and you can have an individual moving parallel to that, in one costume, through a whole series of different scenes with different costumes. I would not, by choice, now select a period for Shakespeare out of time that isn't our own time, or isn't in this eclectic manner, merely to make a parallel. For example, a *Julius Caesar* set in the 1930s: I used to think one could do Shakespeare like that; I could do it; but I don't do it any more. When I say that I chose Regency for *Richard II*, I wouldn't if I were doing *Richard II* on its own do it like that. It's only in relation to seven plays, bringing them to modern times, that I have, if you like, developed costumes, in the political areas, that move over the last 150 years, from Regency to contemporary. In all the low-life and battle scenes I move backwards and forwards all the time. When I deal with *Richard III*, it's modern dress up till the last moment. The fight between Richard and Richmond is in full armour, with long swords. We switched from modern dress to armour, then back to the television studio for Richmond's address to the people. So we slice through the period in which it is set, mediaeval England, to the period in which I'm playing it; and we try to make a parallel between the one-to-one combat where a country's fate is determined by that contest between two individuals, and where we're now at – where the country's fate is determined by electronics, computers, Star Wars. The whole cycle is about aggression and the territorial imperative. I try to make the point right at the end of the cycle, by switching – it's the most eclectic thing of the lot. And I hope everything that I've been trying from the beginning, with the periods and costumes, falls into place. Whether it's successful or not is not for me to judge, but that was the intention.

RB I would like to make a slight widening of the issue and go back to your splendid production of *The Spanish Tragedy* at the National Theatre, a few years ago. That was largely within a period, Spanish Renaissance, was it not?

MB Yes it was.

RB Excluding Revenge from the period?

MB The actor playing Revenge had a contemporary look, yes.

RB So you do accept the idea of a complete social envelope for a production?

MB Yes. Anybody who thinks I'm incapable of mounting anything other than modern dress Shakespeare hasn't seen the period of my life when I was a director of unknown European classics! *Lorenzaccio* was included in that, as well as *The Spanish Tragedy*, and *The Mayor of Zalamea*. But I do find a particular challenge with Shakespeare for audiences. For some reason he's so dense and so difficult that many people do not understand what is happening and they do not want to go to

Shakespeare because they're afraid of not understanding him. They don't want to be baffled. People go just out of duty. I'm not interested unless I can change the nature of the theatre-going. One of the exciting things about this particular project is that we have gathered an enormous number of middle-aged and older groupies, who have travelled the length and breadth of the country, and in some instances have gone abroad to see the plays. I met one wonderful lady in York who said she'd seen them twenty-eight times, up and down the country. We have a mailing list now and we receive a lot of letters. Two thirds of them are from older people, who say that they've had their theatre-going habits changed because of what we've had to offer them.

RB Would it be tactless of me to ask you what you see your Company offering the public that is quite different from the major institutions?

MB I don't know that I can *say* what we're giving that is different. Let me say what we're trying to do. I'm trying to give the public a company that knows, every time it's on stage, what it's doing, what it's saying, why it's there, how every single character and every single line fits into social and political structures. Therefore there is not one single line that has gone by without the analysis going on as to how that character fits into the whole, even if it's a messenger with one line. The Company is all travelling in the same direction: it knows where it's heading with the story and the social structure of the plot. That releases a kind of power, if you get it right, that goes straight to an audience's head; because the audience is listening and understanding, and is not frightened, it is drawn in. If we are providing anything that is exciting audiences, it is because we have achieved this. If we're not providing it, it is because although the intention is there, it hasn't quite worked. But basically, one should be able to say that every company does that.

By stripping the plays down and presenting a series of very stark, clear images with a handful of props and occasionally some colouring in the costumes, and a company that has worked together and also employs twenty-five actors in seven plays and understudies of each other in every role, and is committed to that kind of ensemble playing that you do not see now in this country on that scale – when you get it right over three years, there is understanding by that stage. People can take the plays into another area of feeling. Audiences believe that the actors are inhabiting that world properly.

RB Do you do much cutting?

MB Yes. One has to, though I suspect that I cut the plays less than most directors. Our production of *Richard III* runs to four hours; there are very few productions of *Richard* that run that long now. The reason is that a lot of the stuff that's often cut is excessive to an audience, if they've seen the plays that have gone before. One third of *Richard III* is inaccessible to an audience if they don't know what has gone before. There is so much reference to characters and events. On the other hand, if you have on the same day, on a Saturday as we often have, a *House of Lancaster* in the morning and a *House of York* in the afternoon (our two condensed parts of *Henry VI*), with *Richard III* in the evening, they understand all those references to all those events. And so I haven't cut it as much as I might: I've cut about an hour I suppose. Five hours is a long evening!

RB I understand that Adrian Noble is cutting about 5,000 lines from *The Plantagenets*.

MB It's something you do. I've cut from the *Henry VI* plays – reducing them to two parts – about five and a half thousand lines. But then, we've written about 300 lines to clarify the story and to link, and make sure that things are moving forward. Our *Henry IV* plays run about three and a quarter hours each. For most purposes, that's about a quarter of an hour too long, but it's good stuff and we won't lose it! With *Henry V*, the problem is that we're stuck with the legacy of the Olivier film, where he had to cut about half, some 1,700 lines, in order to get that patriotism and it's the only way you can get it. If you keep in the embarrassing bits, like the battle of Agincourt where Pistol is kicking around one poor Frenchman, you have to quote or refer to the other bits. Subversively, there's a most interesting play in *Henry V*.

RB Yes, Olivier had to cut in 1944.

MB But unfortunately, we've inherited that version of the play. We don't listen to the irony of the Chorus, we don't see how you can turn some of the speeches on their heads so that they mean something quite different.

RB I think of *Henry V* as a great war play embedded in a greater anti-war play.

MB Absolutely.

RB One final question. Where are the frontiers? Where are you headed? What is the next project?

MB I don't know. I have possibly one of my best pieces of theatre in Germany, my production of *Julius Caesar* at the Schauspielhaus in Hamburg. I shall be taking over the Schauspielhaus in 1989. I suspect that I shall do only a couple of Shakespeares there. I will certainly do a *Hamlet* there; I've done *Hamlet* four times and am still moving towards what arc I can bring to it. One of the things I have started doing is this: I started by doing bare-stage Shakespeare, thinking that that was the way I could make the stories most accessible, nothing between the lines at all and everything in modern dress. Pretty soon I realised that a few props and bits of furniture were aids. Gradually I've been expanding that, to clarify what's happening. Even with these pictures, which are very stark, I'm seeing other pictures that I'm quoting with just a few boxes and chairs. In an ideal world, I suspect I would develop that much further.

RB You're headed in the direction of larger, shall I say more lavish production values?

MB Not necessarily more lavish. I want the possibility that if I need an image I can afford to have it. One can have it at the RSC and the National. But having worked in both institutions and having been an Associate Director at the National for much of the time, I needed to free myself from the chains of a building to see how it could be created for myself with a group of people, with Michael Pennington my partner. We wanted to see how we could rise to the challenge of overturning a lot of traditional values and at the same time presenting a repertoire that wasn't traditional, all-day Saturdays. We played the trilogy, all day

Saturday, everywhere in the country. Sometimes we did a full weekend with *Richard II* on Friday evening, the two parts of *Henry IV* on Saturday and the *Henry VI/Richard III* plays on Sunday. It provided the audience with a challenge and us with a challenge. Unless I can do that with Shakespeare, making him clearer and more accessible, releasing the language – language is the most important factor for me, as I've said – I shall stop doing Shakespeare. That is a possibility. Standing still, or treading water, cannot give a challenge to myself and to others. Then I would leave him, at least for a spell.

1988

Index to Shakespeare Plays